MURDER BY NUMBERS

MURDER BY NUMBERS

British Serial Sex Killers Since 1950:
Their Childhoods, Their Lives,
Their Crimes

ANNA GEKOSKI

André Deutsch

First published in Great Britain in 1998
by André Deutsch Ltd,
76 Dean Street,
London W1V 5HA
www.vci.co.uk

André Deutsch Ltd is a VCI plc company

A catalogue record for this title is available
from the British Library

ISBN 0 233 99138 7

Typeset by Derek Doyle & Associates
Mold, Flintshire.
Printed by WSOY, Finland.

This book is dedicated to:
Dad, Mum, Bertie and Steve

Contents

Acknowledgements   ix

1   Serial Killing: A Contemporary Fascination   1

2   Serial Killing: The Wider Context   22

3   John Reginald Halliday Christie   47

4   Ian Brady and Myra Hindley   78

5   Peter Sutcliffe   112

6   Dennis Nilsen   148

7   Robert Black   181

8   Colin Ireland   217

9   Fred and Rose West   248

10 Serial Killing: Some Tentative Conclusions   289

Select Bibliography   305

ACKNOWLEDGEMENTS

The person whom I would like to thank first, and most especially, is my father, Rick. He has taken the time to edit every single page of this book, and has entirely re-written parts of it. He has lovingly believed in me at times when I didn't believe in myself, and without him I would not have contemplated starting this project, nor could I have finished it.

To say that I want to extend special thanks to my father is not to diminish the role my mother, Barbara, has played in the past year. Her nourishment, emotional support, and understanding of all my anxieties have been boundless. And during the last month of writing she proved herself to be an excellent editor and proof-reader.

I would next like to thank Steve, who has had to live with me throughout the duration of this project. He has been patient in contending with my moods, and a constant source of love. His research skills have proved invaluable in various libraries across the country.

I would also like to extend my thanks to Giles Gordon, my agent, for his editing and advice; to Professor David Farrington at the Institute of Criminology in Cambridge for his help with my MPhil thesis, which is where this book originated; to Anthony Storr for kindly listening to my ideas for the conclusion of this book; to Tom Rosenthal for his help in the initial stages of the project; to Louise Dixon at André Deutsch, for her editing and encouragement; to Milena Smith and Polly Rippon for their support and careful proof-reading; to Will Chipperfield, for his photographic skills; to Paul and Rachael Brown for their help in times of computer crisis; to Alison Dunn and Kate Hartshorn for their friendship; and to Bertie Gekoski for his constantly cheerful presence.

Lastly, I am grateful for the help of the staff at the Public Record Office at Kew, Colindale Newspaper Library, the British Library, the Institute of Criminology in Cambridge, and Warwick University Library.

1

SERIAL KILLING:
A CONTEMPORARY
FASCINATION

'No one knows better than he the emotional value of gore and garters. It is a combination the British find absolutely irresistible.'

(Sherlock Holmes on Jack the Ripper, in Michael Dibdin's
The Last Sherlock Holmes Story)

On 31 August 1888, the body of Mary Ann Nicholls was found in Whitechapel, disembowelled, with its throat cut. Between September and November of that year the bodies of four more women were discovered. All the murders were marked by near identical features, one 'signature' clearly stamped upon each: all of the victims were prostitutes and alcoholics, who had been killed on either the first or last weekend of a month in the early hours of the morning. All the women had been soliciting in the same red-light area within a square mile of each other, and had been grabbed from behind and had their throats cut. None appeared to have cried out or made any noise when attacked, and all but one of the murders (presumably due to interruption) had ritualistic elements, with post-mortem mutilations including disembowelment and the removal of organs. None of the victims appeared, in any conventional sense, to have been sexually assaulted.

By the time of the 8 September edition of the *Police News*, it was reported that 'Crowds of spectators continue to visit the scene of the murder in Buck's-Row', as if murder were a form of tourist attraction or spectator sport. Over subsequent issues of the paper, as reports of new murders were covered with a gruesome attention to detail that makes today's tabloids look positively restrained, the 'Whitechapel Fiend' became the obsession of the nation: 'Jack the Ripper', as he was soon to be known, had arrived to an unprecedented fanfare of publicity.

The popular imagination seized upon the image of this mysterious and overpowering figure, who came in the night, alight with unquenchable desire, reminding us of how closely allied are the images of murder and those of sexual obsession. And when one figure came to stand for both the murderous and the lustful it was no wonder that the entire unconscious of a nation shuddered with horror and delight. Indeed, the name 'Jack the Ripper' – the appellation is first used in a letter written to the police, ostensibly by the murderer – ingeniously combines both of these linguistic elements. Though the first edition of the *Oxford English Dictionary* (1933) curiously omits any reference to a 'ripper' as a murderer, the term 'rip' itself is condensed from three meanings into one more complex, newer meaning. In the nineteenth-century, 'rip', used as a noun, can mean either an unchaste woman or a degenerate man; used as a verb, it means to slash or cut up violently. Thus the new coinage (added to the conventional usage of a 'Jack' as a reprobate – as in our current 'Jack-the-lad') is articulate of a brutal, sexually-driven attacker.

Jack the Ripper was hardly the first example of a murderer on such a scale. Indeed, he seems relatively tame compared with prior examples of the type of murderers who have only recently become known as *serial killers.* These include Gilles De Rais, a fifteenth-century French nobleman, who reportedly raped, tortured and killed over 800 children, drinking their blood, eating their flesh and having sex with their corpses; the Beanes of Edinburgh, also in the fifteenth century, who were an inbred family of nearly fifty, living in a cave, killing and eating travellers who passed; Fritz Haarmann, who was said to have sodomized and killed dozens of young boys in Hanover in the nineteenth century; and Herman Webster Mudgett (aka Henry Havard Holmes), in whose self-built mansion and torture-chamber the remains of more than 200 victims were found in America in the 1880s. Yet despite the levels of these excesses, it is Jack the Ripper who epitomizes the age of serial murder, not so much

2

because of the scale of his crimes as the scale of his publicity.

The Ripper has now become an obsession, an enthusiasm, a hobby for millions of devotees. His hold on the popular imagination is attested by the numerous twentieth-century novels, films, documentaries, operas and even computer games that have successfully used the Ripper as their protagonist. Marie Belloc Lowndes' book *The Lodger*, for instance, in which Jack is lodging in an ordinary family house, has been reprinted over thirty times and filmed five times since it was first published in 1913. In Michael Dibdin's *The Last Sherlock Holmes Story* (1978), Holmes is tracking Jack the Ripper, whom he claims is a brilliant professor named Moriarty, a man who has never been seen by anyone but Holmes himself. In a startling twist, where our images of good and evil are plunged into confusion, it transpires that Moriarty is Holmes's alter-ego, and thus that Holmes himself is Jack the Ripper. In the 1979 film *Time After Time* the Ripper is a respected doctor. In *A Wolf in the Fold*, the episode of Star Trek written by Robert Bloch, the Ripper is an alien, immortal being.

Over a century after his crimes, Jack the Ripper continues to be one of the most written- and read-about murderers, as new books continue to be published postulating the *real* identity of the enigmatic killer. A host of different suspects have been credited with the murders including Sir William Gull, Physician-in-Ordinary to Queen Victoria (assisted by the artist Walter Sickert and a coachman by the name of John Netley), Lord Randolph Churchill, James K. Stephen (Prince Albert Victor's tutor at Cambridge), and, more recently, a cotton merchant from Liverpool called James Maybrick, after the discovery of what is allegedly the Ripper's diary.

As the Ripper was never caught, the possibilities are endless. The implication of the works, both true and fictional, is clear, the Ripper could be anyone: a lodger, a detective, a doctor, a Lord, or an alien. This is partly the source of the fascination. As Philip Sugden, author of *The Complete History of Jack the Ripper*, says, 'After a series of horrific murders Jack the Ripper disappeared … He left us, in short, with the classic "whodunnit".' What kind of person, or fiend, could commit such atrocities?

And thus, through our inability to analyse and to categorize him, the Ripper has attained a mythological status. In 1988 England actually 'celebrated' the centennial of Jack the Ripper's murders with T-shirts, badges, mugs and (blood) red cocktails in bars. In America, while modern-day serial killers were roaming the streets waiting to strike, the FBI took the time to draw up a profile of the Ripper to mark the anniversary; in New York you can drink in the Jack the Ripper Pub or eat in the Jack the Ribber restaurant.

With the murders of Jack the Ripper a new phenomenon arose in popular culture: the Ripper was the first murderer-celebrity. And in the inescapable process whereby celebrity tends to glamorize and to idealize, the Ripper inexorably became not a demon but a kind of ideal, a record-holder. In the popular imagination, he was the most famous, the most horrible, had the most victims. Would his records be surpassed? Would we ever see his like again?

Twentieth-century serial killers are, inevitably, compared to the notorious Ripper, and his crimes emulated by them. When Gordon Frederick Cummins killed and mutilated four women, three of whom were prostitutes, during the Second World War, he was nicknamed the 'Wartime Jack the Ripper', or the 'Blackout Ripper'. In 1953 when John Reginald Halliday Christie was on the run, having murdered at least six women, a headline in the *Truth* read 'The Nation-wide Search for a Modern Jack the Ripper'. A similar headline in *People Weekly*, in the 1970s, referring to Peter Sutcliffe (aka the 'Yorkshire Ripper') read, 'Spurned By His Taunts Police Search For Britain's Bloodiest Ripper Since Jack'. Later, while on remand at Brixton prison, Sutcliffe was nicknamed 'JR' by the other inmates – not after the popular *Dallas* star, but after the equally well-known murderer, also a killer and mutilator of prostitutes.

A people equally fascinated by crime, statistics, and fame, Americans are particularly obsessed by their serial killers, who have swiftly risen to celebrity status. Jeffrey Dahmer was on the coveted front cover of *People* magazine in 1992, and when his apartment block, in which he had cannibalized, tortured, sexually assaulted, and killed seventeen men, was pulled down, guards and a barbed-wire fence were put around the property to keep the rubber-necking public at a distance. This did not, however, prevent people from offering the guards up to $75 for a brick as a gruesome memento. Some months later, the refrigerator in which he had kept body parts – including a human heart, in case he fancied a 'light snack' – was auctioned off. In prison, through his lawyer, Dahmer sold the crockery and cutlery that he had used to cannibalize his victims. Most astounding, perhaps, is the fact that while in prison Dahmer received around $30,000, largely donated in small amounts, from people who felt sorry for him. One sent a Bible, inside which were several thousand dollars.

The mind of the serial killer is frequently characterized by egotism and grandiosity. If caught, they frequently embark upon intellectual, and often self-aggrandizing, pursuits. In America, John Wayne Gacy, who killed thirty-three men, sold his otherwise worthless paintings to buyers all over the United States. Jack Unterweger killed a prostitute, and while serving a life sentence for the crime wrote short stories, plays and an autobiography which were all great hits with the Viennese intellectual élite. He was given parole and, while living as a literary celebrity, he carried on killing, claiming the lives of at least nine more prostitutes before he was apprehended. John Gerard Schaefer (who killed more than thirty people) published, in prison, a collection of short stories he'd written about sex and violence, under the title *Killer Fiction*. Robert Hansen, the killer of seventeen prostitutes, says that he wants to write his autobiography and has already been offered contracts by two different publishers. In England, Dennis Nilsen has just written a long account of his murders of fifteen young men, and is demanding a £100,000 advance from publishers. The lesson is clear, if ironic: if you make killers into celebrities, soon enough people will be hanging on their every word.

The press, particularly the tabloids, have played no small part in the glorification of the serial killer. After the emergence of each such killer, the press attach grizzly monikers to them – the Yorkshire Ripper, Stockwell Strangler, Coed Killer, Night Stalker, Skid-Row Slasher, Killer Clown, Angel of Death – and give them publicity which is disproportionate to the frequency of their crimes. The apparent motive for this nick-naming process – to demonize the killer and make him instantly recognizable – curiously has the opposite effect: it depotentizes the power of the words because of the very conventions that they mimic. The killer becomes a cartoon character, or sports star. In this sense the media, in chronicling the rise of the serial killer, has played a vital role in forming both the public perception of the serial killer and also the killer's perception of himself and his actions.

Indeed, it has been speculated that media attention, in the massive coverage of every aspect of the crimes, might actually prolong the killing spree, as the serial killer may feel that the public and press are somehow encouraging him. As David Berkowitz – the 'Son of Sam' – who killed six young women in New York in 1977, told Dr David Abrahamsen, the forensic psychiatrist who examined him after his arrest: 'I finally had convinced myself that it was good to do it, and that the public wanted me to do it ... I believe that many were rooting for me.' While the Yorkshire Ripper was terrorizing women in the north of England, the police appealed to the public for information through the loud-speakers at the Leeds football ground, Elland Road. They were drowned out by chants of 'You'll never catch the Ripper' and '12–0, 12–0', referring to the number of victims claimed by the Ripper at that time. And in the case of Fred and Rose West, who killed twelve young women, one could trace a palpable increase of media attention and excitement as the number of victims located increased, as if some new and implicitly admirable sporting record were being approached. A headline in the *Sun* gleefully screamed, 'THEY'VE LOST COUNT OF THE BODIES'. In the last fifty years, serial killing has come to resemble an Olympic event, with its own heroes and records.

A myth has emerged, and works of fiction are written, films are made, and songs are sung. The Rolling Stones 'Midnight Rambler' is about the killing of Beverly Samans, one of the victims of the 'Boston Strangler' (Albert DeSalvo). Jagger sings 'Oh, don't you do that, oh don't do that'; DeSalvo told police that as he attacked Beverly Samans she kept repeating 'don't do that'. Some years later, Guns N' Roses did a remake of a Charles Manson song on their album *The Spaghetti Incident*, although it is not acknowledged in the list of songs on the cover. When Axl Rose performed the song to live audiences, he wore a Charles Manson T-shirt.

In the 1990s the films *Henry: Portrait of a Serial Killer, Seven, Copycat* and *Kiss the Girls* have all been box-office hits. Yet such works are invariably, and dangerously, misleading. Based very loosely on reality, they contribute to the terrifying (but largely untrue) image of the serial killer as cunning, clever and unstoppable. One of the first such films to convey this image was *The Silence of the Lambs*, written by Thomas Harris (in 1988) and later made into a film (in 1990). It was an instant success with the public. Ex-psychiatrist turned serial killer, the incarcerated Hannibal Lecter was so intelligent, sophisticated and insightful that the FBI turned to him for help on their investigation into a series of murders committed by 'Buffalo Bill'. And as Lecter responded with taunts and complex riddles, he became an instant anti-hero, a role-model, provoking admiration from would-be and actual killers.

One such killer was Colin Ireland, who relates an incident which he calls an example of 'Serial Killer Humour'. Since he was imprisoned in 1993 for the murders of five homosexual men, he has apparently spent much of his time segregated from the other prisoners. During one three-month stretch, he says:

> I decided it might be fun to carry out something I labelled 'reinforcing the stereotype'. I had my radio with me and it would be on for most of the day and on it would be a vast collection of music – until I heard the staff approach the door. On hearing them I would leap up and change the station to a classical one. I would be on the bed before the door opened, my book of paper open, and as the door opened I would glance in a superior fashion around the edge of the reading material. 'Yes, officers?' I would enquire in my best Hannibal Lecter cold, distant, but polite tone.

But actually, as journalist Joan Smith noted in the *Independent*, Colin Ireland, is 'a textbook example of the gulf between the sordid reality of serial killing and its representation in popular culture. He certainly isn't the serial killer beloved of popular culture: charismatic, cunning, outwitting the police at every turn.' As Ireland himself admits, the serial killer's image of his own 'importance and infallibility are both flawed as is shown by the offender's position: he's been caught, his intelligence is similarly flawed'.

The serial killer has become one of the most potent symbols of the modern era: the outlaw unafraid to follow the dictates of his own desire, the existential hero who acknowledges no law save that of his own nature, and the super-star celebrity – all things that make him a glamorous rather than a despicable figure. As psychiatrist Dr Abrahamsen remarks, 'the law-abiding citizen may secretly admire the murderer ... because the murderer carries out in reality what the law-abiding citizen only dares to dream about'. And thus we find that, whilst incarcerated, many killers receive hundreds of letters from adoring women, as if they were pop or film stars. Many want just to correspond with or to meet them; some want – and get – more. In America, for instance, Ted Bundy married a woman who had written to him, and impregnated her during one of their visits. Here in Britain, Peter Sutcliffe has received numerous marriage proposals. Dr Glenn Wilson, reader at the Institute of Psychiatry, explains this phenomenon: 'Women see a man who is completely anti-social, living on the fringes of society, who has a high dose of testosterone. He is the kind of male not to be trifled with.' In these killers such women see uncompromising power and masculinity, plus, of course, the chance to bring some new excitement into their own lives, for to touch celebrity is to acquire some of its power.

However unconsciously, we identify with the unrestrained egotism of the killer, who obeys only his own impulses and pursues only his own pleasures. Not all of us, to be sure, are potential serial killers, but we are all, as the Freudian or Christian will agree, fundamentally creatures of desire. We want what we want – call it the Id or original sin – and only slowly learn that we cannot always have it. But there remains a residual part of the self which holds on to the desire for domination, control, and pleasure, at whatever cost, and the adult self is the arena in which these old impulses have to be tempered by guilt or shame, concern for the welfare of others, fear of censure or of the law. It is easy to see how the serial killer can become a figure of admiration and fascination.

But, as Brian Masters, who has written extensively on murder, says, 'fascination with murder is dangerous. It invites a kind of paralysis of the mental and moral faculties, a blind state of wonderment, featureless and useless. It merely soaks up images and sensations which lodge in the mind and threaten to fester.' He denies vehemently that he, and other serious true crime writers, are themselves fascinated with murder. They are merely interested. 'Interest in murder ... is not only legitimate, but essential. If we do not take the trouble to understand how a man may disintegrate to such an extent that he can terminate the life of another, then we are abandoned in a world of random mischief, which is intolerable.' We should be interested in murder as a human, social and behavioural phenomenon. Under what conditions does a human being become a killer? What goes wrong?

Historically there has been a tradition which sees such killers as one-off freaks of nature – anomalies – possessed by evil spirits or demons. The Ripper murders certainly did nothing to dispel this notion. As the killer was never caught, there were some who continued to believe that the murders were committed by some sort of monster, by a being not only inhuman but the Devil incarnate. The Ripper was not prompted by the Devil, he *was* a Devil, a literal Fiend. We see this notion employed in Peter Ackroyd's novel about a serial killer, *Dan Leno and the Limehouse Golem* (1994). Set in London in the 1880s, it chronicles the fear and fascination of a public that believes the killings are done by a golem, or supernatural spirit. However, in two brilliant reversals, the murderer turns out to be the narrator, who is a young woman.

Yet when the serial killer is imagined as a Devil, he is not merely a repellent figure but, however unconsciously, also an attractive one. By the end of the nineteenth century, in a period of increasing secularization of belief, as religious certainties waned and the moral codes associated with them wavered accordingly, the idea of man himself as God or Devil began slowly to replace the old metaphysical structures. It is arguable that the Christian tradition has always had a greater active engagement with the sensual energy of damnation than with the passivity of redemption: the Devil fascinates; angels bore. Milton's Lucifer is, most surely, a fallen angel. Blake tell us he is 'of the Devil's party', actively associated with energy and the pleasures of the flesh, with the creative power latent in that which is hidden or repressed: with Art. And this suggests complex relations between darkness and light, death and life, murder and sexuality.

Contemporary thought, more psychological than metaphysical, now frequently maintains an image of the serial killer as devoid of control and responsibility. He is labelled not as evil but as insane, out of touch with reality, beyond the bounds of reason: a 'madman' or 'psychotic'. The effect is to distance him from the range of normal human possibility: the serial killer is not a person like you, me, or the man on the Clapham omnibus. This is an attractive enough notion, and has common sense to recommend it: most of us are not Fred West, even in our dreams. We may occasionally wish to murder our boyfriends or bank managers, but not to mutilate strangers.

Yet interviews with serial killers, and official reports, usually deny this putative madness. In the last fifty years in England no serial killer has successfully pleaded insanity, or even manslaughter by reason of diminished responsibility. They have, however, tried: John Christie pleaded 'not-guilty-by-reason-of-insanity' (the NGRI defence) arising from supposed mustard-gas poisoning in the war; Peter Sutcliffe pleaded diminished responsibility, based on a diagnosis of paranoid schizophrenia; Dennis Nilsen pleaded diminished responsibility due to an alleged severe personality disorder. These claims, however, were not accepted by the juries, in spite of supporting evidence from psychiatrists, not to mention the compelling common-sense notion that you'd have to be – as Christie's defence put it – 'mad as a March hare' to commit the crimes in the first place.

Partly, and understandably, juries are reluctant to accept pleas of insanity and diminished responsibility as it makes the killer's release back into the community likely to come sooner rather than later. Influenced by the popular image of the serial killer as a highly manipulative individual, juries are afraid that he will simply trick doctors into believing that he is 'cured' and therefore ready to be released. In America this has led to tragedy on several occasions, when killers prematurely released have killed again, even sometimes warning the authorities that they would do so. As ex-FBI Agent John Douglas says, when it comes down to it, 'jurors realize instinctively that these guys are *dangerous'*.

In England we have yet to find an example of a genuinely psychotic serial killer, although Kenneth Erskine – the 'Stockwell Strangler' who killed seven elderly people in London – had the mental age of an eleven-year-old, and was obviously not entirely *compus mentus* as he sat through his trial with a big smile on his face. There have, however, been cases of serial killing in America in which the killer was obviously psychotic. Richard Chase (aka the Vampire Killer) who was operating in Sacramento in 1978, is an example of such a killer. Chase committed four particularly vicious murders which involved the removal of body parts and organs, the drinking of blood, anal rape, and the insertion of animal faeces into the mouth of one victim.

When apprehended and interviewed, it transpired that Chase believed that he was suffering from what he called 'soap-dish poisoning', a disorder which he seems to have invented. As he patiently explained to (now ex) FBI Agent Robert Ressler: every person has a soap-dish and if you lift up the soap and it's dry underneath then you have nothing to worry about. However, if it's 'gooey' underneath then this means you have soap-dish poisoning. This poisoning apparently turns your blood to powder, and in order to compensate for this you need to acquire more blood from other sources. Chase began his cure by injecting himself with rabbits' blood and biting the heads off birds, but soon moved on to human victims to replenish his blood supply.

Yet Chase is a comparatively rare example. Most serial killers do not display psychotic symptoms. Psychotic murderers tend not to develop into serial killers because they are sloppy and careless in their crimes, and thus they are caught before they can kill again.

In order to obtain a more thorough understanding of the serial killer we need to transcend the traditional stereotypes of the evil or insane. But if the serial killer is neither of these, what sort of person is he? What makes him tick? It is satisfying and reassuring, but misleading, if we imagine a grotesque rather than a recognizable person: as Peter Sutcliffe's brother, Carl, said, 'I imagined him [the Yorkshire Ripper] to be an ugly hunchback wi' boils all over his face.' Yet real serial killers almost always turn out not merely to be sane, but, frequently, tolerably likeable and 'normal' people. A friend of the Sutcliffe family called Peter 'the nice, quiet, sensible type', his mother-in-law said 'there is not a kinder man living'; one of the West's lodgers, Terence Davies, said that Fred 'was a nice bloke as far as I was concerned'; Christie, 'always had a smile on his face' according to one of his old army pals; Robert Black, who killed three girls in England in the 1980s, was referred to by his land-lady as 'a big softie'.

Judge Gerald Sparrow, who attended the Moors Murders trial, commented about Brady and Hindley, that 'their appear-ance of ultra-normality was misleading to an almost gruesome degree'. And Robert Wilson, who wrote a book on the case of the Moors Murderers, remembers how at their committal, 'I stared at them, puzzled, there had been some mistake … that isn't Ian Brady. That isn't Myra Hindley. I still don't know what I expected. But I had never expected this, they looked human.'

Not only are they human, but they are our neighbours, our workmates, our acquaintances. Typically, they do not stand out, or distinguish themselves, in any way. They are certainly not Hannibal Lecter. As Dr Elliott Leyton, professor of anthropology and an authority on the subject of murder, says, the Lecter char-acter is simply 'pure baloney'. Dennis Nilsen told his biographer, Brian Masters, 'The Hannibal Lecter character is a fraudulent fiction ... Lecter is invented to titillate the public, not to give any idea of truth.' The serial killer is not a criminal mastermind, intent on playing games with the police, nor is he mad or possessed. He is a man – and, rarely, a woman – who is driven by a deep-seated and unquenchable lust, a lust not only to kill, but to destroy, to mutilate, to eviscerate.

Before we proceed, though, we need to stop to clarify what we mean by the term 'serial killer'. When Jack the Ripper struck in 1888 his crimes seemed inexplicable partly because there was no category into which they (and thus, he) could be placed. Yet even after a hundred years, and many examples, there still remains some controversy as to how a serial killer is defined. The term, after all, was only coined by Robert Ressler in 1978, in response to hearing that the British refer to a *series* of, for example, rapes, burglaries, or muggings, which he thought was a good way to describe the crimes that had previously been called 'stranger murders'. Thus a *series* of murders became *serial* killings. The FBI take five as the minimum number of victims necessary to 'qualify' as a serial killer. In England, however, where cases of serial killing are less common and the individual killers tend to claim fewer lives, we take the defining number of victims as three. This is not to say, however, that anybody who kills three people is a serial killer. A further requirement is that the murders are separated in time by emotional 'cooling-off periods', which can range from days, to weeks, to years.

Given this stipulation, we see that serial killers are different from 'mass murderers', both in their crimes and in their natures. Mass murder involves the killing of several people in the same general area over a short time by one killer. The mass murderer often has little concern about his own death, and is usually killed in a shoot-out with the police, takes his own life, surrenders, or is quickly apprehended. In contrast, the serial killer may continue undetected for years. Psychologically, the mass murderer, whose life has been a constant battle with frustration, failure, rejection and internalized anger, finally cracks. Unlike the serial killer, the mass murderer usually has psychotic symptoms, and is far more likely to be considered insane. Charles Whitman, the 'Tower-Top' killer in Texas in the 1960s, killed sixteen people by shooting indiscriminately from the top of a building, after which he shot himself. When he was autopsied, it was discovered that he had a large brain tumour, making him susceptible to violent outbursts.

A recent example of mass murder in Scotland, was, of course, the Dunblane tragedy in March 1996. Thomas Hamilton arrived at a Stirlingshire primary school with an arsenal sufficient to kill the entire school population: four guns and 743 rounds of ammunition. After having targeted the gymnasium – where young children were getting ready for their PE class – Hamilton proceeded to shoot 105 bullets from his Browning hand-gun, killing sixteen children and one teacher. The last bullet to be fired was the one with which he took his own life.

Serial killers, in contrast, are not motivated by this simple desire to annihilate large numbers of people. Steven A. Egger, ex-homicide investigator and expert in the area of serial killing, has found that serial killing is 'a compulsive act specifically for gratification based on fantasies'. Because of the compulsive nature of such acts, Brian Masters prefers the term *addictive* killer, to that of *serial* killer: the number is beside the point, it is the addiction to killing which is the essence of such crimes. Furthermore, the obsessive fantasies which the serial killer seeks to satisfy are primarily sexual. The FBI have found that almost all cases of serial killing they have investigated were sexual in nature.

This may mean that there was evidence of rape or other sexual activity with the body; that the victim's sexual organs were exposed; that the body was left in a sexually provocative position; that the victim's clothes were arranged in a suggestive manner; that foreign objects were inserted into the body's orifices; or that there was evidence of other substitute sexual activity or sadistic fantasy. In the mind of such killers, sex may take many forms. John Christie had intercourse with his victims after rendering them unconscious or dead; Gordon Frederick Cummins inserted objects into the vaginas of his victims; Peter Sutcliffe mutilated his victims' sex organs; Dennis Nilsen masturbated over his victims' bodies; Jeffery Dahmer had sex with his victims' viscera.

After a murder the serial killer's appetite will be temporarily satisfied, but some time later the urge to kill reasserts itself, intensifies, and the hunt for a new victim commences. The analogy with the build-up and release of sexual desire is obvious.

Thus victims, like sexual partners, will usually be of certain 'types', rather than randomly chosen: Ted Bundy was very specific in his tastes, targeting female university students with long dark hair parted in the middle. Most are not quite so particular: Dennis Nilsen killed young, often homosexual and/or homeless men, Ian Brady and Myra Hindley killed children, Robert Black killed young girls. In each case sexual pleasure and release accompanied or followed the killing. The sad conclusion is inescapable: victims are not *like* sexual partners, they *are* sexual partners.

In order that the cases with which this book deals should be comparable, we will discount those series of killings in which there was no sexual element, and which were not, therefore, committed out of compulsion and for the satisfaction of lust. Take Beverley Allitt, for instance, the nurse who was found guilty of murdering four children in her care in 1991, and of causing grievous bodily harm to nine others by administering potassium to them. There was clearly no sexual motivation for the attacks, and Allitt was diagnosed as suffering from Munchausen syndrome by proxy. Ordinarily, Munchausen syndrome manifests itself in the overwhelming desire for medical attention, and the sufferer enjoys the concern of the doctors and nurses. Munchausen syndrome by proxy sufferers crave similar attention, but contrive to gain it through the medical misfortune of others. A mother who suffers from this syndrome, for example, may harm her child and then relish the attention given to her by the doctors. Allitt would take pleasure from the praise given to her valiant attempts to 'save' the lives of her victims. Sometimes she was successful, sometimes not.

This type of murder now has a category of its own in the FBI *Crime Classification Manual*: the 'hero murder'. Thus, although Allitt killed more than three people, all of whom were of a specific type, with emotional cooling-off periods in between each attempted murder – meaning that she is palpably some sort of serial killer – she is of an entirely different type to those serial killers who murder through an irresistible compulsion which has its roots in sexual desire.

We similarly discount Donald Neilson (the 'Black Panther')

who killed four people during the course of armed robberies in England in 1974 and 1975. His motivation was not the sexual satisfaction that death brings, but monetary gain. Also excluded is John George Haigh (the 'Acid Bath Murderer') who killed five people and then disposed of their bodies in vats of acid in 1949. He killed not, as he told police, out of a desire to drink his victims' blood (attempting to establish a defence of insanity) but rather to get himself out of debt. Although Neilson and Haigh claimed the lives of multiple victims over a period of time, they have an entirely different psychology to that of the serial sex killer. The act of murder did not, in itself, give the killer pleasure, it was merely necessary to secure other ends.

So it is, in fact, serial *sex* killers whom we are investigating. Their murders will usually contain ritualistic elements which link them together, hence the conclusion that the crimes are part of an obvious series. The victims of Jack the Ripper, with their disembowelment and missing organs, had his unique 'signature' on each of their bodies. The concept of the 'signature' was first developed by FBI Agent John Douglas, and is vital in establishing the link in a series of murders. An offender's signature, in Douglas's words, 'is a unique and integral part of the offender's behaviour and goes beyond the actions needed to commit the crime'. He continues, 'Crime scenes reveal peculiar characteristics or unusual offender input that occur while the crime is being committed'. Such characteristics are the offender's 'individualized "calling card"'.

Peter Sutcliffe's signature, for example, was his frenzied mutilations of his victim's body with various weapons including knives, hacksaws and screwdrivers, on or around the chest, abdomen, neck and vagina. He didn't need to perform these mutilations to kill his victims, as they were already dead from blows to the head with a hammer. He needed to inflict the further injuries to satisfy himself. The compulsion to create the same figuration, and the resulting set of visual images, suggests a nightmarish shadowing of the creative process. Much as a painter's canvases are readily identifiable as the work of one artist, the serial killer's victims are clearly the work of one murderer.

The signature of a serial killer is often confused with his *modus operandi*, or MO. An MO, in Douglas's words, is 'the offender's actions while committing the crime ... learned behaviour that is dynamic and malleable. Developed over time, the MO continuously evolves as offenders gain experience and confidence.' Peter Sutcliffe's MO was stalking solitary women late at night in secluded spots, and rendering them unconscious with hammer blows. This behaviour was subject to some flexibility. If the woman was obviously a prostitute he would approach her and she would willingly accompany him to a deserted area. On other occasions he would simply creep up on his victim and attack her from behind. These slight changes in MO, as the offender learns from past behaviour, are entirely to be expected. We would not, however, expect to see any changes in the signature of a series of crimes: all Sutcliffe's murders were accompanied by the slashing of the victim's body. This was the whole point of the killings, it was where the pleasure and satisfaction came to a climax.

Serial sex killings are often divided into two categories: rape-murders and lust-murders. In the case of the former the primary motivation of the killer is conventional sexual gratification: he rapes the victim and then kills to avoid identification. The killing is purely a matter of utility. The rapist who kills rarely reports sexual gratification from the actual act of killing, and does not perform sexual acts post-mortem. In comparison, the lust-murderer – the type of serial killer with whom we will be concerned – takes sexual pleasure in the *act of killing itself*. Magnus Hirschfield is quoted in Dr Edward Podolsky's article 'The Lust Murderer',

> In genuine cases of sexual murder the killing replaces the sexual act. There is, therefore, no sexual intercourse at all, and sexual pleasure is induced by cutting, stabbing and slashing the victim's body, ripping open her abdomen, plunging the hands into the intestines, cutting out and taking away her genitals, throttling her, sucking her blood. These horrors ... constitutes, so to speak, pathological equivalents of coitus.

The typical lust-murderer kills as a result of recurring compulsions and overwhelming sexual desire, which are temporarily sated by the murder but soon build up again, until he can no longer control himself and must seek another victim. As the 'mentalist' Richard von Krafft-Ebing – who wrote *Psychopathia Sexualis*, the first comprehensive study of sexual perversions in the nineteenth century – said of Jack the Ripper, 'He does not seem to have had sexual intercourse with his victims, but very likely the murderous acts and subsequent mutilation of the corpse were equivalents for the sexual act.'

The term 'lust-murderer' can be further refined into those who are sadistic and those who are not. The sadistic lust-murderer is the killer who becomes sexually excited by another person's suffering. Acts of sexual sadism may include torture – utilizing hammers, pliers, or electric cattle-prods – and repeated stabbing or cutting of the victim, especially of the sex organs. The killer may suck or lick the wounds, bite the victim's flesh or drink their blood. He may even mutilate while the victim is still alive. During these activities he may have an erection or even ejaculate. As one offender said to the FBI, 'she was writhering [sic] in pain and I loved it ... I was alive for the sole purpose of causing pain and receiving sexual gratification ... I was relishing the pain just as much as the sex.' It is not the infliction of pain itself that arouses the killer. Seeing his victim suffer is what excites him – which is why these acts take place pre- rather than post-mortem.

Peter Sutcliffe, Dennis Nilsen and John Christie were not sexual sadists, as their victims were always unconscious or dead when any sexual or violent acts were carried out on them. Colin Ireland, however, tortured one of his victims with a cigarette lighter, which he held to his testicles; and Fred and Rose West were two of the most extreme sexual sadists we may ever encounter. We will never know the exact details of their crimes, but from the evidence available it seems that some of their victims were kept alive for days in their cellar, being subjected to all kind of sexual tortures – possibly including the mutilation and removal of body parts – before they were killed or died from their injuries.

How is it, we wonder, that people with friends and family, frequently liked by those who know them, can commit such unspeakable acts? As always, the darker side of human nature repels, fascinates, and confuses us. It is hard enough to assimilate the notion that some people will kill for gain, or revenge, or to further their political ideals, but at least they have their motives. But serial killers are frequently described as 'motiveless', a term found throughout the literature on serial killing. Yet this seems not just unlikely, but philosophically inconceivable. As the criminologist Edmond Locard said, 'All punishable acts – in fact, all acts – have their cause.' Which is to suggest nothing can, in principle, be motiveless. One thinks, in this context, of Coleridge's description of the 'motiveless malignity' of Iago, which is intended to suggest a presence of pure evil, operating not for profit, but out of the very groundwork of a fallen nature. This is, of course, a misdescription of Iago; just as the term 'motiveless' is a misdescription of the inward world of the serial killer.

This point can be clarified if we think for a moment about rapists. The motives of the rapist combine the desire to pursue sexual satisfaction, and to dominate. Roy Hazlewood, the FBI's leading expert on rape, once dealt with a rapist who acknowledged that the actual act of rape was the least enjoyable part of the crime. He professed that it was the sense of control over his victim that really excited him. Similarly, when Roy Norris and Lawrence Bittaker were apprehended in California for the rape, torture and murder of five teenage girls in 1979, Norris said that 'the rape wasn't really the important part, it was the dominance'.

Rape is not motiveless, and an analogy with the motives of the rapist, rather than those of the traditional killer, helps us to understand how, and why, serial killing is an intensely, indeed overwhelmingly, motivated set of acts. To say that most serial killings are sex crimes, is not to say that sexual desire itself is the primary force which drives the murderer. Robert Berdella, who killed six men in Missouri between 1984 and 1987, said that he wanted to reduce his victims 'to the level of, say, a blow-up doll or clay figure you would make as a kid: moving [them] around, having complete control.' It is now widely recognized, in both academic and law enforcement circles, that serial killing is not about sex *per se* but rather about what it can represent: a means of power and control. As James Fox and Jack Levin, authorities on multiple murder, say, 'Domination unmitigated by guilt is a crucial element in serial crimes with a sexual theme ... the pleasure and exhilaration that the serial killer derives from repeated murder stem from absolute control over other human beings.' The sexual acts are thus a vehicle for the murderer to satisfy other, non-sexual needs, like the desire for dominance and the expression of rage or contempt.

That we so often encounter the term 'motiveless' in the literature of serial killing is thus some indication of the incomprehension of the onlooker, and his need to suggest, however implicitly, the presence of evil. And in the presence of evil, no motivations are traditionally further required.

Analysing serial sex killers, and understanding their motives, must involve some detailed examination of their crimes, however horrifying this may seem. But there is nothing gratuitous or sensational in such close focus. As John Douglas says: to understand a painter you must look at his work; to understand a serial killer you must look at his. And in order to understand why a person has acted as he has, we have to understand who he is, and how he came to be so. An exploration and comparison of the childhoods and upbringings of British serial sex killers will enable us to ask: are there any set of patterns or similarities which prevail in the backgrounds of serial killers generally?

A child, we must assume, is born an innocent, not a potential serial killer. As we shall see, serial killers are made, shaped (like us all) by their backgrounds and formative experiences. Far too little has been written about the childhoods of serial killers. Transfixed by what they have done, rather than by why they did it, we fail to come to any adequate understanding of this phenomenon. Obsessed as we are by the image of the serial killer as 'monster', we are in danger of neglecting the information that might help us to a clearer understanding of the phenomenon that is serial killing. What happened to the child who becomes a serial killer?

This book, then, will ask, and try to answer, the essential

questions: What do we know about serial sex killing? Who were Britain's twentieth-century serial sex killers? What kinds of crimes did they commit? What is known about their formative experiences? And what conclusions can be drawn, what comparisons made, in the light of this analysis? Can we arrive at some general description of the kind of childhood that may produce a serial killer?

To examine the lives and crimes of individual serial killers, however, we need to be aware of the context in which their crimes happen, are investigated, and analysed. Thus we must begin with some awareness of the scope and nature of the problem, not only in Britain but, particularly, in the United States, in which serial killing has occurred more frequently, and been more assiduously studied. Serial killing doesn't happen in a vacuum, and newspaper accounts of it are likely, as we have noted, to distort and to sensationalize. So we need accurate information – to move from image to reality – and a broad canvas against which to assess it. Otherwise, by merely focusing on individual cases, we are likely to fall into the trap of regarding each killer merely as a psychological case study, without reference to the wider social and criminological context, which will be the topic of Chapter 2.

2

SERIAL KILLING: THE WIDER CONTEXT

In January 1987 the beaten and asphyxiated body of Marina Monti, a twenty-seven-year-old prostitute, was found on a patch of wasteland in London; in February 1991 Janine Downes, a twenty-two-year-old prostitute, was strangled and her naked body dumped in a hedge near Wolverhampton; in July 1992 Rachel Nickell, a twenty-three-year-old woman walking on Wimbledon Common with her little boy, was stabbed to death; in 1993 the body of sixteen-year-old Clare Taltman, who had been beaten and sexually assaulted, was found in Kent; in August 1994, twenty-three-year-old Julie Finley's body was found naked in a field in Liverpool; in the summer of 1995, thirty-year-old Vicki Thompson was beaten and hacked to death in Oxfordshire.

Each of these murders generated an immense man-hunt, but in every case the killer went undetected. All of the cases bore the hallmarks of murders committed for sexual satisfaction, and there is no reason to suppose that such killers should necessarily restrict themselves to one offence. In fact, there is every reason to suppose the opposite. Sexually motivated murder is committed for gratification. When the murderer has satisfied himself and then escaped detection, what process of restraint is likely to inhibit him from killing again? His desire will inevitably return and increase, the fantasies of past satisfaction will recur and demand re-enactment. There are evidently sex murderers who have avoided apprehension, but how many? And how many of them have killed more than once? Is it not possible – indeed, likely – that the same individual might be responsible for a number of these unsolved murders? Might it be that there are serial killers operating unknown to public and police alike?

In 1996 Operation Enigma was set up by the English police to study this problem, and to collate and analyse the data pertaining to unsolved sexual murder going back ten years. Operation Enigma is a study of over 200 unsolved cases of rape and murder of 'vulnerable' women, including prostitutes and drug-addicts, exploring possible links between the cases. Based at the National Crime Faculty in Bramshill, Hampshire, experienced police detectives, forensic scientists, fingerprint experts and statisticians are studying the data from unsolved cases, using computers to cross-reference information such as fingerprints, *modus operandi* and photofits. After Operation Enigma has been completed, the plan is to establish a national centre to investigate such crimes in Britain. The Serious Crime Bureau, with a staff of some twenty-six people, and an annual budget of £1.7m, will investigate not only murders and rapes of women, but also those of children, as well as cases of abduction where there is a sexual element, murders of homosexual men and, in the future, all cases of murder. In addition to linking possible serial cases, the Bureau will offer assistance to local police forces who are investigating any of these crimes.

How grave is the problem that the Serious Crime Bureau will address? Are instances of sexual and serial murder, indeed of murder in general, on the rise? The tabloids thrive on provocative headlines and articles chronicling the rise of murder and violent crime, the unsafe streets on which we live, the sex fiends lurking on our street corners. Yet according to Dr Elliott Leyton, murder in England and Wales is still so low as to be considered 'a statistical aberration'. 'The English', he says, 'have an antipathy to murder which borders on eccentricity. It is one of the great cultural oddities of the modern age.' For instance, in England and Wales in 1996 the murder rate was 1.3 people per 100,000 population. In contrast, in the same year Italy had a rate of 1.8, Austria and Sweden of 2.2, Scotland of 2.6, Switzerland of 2.8, Portugal of 3.9, and America of 7.4. In modern times England and Wales (along with Japan, the Republic of Ireland and Belgium) consistently has one of the lowest murder rates in the world.

Yet low as the murder rate may be in comparison with other

countries, murder in England and Wales is undoubtedly on the increase. Over the past thirty years the murder rate has been rising steadily, whereas before this it had been in decline since as far back as the thirteenth century. In 1968 there were 360 deaths recorded by the police as murder, in 1978 there were 471, in 1988 there were 560, and in 1996 there were 681. Thus in 1996 almost twice as many people were murdered as there were thirty years previously.

Furthermore, recent research suggests that the murder rate would be significantly higher each year than it is at present were it not for the quality of modern medicine, and its capacity to save lives that would previously have been lost. According to an article in the *Independent*, in the last twenty years attempted murders have quadrupled, and woundings to endanger life have risen by three-quarters. As Professor Bernard Knight, a leading Home Office pathologist, remarks: 'The murder rate is artificially low now. People say that there were more murders in the old days, but the woundings that happen now would have been murders then.' Dr Lance Workman, a psychologist at the University of Glamorgan, adds, 'our murder rates could quite easily be threefold if doctors were not saving so many people', although of course, as Professor Knight notes, 'there is no way of quantifying it'.

The overwhelming majority of murders are committed by an acquaintance, partner or relative of the victim. In the typical murder a working-class man kills a person he knows in a fit of jealousy, rage, or provocation, most often with a knife. This type of murder accounts for around three-quarters of homicides every year. The remaining quarter are 'stranger murders' – the murder of a person previously unknown to the perpetrator. Interestingly, since the 1970s the murder of strangers seems to have been rising *disproportionately* to other categories of victim. For example, the total number of murders committed in 1990 was six per cent higher than in 1982, whereas the total number of stranger murders in 1990 was forty-five per cent higher than in 1982.

Almost all stranger murders are committed by men who have become involved in a fight, often in a street or a pub, fuelled by alcohol or drugs. Despite the lurid headlines, the sexual assault and murder of a vulnerable woman who has been snatched off the street by a man she doesn't know, is scarce. As a recent report in the *Independent* says: 'Detailed analysis of crime statistics ... reveals that far from being a country over-run by serial killers who strike for no reason and are never caught, most suspects were known to their victims and the majority are jailed.'

Unfortunately there are no official statistics to consult regarding the number of serial killings committed annually. My own analysis of the phenomenon, however, has shown that while serial killing is certainly extremely rare, in the post-war era it seems to have been escalating. In the 1940s two serial killers were operating: Gordon Frederick Cummins and John Reginald Halliday Christie. Between them they claimed the lives of seven victims, four and three women respectively. In the 1950s Christie was still at large, and murdered a further four women before his capture. In the 1960s three serial killers were active: working as a pair, Myra Hindley and Ian Brady killed five children, while Fred West claimed his first victim. Then, in the 1970s, there was a huge increase in the number of victims. Fred West, now with the aid of his partner Rose, killed ten women, while Peter Sutcliffe killed eleven, and Dennis Nilsen murdered two men: a total of twenty-three people. In the 1980s the figures continued to rise, as thirty-three people were victims of eight killers. Peter Sutcliffe killed two more women, Fred and Rose West killed their daughter, Dennis Nilsen murdered a further thirteen young men, Kenneth Erskine claimed the lives of seven elderly people, Robert Black killed three little girls, John Duffy murdered three women, and Michael Lupo killed four men.

Thus far in the 1990s the figures seem to have dropped again, with two killers – Colin Ireland and Peter Moore – claiming nine lives. Interestingly, all their victims were male. On average British serial killers are active for six years, though the Wests managed to escape detection for some thirty years. Therefore it is likely that there have been cases of serial murder in the 1990s that have not yet been officially recognized – the premise upon which Operation Enigma was founded.

Although serial killing has obviously been rising in England and Wales in recent times, looking at serial killing in America puts the problem in perspective. Recent expert opinions differ significantly as to the scale of the problem, estimating that there might be anything between thirty and 500 serial killers at large in America at any one time. The most pessimistic figures suggest that such killers might claim as many as 3,500 to 5,000 victims a year, although 200 is the conservative estimate.

When a man murders his wife or somebody in a pub, he rarely escapes detection. He has killed spontaneously in a fit of rage, which means that there are likely to be witnesses or that he will feel remorse once the anger has abated, and turn himself in to the police. But when he picks a random stranger on a deserted street and sexually assaults and murders her, his chances of escaping increase substantially. Clear-up rates for this type of murder are notoriously poor: the crime lacks an obvious motive, and traditional methods of forensic detection are unlikely to be sufficient. There is obviously the need for a national resource centre to provide specialist help. In time, this will be the job of the Serious Crime Bureau.

The Bureau's work will need to be based on the use of information and methods borrowed from overseas, particularly from America where serious research into serial killing has been pursued for decades. The escalating murder rate in England and Wales in the 1970s followed an international trend which saw the world-wide rise of murder. America was certainly no exception, for there the number of violent crimes being committed had reached gargantuan proportions by the end of the 1970s. Over 20,000 people were being murdered every year, and in 1980 some 23,000 murders were committed – more than sixty-three people a day – approximately double the figure of twenty years before. As Robert O. Heck, a Justice Department official, said: 'Something's going on out there. It's an epidemic.' In contrast, England and Wales had just 549 murders in 1980, making the American murder rate eight or nine times greater, taking into account the difference in population sizes.

We can only speculate why it should be that America has such a proportionately greater problem with murder than England and Wales, and indeed than any other industrial society. The answer must surely lie in the differences in culture between countries. This is particularly evident when we consider the attitudes to, and the increasing desensitization towards, violence in America. It might indeed be claimed that it is a country founded on the necessity of violence: in the ruthless overcoming of nature, the staking out of territory, the subjugation of both the indigenous Indians and the imported Africans, violence was a constant in the forming of the new land. The right to bear arms is specifically protected by the Constitution, and is so deeply rooted in the American psyche that when President Clinton recently supported the Brady Bill, which established a short period of time between applying to buy a gun and being supplied with it, he was widely attacked as being un-American. Given the ease with which arms are available, and how much easier it is to remain anonymous, due to the size of the country and to jurisdictional considerations, it is no surprise that serial killers have taken to the USA like ducks to water.

Unfortunately no reliable or exact figures concerning serial killing in the 1970s can be cited, as at the time there was no national resource centre which stored and linked data regarding all violent crimes occurring in America. However, even by just looking at the cases of serial killing that were emerging in the press, it was obvious that it was becoming an increasingly worrying problem. In that decade, some of the most notorious cases in America included that of Ed Kemper, who killed ten people, including his mother whom he decapitated; the Hillside Stranglers, Angelo Buono and Kenneth Bianchi, who raped and killed twelve women and dumped their bodies on Los Angeles hillsides in 1977 and 1978; Robert Hansen, who raped, tortured and killed seventeen women in Alaska over a period of ten years; Paul John Knowles who killed eighteen victims in just over four months of 1974, with no discrimination between age and sex, in different states and by different methods; Dean Corll who killed and sexually abused at least twenty-seven young men in Texas between 1970 and 1973; Ted Bundy who killed at least thirty young women, many of them students, in several different states between 1973 and 1978; and John Wayne Gacy who tortured and killed thirty-three young men and buried them under his house in Iowa, between 1972 and 1978.

There was clearly a new sort of problem, requiring a new sort of solution. The problem with serial killing seemed to be two-fold. First, the police frequently didn't realize that a serial killer was operating, due to a phenomenon which criminologist Steven A. Egger has called 'linkage blindness'. Second, even when it had been established that a serial killer was at work, it was a difficult crime to solve by conventional methods of foren-sic detection.

Establishing that a serial killer was active was often problem-atic due to the mobility of the offender in a country as large as America. In the most complex cases, murders with identical sexual or ritualistic features were occurring in different cities or states, and the local police departments were unaware that their particular murder was part of a series. Thus they would all be pursuing separate investigations, hence the term 'linkage blind-ness'. (Ted Bundy, for instance, killed his victims over five different states, from Washington to Florida.) It would only have come to light that a serial killer was at work through links being made in newspapers, or by particularly diligent detectives look-ing at murders in other areas. This is not a matter of mere methodological sloppiness: during the wasted time, the victim count could have continued to rise. Local police needed a way in which they could establish whether the murder they were inves-tigating had similar features to any other murders that had occurred elsewhere, in order that the investigations could be combined.

There was clearly a pressing need for a national resource centre, available to all law enforcement agencies, to link, sort, analyse and advise upon all violent crime. As early as the 1950s Pierce Brooks, then a Los Angeles Police Department homicide detective, had seen the problem and proposed a system which linked all the police departments in the state of California by computer. He had evolved this idea while working on the case of the serial killer Harvey Glatman in the mid-1950s. Brooks was convinced that Glatman was responsible for more than the two murders which had been officially attributed to him, so he manually went through police records and newspaper reports in all the surrounding areas. Brooks's efficiency eventually paid off and he was able to link other murders to Glatman, who was apprehended and executed. Brooks realized that a lot of time, effort, and probably lives, could have been saved if there had been inter-departmental computer linkage. The state of California turned down his proposal for such a system, however, due to the huge expense which the project would have entailed, as computers were a relatively new, and very costly, tool.

However Brooks never abandoned the idea, and in the early 1980s he finally obtained a modest grant to study the feasibility of establishing a data-base linking the entire country. Synchronistically, at about the same time the FBI's Behavioural Science Unit (BSU) had been asked by the Attorney General's Task Force on Violent Crime to submit a report outlining what could be done about the increase of stranger murder. The parties met and made plans to establish a National Centre for the Analysis of Violent Crime (NCAVC) which would be run by the FBI's BSU. In 1984 NCAVC began as a pilot project, its primary aim being the 'identity and tracking of repeat killers'.

NCAVC runs four main programmes: research and develop-ment, training, profiling and consultation, and the Violent Criminal Apprehension Programme. VICAP is a nation-wide data information centre which collates information concerning violent crimes from all over the country. It deals specifically with unsolved and solved murders that involve abduction, are random, motiveless, sexual or serial in nature; and unidentified bodies and missing persons where murder is suspected. When confronted with particularly unusual, vicious, sexual or serial crimes, law enforcement officers are encouraged to submit the details of the case to VICAP.

A ten-section questionnaire asks for information about the victim, the offender, the condition of the body when found, the cause of death, forensic evidence, the vehicle used (if any), and details of any related cases. The information is then fed into the computer, which checks the MO of the offender against the MO in all other cases of murder to be found in the system. If the computer establishes links to other cases, the VICAP analysts then decide whether the same offender is likely to be responsi-ble. If they believe this to be the case, the different police departments are put in touch with one another in order that they can co-ordinate their investigations.

Of course it is one thing to know that a new serial killer is on the loose, and entirely another to find him. This brings us to our second problem. In the late 1970s and early 1980s the police lacked experience when it came to dealing with serial killers. Not enough was known about them, and the investigative methods open to law enforcement officers were insufficiently sophisticated. How do you locate a transient killer who has murdered a stranger? What tools do you have at your disposal?

Perhaps the most important step in the history of the identification of criminals was made by Alphonse Bertillon, in the 1880s, in a technique which became known as Bertillonage. His system of criminal classification was based upon taking body measurements of those placed under arrest – including height, length and width of head, ring finger, middle finger, forearm, right ear and left foot – which were recorded at the police station. As no two people have exactly the same sets of measurements, Bertillon's system allowed the police to check whether the criminal had committed any previous crimes. The popularity of Bertillonage in the 1880s, however, soon gave way to the more efficient system of fingerprinting in the 1890s, when it was recognized that no two persons' fingerprints are the same. Fingerprinting allowed for the identification of unknown suspects from prints left at crime scenes (providing, of course, that the offender had previously been fingerprinted). When, in the early twentieth century, a system of blood typing was developed, the tools of detection at the investigator's disposal must have seemed extensive indeed.

Such advances in forensic detection were, and still are, invaluable in aiding the police in the identification of criminals of the more mundane variety: a fingerprint left by a drunk and careless burglar who has made off with the family silver; the blood which a suspect claims to be from a rabbit not only turns out to be human, but of the same type as that of a victim of an assault earlier in the day. But with serial sex killing, these advances often seem useless. The serial killer is rarely caught by a fingerprint or a bloodstain, or even, since the development of genetic fingerprinting in 1984, by analysis of semen or other bodily fluids. He is too careful, too methodical, too anxious to keep killing. In England, the Railway Killer, John Duffy, went to the lengths of using burning tissues to eliminate semen traces; Colin Ireland disposed of any half-eaten food, knowing that dental impressions could be taken from its remains.

Furthermore, even in cases where the serial killer has not been as diligent as he should and has left traces of himself at the scene, the police do not usually know who to test the evidence against. They may have a lock of the offender's hair or a smear of his blood, but as the victim almost certainly wasn't known to the killer prior to being murdered, there is no point of comparison. Thus the police are occasionally forced to genetically test everyone – or all possible males – in an entire vicinity or village. It cannot be long, one suspects, before advocates of National Identity Cards will wish them to include relevant genetic information.

Forensic evidence may later confirm that the right suspect has been apprehended, but it is not often crucial to his capture. In fact, much of the identification and apprehension of serial killers is based on a good dose of luck, though luck comes most frequently to those who work hardest. Sometimes routine policing leads to unexpected rewards. Peter Sutcliffe, for instance, was caught with a prostitute in a car upon which he had attached false number plates, and when he was taken to the station he soon confessed to the series of murders. Similarly, Joe Rifkin, of Long Island, New York, was pulled over by police because he had a missing number plate; the body of his seventeenth victim was in the back of his van.

Luck is not an investigative tool, however, and it slowly became clear that locating a suspect was more likely to be a matter of psychological rather than of physical analysis. If forensic evidence was unlikely to identify a serial killer, might it be possible to narrow down the field of suspects by postulating the *sort* of individual who could have committed such a crime? The Sherlock Holmes archetype who deals primarily with material clues and traditional deductive techniques, has gradually been replaced by the psychological detective: the offender profiler, whose subject is the mind of the serial killer.

Working from the premise that the killer leaves behind him, at the crime scene, traces of his character in the form of his behaviour, the profiler builds up a description of the *type* of person who could commit a given crime. The first principle of detective work, as Edmond Locard said, is that 'Every contact leaves a trace'. He may have been speaking forensically, of physical traces, yet this applies equally, as Professor David Canter says in his book *Criminal Shadows*, to psychological traces: the offender leaves his shadow behind him. In this respect, killers are no different from the rest of us. We fill the world with traces and imprints of our personalities: with unkempt gardens or polished cars, collections of art or of garden gnomes. You can tell a lot about a person from how he manifests himself. Serial killers do so in their crimes. The job of the profile is thus to work backwards, from effects to causes, attempting to establish the typology that would characteristically be associated with a certain pattern of behaviour.

The first successful profile was compiled by Dr James Brussel in the mid-1950s, and has by now reached legendary status in police and psychiatric circles. Brussel's profile of George Metesky – the 'Mad Bomber' of New York – astounded police by its accuracy. He even correctly predicted that the perpetrator would be wearing a *buttoned-up* double-breasted suit when apprehended. But despite this success, offender profiling did not really emerge as an investigative tool in America until 1974, when the first 'official' profile administered by the FBI helped to identify the murderer of a seven-year-old girl named Susan Jaeger. The perpetrator – David Meirhoffer – committed suicide in his cell before he could be brought to trial, but the evidence against him was overwhelming.

From the 1950s to the 1970s the FBI had slowly been refining the art of profiling, moving the emphasis from catching individuals, which involved heavy reliance upon psychiatric reports and conjecture (as performed so successfully by Dr Brussel), to a more scientific and objective technique whereby the crime scene was used as the keystone of the profile, which aimed at identifying the *type* of individual who might be responsible for the offence. In this way police detectives, rather than psychiatrists, could construct the profiles, which would deal less with the perpetrators' psychological condition and more with tangible qualities – his race, age, likely employment, domicillary area, and so on. Dr Brussel, for instance, had conjectured in his profile of the 'Mad Bomber' that since the offender's written *Ws* were flowing with pointed tips (thus representing the female breast), and since some of his bombs were placed in holes cut from cinema seats (which Brussel claimed, somewhat obscurely, were again suggestive of the female anatomy), he might thus have some kind of sexual difficulty which was the cause of his behaviour. Such psychoanalytic speculation would not be found in a profile today.

How is an offender profile constructed? This is a complex question, because there is no set pattern to follow, though a general method is common to most cases. The profiler begins by collating all the information available to him concerning the crime. He looks at the body, the crime scene, police reports, autopsy reports, forensic evidence, and crime scene photographs. He then works this information into a profile of what type of person could have committed such a crime by asking himself the right kinds of questions. Such questions will inevitably include the following:

The victim, pre-mortem:
- What *type* of person was the victim? A professional person? a prostitute? a homosexual? a child?
- Who was the victim specifically? What was their age, physical appearance, habits, job, daily routine? Who were their friends and family?
- What did they do on the day of the murder? By whom were they last seen, and where?
- Was the victim a high or low risk one? That is, were they in a location which made them vulnerable? Did their occupation make them more open to attack?

The victim, post-mortem:
- *How* did the victim die? What was the ultimate cause of death?

- What other injuries or wounds were found?
- Was there any evidence of torture?
- Was the victim raped, or subjected to any other kind of sexual activity or acts of sexual substitution? Were these before or after death?
- Were any restraints used to control the victim?
- In what position was the body left? Was it covered up? naked? on display? hidden?

Time scale and locations:
- When and where was the victim abducted or last seen alive?
- Was the victim killed straight after abduction, or kept alive for some time before death, and if so, for how long? and where?
- When and where was the victim's body finally disposed of? Was it kept for any time after death? Where and how was it kept and treated?

The crime scene:
- What forensic evidence was left at the crime scene? Were there, for instance, any finger or foot prints, blood, semen, hair, fibres, or weapons?
- Did the killer take anything from the crime scene or victim?
- Was the crime scene where the victim was actually killed?
- What overall impression was given by the crime scene? Was it in disarray or was it neat?
- Did the scene show evidence of ritualistic traits or compulsive behaviour?

Armed with the answers to the above kinds of questions, the profiler is now in a position to make an important distinction between two types of serial offender. In extensive studies of crime scenes and offenders the FBI have come to distinguish between those killers who are *organized* and those who are *disorganized*, and to recognize the different crime scenes produced by each personality type. Of course, these are not rigid categories (how much easier it would be if they were), as some crime scenes display mixed characteristics, though this too tells us something about the offender's personality.

Let us suppose that we are faced with a serial killer whose crimes have some or all of the following characteristics: (1) the victims were strangers to the killer, and were all of a certain type, perhaps blondes or prostitutes; (2) the victims were not abducted by brute force, but were lured by their killer by conversation, or were tricked into helping him; (3) constraints were used to control the victims; (4) there was evidence of compulsive rituals at the crime scenes; (5) the murder weapon was brought to, and taken from, the scenes; (6) a minimal amount of forensic evidence was left; (7) violent and/or sexual acts took place prior to death; (8) the victims' bodies were moved after the murders; (9) there was some attempt to hide the bodies; and (10) the scenes themselves had some semblance of control and order.

This type of crime scene is typical of the sort of killer that the FBI have classified as *organized*. The organized killer's crime scene – with its obvious methodical planning – reflects a highly orderly personality. This kind of serial killer, it has been found, is likely to be of average or higher than average intelligence. He is socially and sexually confident, and often lives with a spouse or girlfriend. He has his own transport, which is usually a car that is kept in good condition. Often the eldest child, he had a father in stable work, but was subjected to inconsistent discipline in his early years. Before the killing there will be evidence of some sort of emotional or situational trigger; during the crime the murderer is controlled and calm; afterwards he will read press accounts of his murder.

In contrast, the disorganized offender's crime scene shows evidence of frenzy and lacks orderliness, reflecting his less controlled personality. The crimes of a disorganized killer might look like this: (1) the victims were known to the killer, and were killed spontaneously; (2) there was little conversation between killer and victim; (3) the victims were captured by the killer in an act of sudden violence, with no need for restraints; (4) the victims were subjected to aggressive or sexual acts after death; (5) the bodies of the victims were left where they were killed; (6) there was no attempt to hide the bodies; (7) the weapon was one of opportunity, found, and left, at the scenes; (8) the crime scenes looked disordered, as if the killings were the result of random impulse, sudden rage or frenzy.

There is nothing planned about such attacks. Experience shows that such a killer is usually a socially inept person who lives close to the crime scenes, alone or with his family. He is likely to be sexually inexperienced and inadequate, and of below average intelligence. He will have older brothers and/or sisters, and will have been harshly disciplined as a child, most likely by a father who was in and out of work. Unlike the organized killer, he is likely to be unemployed. He will have been in a confused, anxious and distressed state at the time of his crimes, and will take no interest in accounts of them afterwards.

From the crime scene the profiler may be able to make suggestions to the police about some or all of the following factors: physical characteristics of the offender, age, race, appearance/grooming, employment, marital status, habits, IQ, school/college performance, demeanour, life-style, where the offender lives in relation to the crime scene, how the offender interacts with other people, pre- and post-offence behaviour. To do this the profiler calls upon his experience in similar cases, on research studies, on recognized statistics, and on intuition. Although a computer programme – PROFILER – has been developed that can produce a profile of what John Douglas calls the UNSUB (unknown subject) when supplied with relevant data, this will never take over from the skilled human profilers, as much profiling is based on intuition grounded in years of experience. There is no check-list – which Robert Ressler says he has been asked for – which exactly matches certain crime-scene characteristics with particular character traits, so we must try to grasp how a profile is constructed by looking at an example of how the idea works in practice.

In recent years, South Africa has produced some of the most prolific serial killers. Since 1994 alone the country has contended with the 'Hammer and Wemmer Pan Murderer' who is believed to have killed forty people; the 'Phoenix Killer' who claimed twenty-two lives; the 'Kranskop Killer' who murdered five people; the 'Donnybrook Killer' who claimed eighteen victims;

and the 'Cape Town Strangler' who killed nineteen boys.

Between May 1994 and October 1995 there was a serial killer operating who claimed approximately forty victims. The killings were soon dubbed the 'ABC Murders' by the press, the letters corresponding to the different areas in which the bodies had been found – Atteridgeville, Boksburg and Cleveland. The victims were all black women, mostly aged in their twenties and thirties. Some of these women went missing on their journeys to work, but most were unemployed and were abducted while searching for jobs. The victims seemed to vanish without trace: there were no witnesses to the abductions and no evidence of any struggle. Although in every case the woman was raped and then strangled, the crimes became more elaborate as they progressed. The earlier victims were manually strangled, later ones were strangled using their own underwear or a handbag strap, and in the last cases a garrotte was used, fashioned out of the victim's clothing and a stick or pen. If the victim had been strangled with her underwear she would be left at least partially naked; if she had been strangled with her handbag strap or a garrotte she would be left clothed.

The dumping sites were over three general areas, all of which were remote: a field, an industrial mine area, or some disused land. In the earlier cases it seemed that the killer had murdered his victim before transporting her to the dump-site; in later cases the evidence suggested that the killer took his victim to the site while she was still alive, possibly to show her the undiscovered bodies of previous victims. After the murder, the killer would often take some of his victim's clothing and personal items away with him, as trophies or perhaps to delay identification. There was evidence to suggest that the killer returned to the sites, probably to masturbate over the memories of his crimes.

In response to the extraordinary pace at which the killer was working, the South African police quickly put together a task force. One of the key figures in the investigation was Micki Pistorius, who had been recruited by the police in 1994 while she was doing her doctorate in psychology, examining how psychoanalysis can aid in the understanding of serial killers. That year she successfully profiled the Cape Town 'Station

Strangler' (Norman Simons) who claimed twenty-two victims. Pistorius is now a senior superintendent, the equivalent to a 'colonel' under the military rankings which the South African police have recently dispensed with. Pistorius herself drew up a preliminary profile of the perpetrator of the ABC Murders – the 'Atteridgeville Strangler' – and she also persuaded her superiors to call in a more experienced profiler. Since leaving the FBI, Robert Ressler has continued to draw up profiles of serial offenders for police departments all over the world and, working closely with Pistorius, Ressler compiled a profile of the type of person that would be responsible for the ABC Murders:

1) The killer – or possibly killers, given the rate of the murders – would be a black man in his late twenties to early thirties, said Ressler. Experience has shown that serial sex killings are almost exclusively committed by men, and are nearly always intraracial: white on white, black on black. In postulating the age of the offender, profilers usually take twenty-five as a starting point, as statistics show that serial killers commit their first murder between the age of twenty-five and thirty. They then add or subtract years from this figure depending upon the kind of 'experience' reflected in the crime. As the experience seemed to be considerable in this case, the killer was placed at the older end of the spectrum.

2) Ressler further predicted that the offender was likely to be local to the area which encompassed the dumping sites. He seemed sure that he would not be interrupted while assaulting his victims or leaving their bodies, which implied that he knew the area well. Perhaps he had grown up there, or visited frequently for some other reason, such as his work. As the times that his victims were abducted varied, he was unlikely to be in a job with conventional hours where his absences would be missed. He would, however, probably be working as he was obviously intelligent, which was attested by the methodical planning and execution of his crimes. He might, therefore, be self-employed, able to keep to his own hours.

3) Because there had been no signs of an abduction or a

struggle in any of the cases, and as the victims were often unemployed and looking for work, it was possible that the killer had lured them into his car with offers of employment. If this was the case, Ressler postulated that the killer would be upper middle class, sophisticated, socially confident, plausible, financially well-off, and well dressed.

4) The ease with which he abducted his victims implied a confidence around women, so he was likely to be either married or divorced, Ressler said. The extent of his sexual assaults suggested that he would have a high sex drive, and would utilize pornography which had aggressive themes. He would see woman as objects to be used as he wanted, and his victims would be symbolic of a woman in his life who he believed had wronged him in some way.

5) Furthermore, the killer would be manipulative, confident and arrogant. The bodies were dumped close to one another, and in Boksburg he even left his victims beside the prison: he was taunting the police, who he believed could not catch him. Furthermore, the bodies were openly displayed, not hidden: they were meant to be found, and perhaps to elicit shock. The killer was also thought to have telephoned two of his victims' families after their deaths, and he later made contact with a newspaper. He was thriving off the publicity which he had created for himself; he would almost certainly follow his crimes closely in the press.

6) The relative lack of forensic evidence at the crime scenes, and the fact that the killer seemed to have swapped his victims' clothing on some occasions to confuse the police, suggested both that he was of above average intelligence and that he had some knowledge of police investigation techniques. He would probably have gained this knowledge through the media or by reading true crime books, particularly ones about serial killers.

Ressler outlined his profile to the South African police in September 1995; in October a suspect was identified. When the police went to question Moses Sithole he turned on one of the officers with an axe, forcing the officer to shoot him. The injuries to Sithole's foot and stomach were non-fatal, however, and he was subsequently charged with thirty-six counts of murder.

The profile proved to be very accurate: Sithole was a local thirty-one-year-old black man who was self-employed. He ran a charity called 'Youth Against Abuse', counselling young people. He had used his position to approach his victims and to offer them help in finding jobs. He knew how to relate to young women, and was confident and comfortable in their company, he inspired their trust. But his caring demeanour was a façade: he was a highly manipulative man, described by one person who knew him as 'cunning and clever' and he had up to six different aliases. His killings had begun after he had been released from a fourteen-year prison sentence for a rape which he claimed not to have committed. He later said that his victims reminded him of this woman.

The South African police have recently established a National Police Force, akin to the FBI's Behavioural Science Unit. Following the spates of serial killing in the past few years, they now have plans to found a unit of police officers who are specially trained in the investigation of serial rape and murder. In England, while it is becoming increasingly common for a psychologist to aid the police, there is as yet no national resource centre which specializes in profiling techniques. Perhaps once the Serious Crime Bureau has been established there will be a move in this direction.

Profiling was first successfully employed in Britain in 1986 when David Canter – now a Professor of Psychology at the University of Liverpool – helped the police in their investigation into a series of rapes that eventually escalated into serial murders.

Between 1982 and 1986 the so-called 'Railway Rapist' (he usually attacked his victims near railway lines) was at large in London. The man (or men, as the Railway Rapist sometimes worked with a partner) would typically stroll past the victim, make some remark to her, then grab her from behind and subdue her by threatening her with a knife. Before the rape was carried out, the woman's hands – or thumbs – would often be tied behind her back, frequently using her own tights. After the rape the victim would be engaged in conversation, almost as if a relationship had been established between them. Astonishingly, one was asked if she had ever thought of learning self-defence, while others were asked about their boyfriends, or where they lived and given directions home.

Initially the rapes were committed by two men working together, but as the series progressed the railway rapes were increasingly perpetrated by a lone offender. When, in July 1985, there were three rapes in one night, all thought to have been committed by the Railway Rapist, 'Operation Hart' was set up by the police. The operation was to become, as *The Times* put it, 'the biggest manhunt since the Yorkshire Ripper', involving four separate police forces, and a computer-based inquiry, that eventually cost some £3m.

The next month, in August 1985, John Francis Duffy was charged with the rape of his wife at knife-point. He was released on bail. Given the nature of the offence he was routinely entered as an Operation Hart suspect, but there was no compelling reason to suppose that he was guilty of the crimes under investigation.

In January 1986, nineteen-year-old Alison Day was forced off a train and taken to some flats in Hackney. There she was garrotted using a 'Spanish windlass', a type of tourniquet used by carpenters, made out of her shirt and a stick. Her body was found seventeen days later in the River Lea. Given the time it had been in the water, it was impossible to tell whether she had been sexually violated.

Just three months later, in April, fifteen-year-old Maartje Tamboezer was on her way to the shops near her home in Surrey when she was approached by a man as she cut through the woods. After raping and strangling her, the man set alight a handkerchief, which he put in her vagina in an attempt to eliminate forensic evidence. He was not successful, however, in eradicating all traces of semen, and it was later established that Maartje's murderer had the same blood group as the Railway Rapist. Her murder was also linked to that of Alison Day and the respective investigations were combined.

Operation Hart had been on the verge of closing, due to a lack of leads, but it was now stepped up with a fierce intensity. The first list of suspects generated by the operation comprised every man in England who had ever been guilty of violence against a woman. It was cut down to 5,000 names after the blood group of the man who was now being called the Railway Killer was established. The list was further reduced to 1,999 after the names were rigorously cross-referenced with MO, links to railways, and physical descriptions and ages.

But as fast as the police were working, the Railway Killer was still one step ahead. In May, just a month after Maartje's murder, he claimed his third victim, thirty-three-year-old Anne Locke who was assaulted as she was returning home from work, walking through Brookman's Park in Herefordshire. Like Maartje, she was raped and strangled, and once again the murderer tried to get rid of traces of semen with burning tissues. The Railway Killer's MO and signature were consistent: all three women were asphyxiated, two (at least) were raped, their hands were tied behind their backs, their clothes were torn to make gags, and two of the victims had had burnt tissues stuffed inside them.

After the cross-referencing of the suspect list was complete, John Duffy was amongst the 1,999 suspects and, routinely, in July 1986 he was interviewed. He offered an alibi to the police for the night of Alison Day's murder, and yet when he was asked to give a blood sample he refused to do so, as was his right. The very next day he admitted himself to a psychiatric hospital, claiming that he had been beaten up and was, as a result, suffering from amnesia.

Meanwhile, the police were becoming increasingly anxious: the Railway Killer was working quickly and methodically, leaving them few leads. They decided to enlist the help of Professor David Canter who, in October, drew up a profile of the type of person who could be responsible for such crimes:

- Canter postulated that the murderer would live in the Kilburn/Cricklewood area of London. 'His initial attacks,' said Canter, 'would have been when he was exploring the possibilities close to home ... when he was not yet committed to being a "rapist".'
- He would probably live with a partner, a wife or a girlfriend,

Canter deduced. He spoke to his rape victims both before and after the attacks, which suggests that he was used to, and comfortable in the presence of a woman.

- He would probably have no children, however, as people who make attacks on minors (Maartje was only fifteen-years-old) are frequently childless themselves.
- He would be in his mid- to late-twenties, Canter further told police, as the manner in which the crimes were carried out, and the avoidance of capture, were indicative of a more experienced man, who had progressed from less serious offences into violent crimes.
- The care and planning that went into the attacks also suggested that he was man who was most likely to be employed in a skilled or semi-skilled job, as his mental capacity was adequate to learning a trade.
- As criminal careers don't often begin with serious crimes such as rape and murder, he would probably have been arrested in the past. In addition, his forensic awareness – the attempt to rid the bodies of semen traces – indicated some knowledge of police investigation techniques.
- He would most likely be something of a loner, with just a couple of close male friends, and little contact with women aside from his partner.
- He would be knowledgeable about the railways, since the attacks occurred near them.
- His sexual experience would be likely to be substantial, due to the variety of sexual activities in which he forced his victims to participate.

When Canter's profile was run against the list of suspects, John Duffy's name came up as a match. Due to his refusal to give blood, his suspicious story about contracting amnesia, his previous charge of raping his wife at knife-point, and his physical appearance, he was put under police surveillance. When he was followed into Copthall Park (where one of the 'Railway Rapes' had occurred), apparently preparing for a new attack, the police brought him in for questioning.

Five of the victims of the Railway Rapist positively identified

Duffy in a parade, and evidence quickly mounted against him. Fibres found on the body of Alison Day matched those found on items of Duffy's clothing. He had used a rare type of string on some occasions to bind his victims, and an identical ball of string was found at his home. And a box of Swan Vesta matches and some tissues, just like those utilized in Maartje and Anne's murders, were also found.

And the profile fitted: Duffy was twenty-nine-years-old when he was arrested, living in Kilburn, married, childless, and working as a travelling carpenter for British Rail. He had been arrested before for raping his wife at knife-point, and he was something of a loner, described variously as 'insignificant', 'almost invisible', 'weak' and 'immature'. An impressed Chief Superintendent Vincent McFadden told Canter 'I don't know how you did it, or if it was all flannel, but that profile you gave us was very accurate and was very useful to the investigation.' The Railway Killer – whom Mr Justice Farquharson described as a 'predatory animal' – was subsequently found guilty on two counts of murder and five of rape, and received a life sentence on each count.

Despite the numerous successes of the profilers, however, we must be careful about having too much faith in the technique. Newspapers, films, television and popular novels now regularly depict profilers as magicians, able to produce serial killers like rabbits out of hats. When Thomas Harris's *The Silence of the Lambs* introduced profiling to a public who were instantly riveted, the FBI received baskets full of letters asking how to become a profiler. More recently, the British television series *Cracker,* featuring Robbie Coltrane as a psychologist-detective, who tracks criminals by means of profiling techniques, has attracted huge audiences. While our fathers wanted to be footballers, their sons – and, interestingly their daughters too (a nice index of social change) – seem to want to be profilers.

Yet profiling is undoubtedly more of an art than a science, relying heavily upon intuition and experience. Predictably, in accounts from profilers the emphasis tends to be more upon their successes than their failures. But profiles can be completely misleading. For instance, one case generated a profile by the FBI that turned out to be entirely inaccurate. The police were told to look for a man who came from a broken home, had dropped out of high school, held an unskilled job, spent a lot of time in bars, and lived far away from the crime scene. When the offender was later apprehended it transpired that he was not from a broken home, had a degree, was an executive in a financial company, never drank alcohol and lived just by the scene of the crime.

When profiles were just beginning to be used in America, the criminologist C. Campbell claimed that they were hardly better than information that could be obtained by the local barman, and that psychologists were simply playing educated guessing-games. In England the Lord Chief Justice once disparagingly referred to profiling as 'guesswork [and] conjecture'. Yet this seems too harsh, given the obvious progress that profiling has made, the successes it has enjoyed, and the contribution that it has made to more traditional methods of detection, which are often inadequate to identify serial offenders. The FBI and other profilers warn police to take the profile simply as a guide, to be used to prioritize suspects and centre the investigation, not to identify individuals. Profiles are best seen as devices to be used in conjunction with traditional investigative techniques.

Thus we must proceed with extreme caution, at least until the art of profiling can be based upon a stronger foundation than intuition and experience. And to approach the status of a science more research needs to be done, not least on the killers themselves. We need to know what sort of people they are, and this inevitably involves a study of where they came from, how they formed and developed. And so we return to the topic of this book, which may be of interest to the professional profiler and to the student of human nature alike, both of whom may wonder how the serial killer came to be as he is.

There seem to have been fourteen British serial sex killers over the last fifty years: Gordon Frederick Cummins, John Reginald Halliday Christie, Myra Hindley and Ian Brady, Peter Sutcliffe, Dennis Nilsen, Kenneth Erskine, John Duffy, Michael Lupo, Colin Ireland, Robert Black, Fred and Rose West, and Peter Moore. Of the above, nine case-histories will be considered in detail. Unfortunately five have had to be excluded: Michael

Lupo committed his crimes in England, but was born and raised in Italy, so is not truly a British serial killer; the cases of Gordon Cummins, Peter Moore, and Kenneth Erskine, are insufficiently documented to enable us to compare their lives to those of the other offenders; and John Duffy's case has already been examined in this chapter.

While nine offenders is not a number from which we can draw statistically significant results, it is, nevertheless, three quarters of the population of British serial sex killers over the past fifty years. Thus if we find similarities within this sample, it is not over-reaching ourselves to say that we should be able to generalize about British serial sex killers as a group. So let us proceed by examining, in detail, the childhoods, lives, and crimes of our nine serial sex killers, and see what emerges.

3

JOHN REGINALD HALLIDAY CHRISTIE

John Christie had happy memories of his childhood. According to his own sunny account (published in the *Sunday Pictorial* after his arrest) he always enjoyed school, where he was a good all-rounder who excelled at maths and algebra, was capable at games and sports – particularly football – and an active participant in after-school activities, being a member of the church choir and eventually becoming an Assistant Scout Master. One of his loves as a boy, which endured all of his life, was for animals, and he had a dog and a cat of his own whom he adored. Locally, his reputation as being knowledgeable about animals prompted, on more than one occasion, neighbours to bring their sick pets for Reggie (as he was commonly called) to look at. Animals, he said, appeared to understand him, humans did not.

Behind John Christie's rosy story of his childhood, however, there were aspects that he was more reluctant to acknowledge. Born on 8 April 1899, the fifth child of Ernest John and Mary Hannah Christie, née Halliday, Reggie was born in a secluded house, called 'Black Boy', on High Sunderland moor, a few miles outside Halifax in Yorkshire. From an early age he was an anxious boy. At bedtime he was terrified of the dark; he used to see what he later described as a spot of light in front of his eyes and would hide under the sheets to escape from it. His peers remember him as being slightly odd. He used, for instance, to wash his hands more than was normal. He was also a great hypochondriac, always complaining of various illnesses, and exaggerating his ailments, although he had a perfectly healthy constitution. He was, in addition, inordinately fussy about what foods he would eat.

All these childhood symptoms were signs, in retrospect, of a serious personality disorder in the making. Compulsive hand-washing, with its incessant and unappeasable fear of dirt and germs, means that the world is constantly regarded as unsafe, and a source of contagion. (Though the washing rituals may be interpreted as an attempt to rid the self of the unacknowledged dirty side of one's nature, which has been projected onto the world.) Such a symptom is often allied to hypochondria – yet another manifestation of the feeling of being at constant risk of infection, while the fastidiousness with regard to eating suggests, once again, the sense of fragility and exposure to contamination.

In contrast to Christie's own image of himself as well-rounded and popular at Boothtown Council School and the Holy Trinity School, he is remembered by others as a small and puny child – provoking the inevitable taunts of 'sissy' and 'weakling' – who never made any good friends. He was always on the edge of the crowd, estranged from the other children, who thought of him as moody and malicious. As they began to be interested in the opposite sex, and started to swap 'dirty' jokes and learn swear words, Reggie alienated himself further by being surprisingly prudish for one so young.

Reggie always seemed a boy too old for his years, a trait which probably came from his desire to be more like his arche-typical Victorian father, Ernest Christie, or 'Mephistopheles', as he was nicknamed at work due to his distinctive goatee. A carpet designer by trade, Ernest was a severe, forbidding man, traits which earned him respect in the local community and provoked fear in his home. He was the sort whom friends and neighbours praised as a good family man, a church-goer, an upstanding member of the community, an active participant in local activi-ties (Ernest was the Halifax Conservative Party's founder, and he was involved in the scouts, the Boys' Brigade and the St John's Ambulance Brigade). But they didn't witness the dark and often violent side which accompanied, indeed generated, such morally strict standards: the tyranny, the dominance, the rigidity.

At home Ernest's children were 'in dread' of their father's

temper, which flared up at the slightest provocation, and led to cruel beatings. Christie himself recalled a time when his father thrashed him after he denied pinching one of his tomatoes, although tomatoes were one of the foods which Reggie refused to eat (when Hannah later told Ernest that Reggie was innocent Ernest gave his son a shilling in recompense). On a different occasion, Reggie was beaten by his father simply for rocking on a park bench with his little sister; and Christie remembered how he and his siblings used to be taken on long hikes by Ernest on Sundays, and made to march like soldiers. The control that his father exercised over the household meant that Christie was denied the natural, and necessary, outlet of the expression of negative feelings, which were internalized and left to accumulate.

As there were only two boys out of the six children, Reggie seemed to get more than his fair share of beatings, which may have been subconsciously triggered by Ernest's frustration at the small and weak boy he had produced, so unlike himself. Perhaps a good thrashing would toughen him up a bit? Nevertheless, while Christie maintained that they lived in dread of Ernest, he later turned this temper and cruelty into a virtue. Harsh physical and mental discipline were necessary constituents of a proper Victorian man – strong, uncompromising, respected. In retrospect, for Christie, Ernest was a figure to be admired, a man who was 'brilliant' at his job and also in his ambulance work and medical knowledge. This seems to have been a denial of his negative feelings: in extolling the virtues of his father, he both denied his anger at him and identified himself with the role of the oppressor rather than that of the victim. Ernest was allegedly known locally as 'Dr Christie' as he diagnosed, and prescribed for, his friends' and neighbours' conditions. Years later John Christie was still proud of this, bragging – quite falsely – to anybody who would listen that his father was 'a specialist, who had trained other doctors'. He looked up to his father: Ernest was admired by others, and always in control.

As an adult, Christie would emulate his father by pretending to have medical training, and after his capture many witnesses told of having met Christie in cafés where he would offer strangers cures for their ailments. One of Christie's victims was certainly lured to his home at 10 Rillington Place with the promise of medical treatment. (And at least one further woman made a lucky escape. Margaret Forrest made a date with Christie for him to cure her migraines by use of an 'inhalant'. If she had not thought better of keeping the date, she would almost certainly have been murdered.) Impersonating a doctor, whom he may have thought of as God-like, having the power of life and death, gave Christie a feeling of grandeur, of omnipotence.

While with hindsight Christie respected and admired his father, to a frail and nervous boy Ernest's fearsome temper must have been frightening, and would certainly have undermined Christie's own development. Hannah, a kindly woman, in trying to protect her children from Ernest's temper, compensated for her husband's behaviour by being over-protective towards her son, who seemed to need more care and attention than the other children due to his general frailty. In escaping the dominant male influence, Christie's manhood was further diminished by the cosseting of his mother. And so he eventually came to identify with the womanly, the gentle, the helpless, but the figure of the overbearing male tyrant remained latent in him, to erupt violently in later life.

When he was eight years old Reggie had his first contact with death. When his grandfather died, he saw the body laid out in the house for visitors to pay their last respects. However, far from feeling devastated over his death (Reggie had never really liked his grandfather, an intimidating man like his father) when he saw the body he felt both interest and pleasure. He was not only happy that his grandfather wouldn't be coming back, but he also felt that death didn't seem a disagreeable state – on the contrary, it seemed restful. As Ludovic Kennedy, author of *10 Rillington Place*, points out, seeing the figure who had rendered Reggie fearful, finally silent and still, unable to chastise him any more, was understandably a pleasurable feeling. After this event, the boy soon began to play in the local cemetery, where he seemed to enjoy looking at the graves. A morbid interest in death had begun.

Having grown up in a household of five women, where his mother stifled his masculinity and his sisters, he remembered, 'were always bossing me about', Christie's initiation into sexual activity was unsuccessful. He later claimed that he neither masturbated nor had wet-dreams as an adolescent, a denial which is unsurprising (although probably false) given his general sanctimonious and prudish demeanour. At the age of fifteen, when his peers were beginning to experiment with sex, Christie tried but failed to have intercourse with one of the local girls, whose greater sexual experience seemed to render him incapable. He was simply not used to acting, or performing, like a man. Rumours started: the girl told a friend about the incident, and that friend told a friend, until soon everybody knew. As Dr Hobson – a psychiatrist who examined Christie after his arrest in 1953 – later euphemistically put it: 'he was given a nickname which implied that he was not quite a man': 'Reggie-No-Dick' and 'Can't-do-it-Christie'. This first failed attempt at sex would shape, and blight, Christie's sexual development.

Although he had won a scholarship to Halifax Secondary School and was considered intelligent during his years there, Christie left at the age of fifteen, in 1913, without qualifications. He began work as an assistant cinema operator, the first in a long string of unambitious jobs which later included clerical and factory work. That same year he left the cinema and became a clerk with the Halifax police, but was soon unemployed again after being given the sack for pilfering. His next job, in his father's carpet factory, was also quickly terminated when he was sacked for petty theft. This pattern of rapidly changing jobs, with repeated dismissals for minor, but criminal, offences was to persist throughout his life.

In 1916, after at least three unsuccessful jobs, at the age of eighteen Christie decided to join the army. Here he was remembered as efficient, good at his work and an example to others. Christie was probably exaggerating, however, when he later told Dr Matheson (who examined him at Brixton Prison after his arrest) that he was offered promotion three times but turned it down because he wanted to stay with the friends he'd made. In 1918 Christie saw his first – and last – action when he was posted to France. In June a mustard-gas shell exploded near to him, rendering him unconscious. He later claimed that the gas left him blind for some months and dumb for three and a half years. There was, however, no record that he was blinded at all and although it is true that he lost his speech for a time, this was due to psychological rather than physical reasons: he was diagnosed as having functional aphonia. In fact, just seven weeks after the event he was declared fit for duty.

Although it has been suggested that this physical trauma might help to account for Christie's later behaviour, the incident was really no more than an example of his nervous and highly strung disposition. As Dr Matheson said, Christie's loss of voice was an 'hysterical manifestation'. Throughout his life Christie 'readily in the face of difficulties took refuge in physical illness'. Dr Odess, Christie's doctor from 1934 to 1952, later described Christie as 'a very, very frequent patient of mine' who was a 'neurotic' and 'a nervous man'. He consulted Dr Odess about a whole range of symptoms, most of them psychosomatic, including insomnia, depression, back pain, stomach pain, memory loss, diarrhoea, and eczema. Christie visited Dr Odess thirty-two times in the first eight months of 1952, and 173 times in total, but for almost all of his complaints Dr Odess could prescribe nothing other than tranquillizers, sleeping pills and a good holiday. Dr Odess finally referred Christie to Dr Petit, a psychiatrist, as he was consistently unable to find anything physically wrong with him. Dr Petit said he believed that Christie would benefit from treatment for his anxiety as an out-patient in a psychiatric hospital, and referred him to Springfield Mental Hospital in the spring of 1952. Unsurprisingly, Christie refused to go. Like many neurotics, he was convinced that there was an underlying physical cause for his symptoms.

Christie met his wife-to-be, Ethel Simpson, after he had left the army in 1920, and they married the same year. Ethel was a passive and unprepossessing sort of girl, who didn't smother him as his mother and sisters had done. But Christie was still very unsure of himself sexually. He told Dr Matheson that he and Ethel didn't have sex during their courtship, and that for the first three years of their marriage he always had difficulty with intercourse. After this time they began to have sex about once a week, until they stopped altogether two or three years before Ethel's death in 1952. They had apparently never used any form of contraception but Ethel – to their disappointment, Christie claimed – had never conceived. If this is true, it would have further reinforced Christie's negative image of himself. He had trouble with intercourse, and could not impregnate his wife. It cannot have helped an already uncertain self-image, and may well have triggered anger at the woman who had elicited the inadequate behaviour.

Before his marriage Christie's sexual experiences had been largely with prostitutes, whom he visited frequently while he was in the army. These were women to whom he didn't have to prove anything, or to worry about pleasing. It seemed that Christie was only able to achieve erection and penetration when his partner was entirely undemanding and passive. He discovered later in life that the best way to achieve this was with a corpse: the ultimately unresponsive sexual partner. A dead body has no needs, it cannot be disappointed, nor can it mock.

The Christies' marriage was turbulent from the start. This was partly due to the fact that Christie couldn't seem to hold a job down for long, despite the intelligence which had been noted at school. His frequent prison sentences did nothing to further his job prospects, nor to improve marital harmony. The year after he married, in 1921, Christie was imprisoned for the first time, having been found guilty of stealing postal orders while he was working as a postman; the police found sacks full of unopened mail in his room. Two years later, in 1923, he was charged with obtaining money by false pretences and given twelve months probation. Just the next year he was found guilty of stealing goods and money, for which he received nine months hard labour. Ethel finally left her husband in 1924: he had been recently released from prison, was unemployed again, and it was rumoured locally that he was seeing prostitutes. They remained separated for nine years until Christie wrote to her in 1933 when he was once again in prison (for stealing a car) and asked her to come and see him. Lonely, and obviously forgetful, Ethel agreed, and after Christie's release they decided to live together once again.

The next year, in 1934, Christie was hit by a car while he was cycling. He was taken to hospital, where he had to have an operation on his knee and part of his collar-bone removed. He later claimed that he had been knocked unconscious for over an hour, but hospital records do not corroborate this claim. It is true, however, that when Christie was given an EEG after his arrest, Dr Matheson reported that the results were slightly abnormal. In his report for the Crown, Dr Matheson said that, 'It is possible that the pattern is a result of brain damage suffered earlier in life but ... I think this mild abnormality may be constitutional rather than acquired.' In court, Dr Hobson (for the defence) concurred with Dr Matheson, saying, 'I do not feel that any psychological symptoms he [Christie] exhibits at the present time result from head injury, though the minor abnormalities on the EEG are said to be such that could have been caused by slight head injury.'

In 1938 the Christies moved to 10 Rillington Place in Notting Hill. Rillington Place was – it no longer exists – a cul-de-sac in which number ten was at the end on the left. Although Christie always fancied himself as a class above the ordinary working man, the living conditions at Rillington Place were spartan and Christie used to lie to Ethel's family about the area in which they lived. Shortly after they moved, Christie became a Special Constable in the War Reserve Police, stationed at Harrow Road, where he received two commendations for the 'efficient detection of crime' during his four years there. But he was known locally as a bully who abused his position, and his neighbours began to dislike him, as he was forever charging people with the pettiest of offences. For Christie, it was an ideal opportunity to be dominant, to finally seize control and be more like his father.

It was during this time that Christie began surreptitiously to go out with a married woman from the station, although it is not known if they had sexual relations. In 1943, her husband caught them together, and gave Christie a beating. This, it has been speculated, was the trigger that started Christie on his murderous spree, as he killed his first victim later the same year. After forty-five years of submission and inadequacy, a murderous rage that had been festering since childhood finally erupted.

*

The results were horrifying. Ten years on, on 26 March 1953: the headlines told the story – the *Mirror* screamed of 'THE HOUSE OF MURDER', the *Express* told its enthralled public of 'MURDER UNLIMITED – STARING EYES MAN HUNTED', three days later *Truth* described 'THE NATION-WIDE SEARCH FOR A MODERN JACK-THE-RIPPER'. The bodies of six women had been found in a house in Notting Hill. In late March of 1953 the hunt began for the 'Monster of Rillington Place', fifty-five-year-old John Reginald Halliday Christie. He had last been seen at home in mid-March, when he sub-let his flat at 10 Rillington Place to a young couple, Mr and Mrs Reilly. He told them that he was being transferred to British Road Services in Birmingham and that his wife had gone on ahead.

In truth, Christie's situation must finally have become intolerable to him. Not only was he unemployed and without any furniture (it had been sold to raise enough money to live on), but his flat had four corpses in it, and two more bodies were buried in his garden. Later, when asked in court, 'Were you conscious of the fact when talking to the Reillys that on your premises there were four dead bodies?', Christie characteristically replied that 'I never gave it a thought.' The Reillys recalled that the flat had had a most unpleasant smell about it.

When Charles Brown, the landlord of 10 Rillington Place, returned on 21 March, he was unimpressed to find that Christie had disappeared and that new tenants had been installed in one of his flats, as sub-letting was strictly forbidden. He asked the Reillys to leave and gave Beresford Brown, another of the tenants, permission to make use of Christie's flat himself. On 24 March, Beresford Brown was cleaning out the flat and looking around the kitchen for somewhere to attach brackets for a wireless set. In his statement to the police, he described how he 'went to the back wall of the kitchen and tapped the wall to find a solid place, to which I could fasten the brackets. I noticed the top part of the wall was sounding solid but when I tapped the wall about four feet up from the floor it sounded hollow.' Investigating further, he pulled off some of the wallpaper, shone a torch in the hole he had uncovered and – to his shock – saw what was unmistakably 'the bare back of a human being'. He rang the police immediately and Police Sergeant Leslie Siseman arrived soon afterwards, who in turn called Detective Chief Inspector Albert Griffin from Scotland Yard, who arrived at Rillington Place accompanied by pathologist Dr Francis Camps. In the hollow behind the wall they soon made the gruesome discovery of not one, but three, bodies.

The first body was that of twenty-six-year-old Hectorina MacLennan who, according to the police report, had been left 'in a sitting position, back to the wall, with her head and shoulders hunched'. According to Dr Camps's later report, she was partially dressed in a white cotton jacket, a black jumper, stockings and suspender belt, and a blue bra which had been pulled up so as to leave her breasts exposed. Her wrists had been tied together with a handkerchief, mould was growing out of her nostrils, the area around her mouth and nose was discoloured, her eyes were swollen, there was secretion coming from her breasts, soiling between her legs, and there was sperm leaking out of her vagina. There was also a linear mark around her neck.

Dr Camps concluded from his post-mortem examination that the cause of death had been asphyxia due to strangulation by a ligature (which was apparent from the mark around her neck and from haemorrhaging in the body, due to the oxygen supply being cut off), associated with carbon-monoxide poisoning (which was identifiable from the colour of the blood and tissues). He estimated that she had been killed some four weeks earlier.

Behind her body they found the corpse of Kathleen Maloney, who had also been twenty-six years old. Kathleen's body was leaning against the wall, wrapped in a flannelette blanket; a piece of cloth covered her head, secured by a stocking tied around her neck. When the blanket and cloth were removed, Kathleen was dressed only in a white cardigan and vest. Between her legs another vest served as a sort of home-made sanitary towel for catching the sperm which had leaked out of her vagina. There were, however, no marks around her neck, except those which had been made by the pressure of the stocking which had kept the cloth over her head in place.

Despite the lack of external indications, it was obvious upon post-mortem examination that the cause of death had been the same for both victims: asphyxia due both to strangulation and carbon-monoxide poisoning. The time of death was estimated at between four and eight weeks previously.

The third body behind the wall was that of twenty-five-year-old Rita Nelson. She too was wrapped in a blanket, a piece of material and bloodstained towelling around her head. She was wearing a blue cardigan, a fawn-coloured dress, stockings, a pink slip, two vests and a pink bra. Like Kathleen, Rita also had what Dr Camps described as a kind of 'diaper' between her legs to absorb the semen. Due to the changed condition of her skin in death (it had grown mouldy as she had been dead some two months) it was impossible to tell if there were marks around her neck, but the post-mortem confirmed that the cause of her death was the same as in the previous two cases. To make matters worse – if that were possible – the post-mortem confirmed that Rita Nelson had been six months pregnant. The foetus had not been interfered with.

A thorough search of the rest of the flat was promptly conducted, during the course of which Chief Inspector Griffin noticed that some floor boards in the front room were loose. Underneath them, partially hidden by earth, was a fourth body – wrapped first in a silk dress and then in a blanket. The identity of the body was another shock: it was that of Christie's wife, Ethel, who had been 'missing' since December. Christie's various explanations to concerned friends and neighbours (that Ethel had gone to Birmingham for a 'women's operation' or to await his work transfer, or to Sheffield to 'look after her mother') were now exposed as lies. The signature of the murder was different to that of the other three in two important ways: this time there was no semen to indicate sexual assault, although the home-made 'nappy' was still in place; and while the cause of death was again determined to be asphyxia, on this occasion there was no evidence of carbon-monoxide poisoning. Ethel had been dead the longest of the four women, Dr Camps estimating that she had been killed twelve to fourteen weeks previously.

Along with the bodies a tin containing four clippings of pubic hair was found. Experts later testified that the hair did not belong to any of the women in the cupboard. It might have been from the prostitutes that Christie had frequented, or perhaps from other victims. Retaining some sort of trophy from their victims is a phenomenon not uncommon among serial killers. Sometimes this trophy might simply be the victim's watch, a purse, a piece of clothing or a lock of hair. At the other extreme the killer might remove and take with him a body part, like Jack the Ripper, who removed a kidney from one of his victims. Taking a trophy allows the killer a symbol of his power over his victim, and facilitates the rebirth of the murders in his mind. When he looks at his trophy, he may masturbate over it, remembering his crime and planning the next one.

Four bodies had been discovered, yet there were still more to come. On 27 March – three days after the initial discovery – police began to search the garden of number ten, of which the Christies had sole use. In the ashes of an old bonfire a number of bones were found and propped up against the trellis was a thigh-bone. The bones were taken to Professor Richard Harrison to be examined, and Christie's first two victims – killed almost ten years before, in 1943 and 1944 – were identified as twenty-one-year-old Ruth Fuerst and thirty-one-year-old Muriel Eady. Their skeletons were almost complete, although Muriel's skull was missing.

There was little mystery as to who the killer of these six unfortunate women was, but nobody had seen Christie since he had left his flat over a week before the discovery of the bodies. The police promptly began a national manhunt for the bald and bespectacled man whom his neighbours knew as a quiet, respectable, religious and knowledgeable gentleman, with impeccable moral values and a medical background. They searched the entire country, on tips from letters that had flooded in, some of which were from the inevitable cranks who seem to come out of the woodwork whenever a murder has been committed. (There was one letter from a 'psychic' who said that Christie had disguised himself as an old man and was wearing dark glasses; another from somebody who said that Christie's 'prominent ear' was the key: a trait apparently found in all 'potential' murderers.)

While the police were sifting through their various leads –

such as they were – Christie himself was ambling unabashed around London, staying in cheap lodgings and frequenting cafés, cinemas and billiard halls. Later he told the court that he remembered seeing a headline on a billboard that read, 'WILL THE KILLER STRIKE AGAIN?' and he heard people talking about the murders, but he felt strangely removed from the events, making little effort to hide himself away. In his lodgings at Rowton House on the Kings Cross Road, the register shows that he even gave his correct name and address.

The hunt for the man who was already known as one of the most infamous murderers in British history lasted just over a week. On 31 March, Police Constable Thomas Ledger recognized and stopped Christie on the Embankment (looking 'rather down and out of condition') as he was making his way to Putney Bridge from Rowton House. When Ledger enquired as to Christie's name, Christie replied that he was John Waddington – Waddington was Ethel's maiden name – of Westbourne Grove. The constable, however, was unconvinced and asked Christie to remove his hat. Now certain that he had found Britain's most wanted man, PC Ledger asked Christie if he would accompany him to Putney Police Station. As luck would have it, at that moment a police van happened to pass and as PC Ledger and Christie climbed inside, Christie, knowing the game was up, admitted his real identity.

Over the next few months Christie made three separate confessions to the police to the murders of seven women spanning ten years, from August 1943 to March 1953. Yet while Christie admitted culpability for each of the murders, he was far from candid in his confessions which were, as Ludovic Kennedy says, true in substance but false in detail. In each subsequent version details were altered, embellished and forgotten. (In Christie's account of his life and crimes in the *Sunday Pictorial* he went as far as to sensationally – and untruthfully – claim that a mysterious and powerful force, out of his own control, had led him to commit the murders and that it had been his mission to kill ten women.) Having admitted to the murders only when presented with incontrovertible evidence, Christie then strove to morally redeem himself and to cast himself in the best possible light that the circumstances allowed. He may have killed, yes, but he was forced into it, it was their fault. He was, after all, a good and respectable man.

According to Christie's statement he met his first victim, twenty-one-year-old German prostitute Ruth Fuerst, while he was working in the police War Reserve in 1943. They had apparently met in a snack-bar which Christie had gone into on police business, although he was off duty at the time. After this initial meeting they became friendly and started seeing each other regularly. One day in August, Christie took Ruth back to Rillington Place while Ethel was away visiting her family in Sheffield. According to Christie, they were in the bedroom when all of a sudden:

> She undressed and wanted me to have intercourse with her. I got a telegram while she was there, saying that my wife was on her way home. The girl wanted us to team up together and go right away somewhere together. I would not do that. I got on the bed and had intercourse with her. While I was having intercourse with her I strangled her with a piece of rope.

Christie prided himself upon being a man of unquestionable moral character, and Ruth's behaviour had been offensive to him. She had got what she deserved. Christie put her body under the floorboards, and the next day he buried it in the garden, burning her clothes.

Although there is no way of verifying Christie's version of events, as it was impossible to determine the cause of Ruth's death from her skeleton, it is highly probable that Ruth (and Muriel) died in the way that he described, in the same manner as his other victims: strangled, and possibly gassed, while Christie raped them. Serial killers rarely change their method of killing as they are acting out fantasies which, while they may escalate, nevertheless have that unmistakable personal signature. Ruth was killed because this was the only way in which Christie was able to have intercourse with her: by first rendering her unconscious, and thus unthreatening. From the time that he was mocked as a boy for his first unsuccessful attempt at penetration, through to his adult relationships and his marriage, Christie had been largely impotent. As Dr Matheson later said:

> as a young man he received no sex instruction. He picked it up in Halifax and found himself unable to behave as his young friends behaved and that gave him a feeling of inferiority. That started, I think, a feeling all through his life, that sexually he is not so mature or capable as he should be.

Finally these feelings escalated to such an extent that Christie was incapable of satisfactory intercourse with a living and demanding woman. He had reached the stage whereby the only way in which he could achieve sexual gratification was with an unconscious, or dead, body. As Dr Matheson said: 'Christie has a very weak sex instinct and to complete the sexual act he needs considerable stimulation by adopting perverse practices. He had to render the woman with whom he was going to have intercourse, unconscious before he began, lest he prove impotent.' The name for this aberration is, of course, necrophilia, and Christie is an example of the most commonly referred to, and most extreme, type of necrophile, the sort who has sexual intercourse with dead bodies.

While Christie was working at the Park Royal radio factory in 1944, he met his second victim, Muriel Eady. They soon struck up a friendship and Christie invited Muriel and her boyfriend around for tea with himself and Ethel on several occasions. During one such visit Muriel complained to Christie of her catarrh problem, which he assured her that he could cure, no doubt telling her of his bogus medical background. He invited her to Rillington Place one day when Ethel was away. Christie's account of Muriel's murder was the only confession in which he did not try to shift the blame onto his victim. He described to Chief Inspector Griffin how he had used a home-made inhalant device (which he told Muriel would cure her ailment) to render her unconscious. The *Daily Mail* was later to call it 'A Death Machine'; the *Telegraph* a 'home made death mask'. In his report, Chief Inspector Griffin recounted the process Christie described to him:

This inhalant [Friar's Balsam] he put in a square glass jar with a metal screwtop lid. He made two holes in the lid and through one of the holes put the end of a length of tubing from a gas point. The end of this tubing went into the liquid, and through the other hole in the lid he inserted another piece of tubing which did not touch the liquid. The woman inhaled the stuff through the tube.

After Muriel became 'sort of unconscious' Christie tied a stocking around her neck, strangling her as he penetrated her body. That night he put her body in the washhouse, and the next day buried her in the garden, along with Ruth Fuerst.

Beryl Evans was Christie's third victim, yet it was her husband who was hanged for her murder. The six bodies that the police found in March 1953 were not the first bodies to have been discovered at 10 Rillington Place. On 2 December 1950, two bodies had been found in the washhouse in the garden: the top-floor tenants Beryl Evans and her fourteen-month-old daughter Geraldine, the wife and daughter of Timothy Evans. Dr Teare, the Home Office pathologist who was called to the scene, determined that Beryl and Geraldine had both been murdered some three weeks before; the cause of death in both cases was ligature-strangulation. At the time, Timothy Evans – who had the mental age of a child – confessed to the murders, and although he subsequently retracted his confession and blamed the murders on Christie, he was charged with the crimes. After all, Christie was an upstanding member of the local community, an ex-soldier and policeman, and it has always been statistically far more likely that a murder victim has been killed by somebody intimate with them.

In the 1950s lust-murder was a scarce phenomenon, and the term serial killer would not even be invented for another twenty-five years. Certainly there had been Jack the Ripper and The Blackout Ripper but they were surely anomalies, freaks. When the case came to trial the jury had no cause to believe that the reason for the murders might have been sexual, as this evidence never came out in court. If the jury had been in full possession of all the facts the outcome of the case might have been different. Dr Teare had found a bruise inside Beryl's vagina which, he said, 'could have been caused by an attempt at forced intercourse or in a struggle', although this attempt had been made *ante-mortem*, that is, before death. At the time Dr Teare had suggested taking a swab, but 'others thought it unnecessary'. Arguably, if this had been done the life of Timothy Evans might have been saved. If a sexual element to Beryl's murder had been established, through the presence of sperm, (although there was no genetic fingerprinting in the 1950s that could have linked it to Christie through DNA) the murder would have been cast in an entirely different light. It would have been plausible that Beryl had been killed for sexual gratification. And why would a man who was having a murderous argument with his wife have sex with her?

After Christie's arrest in 1953 the truth began to emerge, although Christie, typically, never gave a frank version of events. On questioning, he admitted to murdering Beryl, although he maintained his innocence over the murder of Geraldine. In his statement Christie told the police that in the time leading up to her death, Beryl and Timothy had been arguing frequently and that after one such occasion he caught her trying to commit suicide, lying in front of the fireplace with the gas on. Christie claimed that he opened the door and window to disperse the gas and made Beryl a cup of tea to comfort her. The next day she allegedly came to him to ask if he would help her end her life: 'she said she would do anything ... I think she was referring to letting me be intimate with her'.

> I turned the gas tap on and as near as I can make out I held it close to her face. When she became unconscious I turned the tap off. I was going to try to have intercourse with her but it was impossible. I couldn't bend over [because of his bad back]. I think that is when I strangled her.

When Timothy Evans came home, Christie claims to have told him that his wife had committed suicide but that, 'no doubt he would be suspected of having done it because of the rows and fights he had with his wife. He seemed to think the same.'

What then was the real story? The widely agreed version of events now is that Timothy Evans's eventual defence in court was the truth. Beryl was pregnant and wanted an abortion, so when Christie offered to perform the procedure, telling her that he had experience in such matters, she agreed. On the day of the 'operation' Timothy went to work as usual, showing his displeasure at Beryl's decision to terminate her pregnancy. After Timothy had left, Christie asked Beryl to lie down and remove her underwear. He then gave her gas, telling her it would help with the pain, and inserted something into her, a finger or some implement. At around this time Christie became aroused by the sight of Beryl, who was vulnerable, semi-conscious and at least partially naked, and strangled and raped her. When Timothy got home Christie told him that his wife had died during the procedure and he would be blamed as they had been fighting. Timothy, who was slightly mentally deficient, panicked and went along with Christie's plans for disposing of Beryl's body. His guilt over letting Christie carry out the procedure may have led him to the conclusion that he was morally to blame for the murders, which led to his first confession. When he later retracted his confession, it was too late.

What of baby Geraldine? Both men denied killing her. If Christie committed this murder, why did he not confess to it, as he had to the other seven murders? Ludovic Kennedy argues that Christie killed Geraldine after he had killed Beryl, telling Timothy that he had taken his daughter to friends of his who would look after her. Christie never admitted to this murder as 'there could be no possible justification for the murder of a helpless baby'. He could hardly claim that she had sexually provoked him, like Ruth; nor that it was a mercy killing, like that of Beryl. But he needed to dispense of Geraldine in order to divert suspicion of foul play. If both mother and baby disappeared it would simply look as if they had left Timothy. But if Timothy and his daughter were left without Beryl it would look odd, as what mother would leave her baby? Questions would soon be asked, and these might eventually incriminate Christie himself.

Thus his motive for the murder of Geraldine was not sexual

but practical, to eliminate any threat to himself. Furthermore, although Christie always officially denied the murder of Geraldine, he privately admitted the killing to a hospital officer, Mr J. A. Roberts. In 1953, after his trial, Christie said to Roberts, 'If the police only knew that they could charge me with the murder of the Evans' baby girl.' Really? asked Roberts. 'More or less as far as I remember,' said Christie, 'but they can't do anything about it now.'

Christie's next victim was his wife, Ethel, whose murder, he claimed, was another mercy killing. In fact, it was simply a matter of necessity, committed in order that he could indulge his lust for killing for a while longer. Christie told the police that Ethel had been very depressed and anxious for some time before her death, due to persecution and assault by the black people who were living in their building. On the morning of 14 December 1952, Ethel allegedly woke Christie in serious distress.

> I was awakened at about 8.15 a.m. I think it was my wife moving about in bed. I sat up and saw that she appeared to be convulsive. Her face was blue and she was choking. I did what I could to try to restore her breathing but it was hopeless. It appeared too late to call for assistance, that is when I couldn't bear to see her, so I got a stocking and tied it round her neck to put her to sleep.

Christie claimed that at the time he didn't know what had caused his wife's attack, but when he got out of bed after she was dead he 'saw a small bottle and a cup half-full of water on a small table near the bed. I noticed that the bottle contained two pheno-barbitone tablets and it originally contained twenty-five. I knew then that she must have taken the remainder.' Ethel and Christie had indeed both been prescribed pheno-barbitone tablets to help them sleep, but Dr Camps found no trace of pills in Ethel's stomach at the post-mortem.

When a serial killer murders a family member – which is rare – it will usually be for entirely different reasons to the other murders in the series. Hence, Ethel's body was the only one not to show signs of sexual activity, which was the motivation for the other murders. Christie didn't need to kill his wife in order to have intercourse with her, as she didn't intimidate him, and render him incapable of arousal as other women did. Ethel was killed for functional reasons. She had reportedly told a friend after Beryl's murder, 'My husband killed that woman. I know it.' The sudden rise in the number of victims after Ethel's death – three in as many months – suggests that Christie's fantasies had been escalating. He needed to get rid of Ethel in order to carry on satisfying his lust.

Rita Nelson, like Ruth, had allegedly propositioned Christie. According to his statement, he encountered Rita, who was a prostitute, in the street in January 1953 where she demanded that he give her thirty shillings in return for sex: 'I said, "I am not interested and I haven't got money to throw away". I'm not like that. I haven't had intercourse with any woman for over two years, my doctor will tell you that ... I walked away.' But Rita was very insistent, and she followed Christie back to Rillington Place.

> When I opened the door she forced her way in ... I tried to get her out and she picked up a frying pan to hit me ... There was a struggle ... I don't remember what happened next but I must have gone haywire. The next thing I remember she was lying still in the chair with the rope around her neck.

The post-mortem examination showed that Rita had been gassed, strangled, and raped while she was dying: Christie had not 'gone haywire', the acts were deliberate. Afterwards, he made himself a cup of tea and retired to bed. After getting up in the morning, washing, shaving and making some more tea, he dealt with Rita's lifeless body. It was the first to be put behind the wall in the kitchen, where it was to remain for two months.

Christie told the police that he had met Kathleen Maloney in a café in Notting Hill in January 1953, a matter of days after he had murdered Rita. The café was apparently crowded, and Christie was obliged to share a table. The two young women who were seated there – Kathleen and her friend – were talking about renting accommodation. Christie claimed that Kathleen had asked him for a cigarette and then struck up a conversation. During the course of this conversation Christie mentioned that he was soon to be leaving his flat, which prompted the young women to ask if they could come round that evening to see if it might be suitable for them. According to Christie's statement, that night Kathleen came round to view the flat, alone.

> She said it would be suitable subject to the landlord's permission. It was then that she made the suggestion that she would visit me for a few days. She said this so I could use my influence with the landlord as a sort of payment in kind. I was rather annoyed and told her that it didn't interest me. I think she started saying I was making accusations against her when she saw there was nothing in it ... I believe it was then that she mentioned something about Irish blood. She was in a violent temper ... she started fighting ... I am very quiet and avoid fighting ... I know there was something, it's in the back of my mind. She was on the floor. I must have put her in the alcove straight away.

The post-mortem evidence again disproved Christie's story of sudden provoked violence: like Rita, Kathleen was killed by gas and strangulation, and was sexually assaulted.

Christie's last victim was Hectorina MacLennan, whom he met as she was coming out of a café with her boyfriend, a Mr Baker, on 3 March 1953. When Baker went across the road to talk to a friend, Christie and Hectorina struck up a conversation, during the course of which she told him that she and Baker were looking for somewhere to stay as they had just been evicted from their flat. Christie offered them accommodation for a few days until they could find somewhere else. Apparently, after three nights at Rillington Place, on 6 March:

> I told them they would have to go as he was being very unpleasant ... they left ... the girl came back alone ... she asked if he had called ... She said she would wait but I advised her not to. She insisted on staying in case he came.

I told her she couldn't ... she must go and that she couldn't stay there alone. She was very funny about it, I got hold of her arm and tried to lead her out. I pushed her out of the kitchen. She started struggling like anything; and some of her clothing got torn. She then sort of fell limp as I had hold of her. She sank to the ground, and I think some of her clothing must have got caught round her neck.

In court, when asked if he had strangled Hectorina, Christie said, 'I must have done', although he claimed not to remember. As in the previous two cases, Christie did not admit to gassing his victim: this admission would have shattered his claims of self-defence and provocation. After penetrating her body, Christie put her in the cupboard behind the wall.

The scenarios which Christie presented to the police were largely inaccurate. The post-mortem evidence and the stories of other women who had encountered Christie attest to this. Mary O'Neill's and Helen Sunderland's statements to the police are helpful in establishing the way in which Christie approached and elicited the trust of his potential victims.

Mary O'Neill met Christie on 23 January 1953 at Ladbroke Grove Station where they got talking, at Christie's instigation, and travelled together. Mary had her baby with her, and Christie gave her £1 to help her and her child financially. After this initial meeting Mary used to go to Rillington Place – at Christie's suggestion – to visit him, where he regularly gave her money and possessions of Ethel's, whom he told her had died. Just over a week after meeting Mary, while they were at Rillington Place, Christie pulled her on to the mattress. When Mary began to struggle vigorously and threatened to scream, Christie let her go. Despite this incident, Mary continued to visit Christie who, on another occasion, told her that he expected some return on his money and asked her to stay the night, telling her ominously that she 'wouldn't be missed'. We suspect that she only got out of the situation alive by telling Christie that she had told a friend his name and address. Unwilling to take the chance that she was telling the truth, Christie had little choice but to let her go.

Helen Sunderland was also approached and befriended by

Christie who sometimes helped her financially and gave her presents. She used to visit him at Rillington Place – he seemed harmless enough and, besides, she needed the money. She insisted that the relationship had not been sexual. As he had done with Mary, after they had got to know each other, Christie forcefully propositioned Helen. A well-aimed kick gave her enough time to escape.

Both Mary and Helen would almost certainly have been raped and murdered had they not escaped by wit or by force. It is likely that Christie's victims were approached in similar ways to Mary and Helen, and offered money and presents. After he had earned their trust, he would attack and kill them. There was no element of provocation in Christie's murders, no question of self-defence: he manufactured accounts of his victims' predatory sexuality and violence to justify, and to validate, his necrophilious urges and behaviour.

John Christie was the first person to be tried at the Old Bailey after its restoration from damage by bombing during the war; a queue for seats in the public gallery had begun to form some fourteen hours before the trial was due to start on 22 June 1953. Mr Justice Finnemore was presiding; for the Crown was the Attorney-General Sir Lionel Heald, Mr R. E. Seaton and Mr Maxwell Turner; for the defence Mr Curtis-Bennett, QC and Mr Colin Sleetman; the jury comprised three women and nine men. Christie was charged only with the murder of his wife, Ethel Christie, despite the fact that he had confessed to an additional six murders. Unlike today, in 1953 it was only possible to be tried for one murder at a time.

To the charge of murder the defence had entered a plea of 'guilty but insane'. Christie readily admitted that he had killed his wife, there was to be no disputing the *actus reus* – the actual physical act – it was Christie's state of mind that was in question. The burden was not upon the Crown to prove a case of murder, as this had already been established, the burden was upon the defence to prove that at the time of the murder Christie had been insane within the McNaughten Rules. As Mr Justice Finnemore pointed out, 'every person is presumed to be sane unless or until the contrary is proved. Therefore everybody is responsible if he breaks the law unless it is proved that he was insane.' For Christie to be considered insane within the McNaughten Rules it was necessary for the defence to prove that at the time he murdered Ethel he was 'labouring under such a defect of reason, from disease of the mind' that (1) he did not know the nature and quality of the act he was doing; or if he did know it, then, (2) he did not know that what he was doing was wrong.

The Crown's case was simple. Christie had killed his wife, Ethel: Christie's statement and the pathologist's report were read out as proof of this. And he had done so intentionally, calmly, deliberately and in full knowledge of what he was doing and that it was wrong. Furthermore, the Attorney-General told the court, there is no such defence in law as 'mercy killing'. Therefore, even if the court did believe Christie when he said that he killed Ethel in order to relieve her suffering (although the forensic evidence was in direct contradiction to this) it was still a case of murder, and Christie should be found guilty as charged. The facts of the case, he said, would surely satisfy the court that Christie's behaviour directly after Ethel's death was that of a deviant and cunning man with a crime he must conceal at all costs, not that of a madman. At this time, Christie deliberately set out to deceive various people as to the whereabouts of his wife, in order that they would think she was still alive.

The month after Ethel's death, on 26 January, Christie wrote to the bank in Sheffield where Ethel had her account, forging his wife's handwriting and signature, and requesting them to close the account and send on the money. The bank manager sent £10 and received a receipt signed 'Ethel Christie'. Christie also sold the furniture from his flat to Mr Hockway, explaining to him that his wife had gone to Northampton and that he was going to join her there shortly. To neighbours and friends Christie explained that Ethel had gone away. He spoke to Rosina Swann, a neighbour of his, twice on 19 December: on the first occasion Christie told her that Ethel was visiting family in Sheffield, on the second he said that he had had a telegram from Ethel which allegedly said 'Arrived safely, and love to Rosie'. About a week after

Christmas he told Mrs Grimes, another neighbour, that Ethel was in Birmingham looking after her sick sister, which was the same story that he told to Mr Stuart, another tenant at number 10.

The real problem, however, was with Ethel's family, particularly as it was Christmas time. How could he explain Ethel's not getting in touch? Ethel had actually written a letter to Mrs Bartle, her sister, on 10 December which she had not got around to posting. On 15 December, the day after Ethel's death, Christie decided to post it himself to allay suspicion, writing on it that 'Ethel has no envelopes, so I posted it for her from work. Reg.' Nearer Christmas, Christie sent Ethel's family a gift of a box of stationery and a card saying that Ethel had asked him to write in her place as the 'rheumatism in her fingers is not so good just now ... I am rubbing them for her and it makes them easier. We are in good health and as soon as Ethel can write ... she is going to send a letter.'

Christie had killed Ethel, and he had done so in full possession of the knowledge that it was wrong, there was no doubt about it. Why attempt to cover it up otherwise? 'Whatever else may be open to discussion in this case,' said the Attorney-General, 'there was no doubt a deliberate series of deceits, lies and eventually forgery designed to conceal Mrs Christie's death.' Thus, the implication was, he must be sane.

The defence, the Attorney-General said, were going to ask that the jury find Christie guilty but insane: either he did not know what he was doing at the time of the murder, or he did not know that it was wrong. But, said the Attorney-General, 'Whatever evidence is given by the defence, the facts of the case negate both of these propositions which I have told you must be established ... There is every possible proof that he knew he had done wrong and was making every effort to conceal it.' Furthermore, it was the murder of Ethel Christie alone that should concern the jury. The defence, he said, would present evidence as to other murders Christie had committed but 'the state of mind of Christie when he killed his wife is the only relevant state of mind'.

It was now the turn of the defence. The charge before the

court today, said Mr Curtis-Bennett, was indeed only for one murder, yet when the case first appeared before the magistrates it was for four murders. It was only fair, he continued, that the court be aware of, and hear evidence regarding, these other cases. Obviously, if the defence were trying to prove that Christie had been insane at the time of Ethel's murder they had a better chance of doing so if he had killed other women, in seemingly motiveless attacks. As Christie himself said to the prison chaplain: 'The more, the merrier'; the more bodies, the greater the chance of a finding of insanity.

When Christie murdered his wife, said Mr Curtis-Bennett, he was insane – 'mad as a March hare', 'a raging lunatic', 'hopelessly and utterly mad' – within the McNaughten Rules, and indeed within any rules. Christie did know what he was doing at the time, he did not, however, know that what he was doing was wrong, maintained the defence. Mr Curtis-Bennett told the court that, 'By the time he has finished [testifying] … you can have no doubt, doctors or no doctors, that at the time he did each of these killings, including that of his wife, he was mad in the eyes of the law.'

Mr Curtis-Bennett then called Christie to the stand to tell his 'terrifying story'. Throughout his testimony, which covered his background, the murder of Ethel and his other murders, Christie came across as rather a pathetic figure. He mumbled inaudibly through most of his answers, frequently refused to speak, and answered many questions – particularly those concerning the more distasteful details of the murders – with the words, 'I don't know', 'I cannot recall', 'I cannot remember'. The judge constantly had to ask him to speak up, although Mr Curtis-Bennett had asked the court to be patient with Christie, as his voice had been damaged in the war. Finally a microphone was installed so that his testimony could be adequately heard. Christie openly wept on at least two occasions, both when he looked at the oath and when he recounted the story of his wife's murder. Were the admissions, behaviour and demeanour of the man whom the jury saw before them, Mr Curtis-Bennett asked, really those of a sane man? 'You saw him in the witness-box. Didn't you think that he exhibited every sign a layman can see of being mad? This man leaves those bodies in this house and gives evidence like a madman.'

Then came the crux of the case for the defence: the evidence of the psychiatrists who deemed Christie to be insane. Dr Hobson (a consultant in psychological medicine at Middlesex Hospital), who had examined Christie on ten or twelve occasions while he had been on remand, testified that the defendant was suffering from the mental disorder known as hysteria. 'Christie's personality, characteristics, his past medical and personal history, the psychiatric symptoms and signs he exhibits at the present time, are quite typical of what is seen in the mental illness to which we attach the label hysteria.' Furthermore, Dr Hobson said, he was suffering from this condition to a 'gross degree' and that in this severe form of the illness it might only be possible to treat it by care within a psychiatric institution.

Dr Hobson testified that the 'first definite signs' of this hysteria had been apparent as far back as 1918, when Christie had suffered mustard-gas poisoning, which he claimed had rendered him blind and dumb. The psychiatrist also referred to Christie's continual visits to his doctor, who had described Christie as a 'neurotic' and 'nervous' man who visited him for a diverse range of psychosomatic symptoms. Dr Hobson said that Christie had been suffering from attacks of hysteria for so long now – almost his entire life – that his mind had become affected with the disease of hysteria. Furthermore, he told the court that 'I regard Christie as one of the most severe hysterics that I have met in my psychiatric practice. In my opinion these severer forms of hysteria should be regarded as "disease of the mind" of the McNaughten Rules.'

When asked to relay to the court what the symptoms of this disease were, Dr Hobson said that Christie had an 'abnormal memory'. He often made contradictory statements which he himself thought made perfect sense, he described embarrassing situations pertaining to himself as if he were talking of a third person, and he constantly strayed from the point when it suited him. These were tactics to preserve Christie's self-respect, said Dr Hobson. The disease had particularly affected Christie's powers of reason, so that while he knew what he was doing when he killed Ethel, it was *highly probable* that he didn't know that it was wrong. As a consequence of the disease Christie displayed 'falsification of memory', that is, he 'forgets or falsely remembers' very easily. Thus, when he killed Ethel he had 'forgotten' that it is wrong to kill.

But what of Christie's deceitful and calculating behaviour after Ethel's murder? In answer to this, Mr Curtis-Bennett told the court that the defence weren't contending that Christie was mad *all* of the time, just at the times when he committed the murders. 'When he comes out of his lunacy he knows what he is doing and what he has done. Then, being a human being, it is not in the least unnatural that he should do his best to cover up what he has done.'

The Crown then called psychiatrists in rebuttal, who testified that, in their opinion, it was not that Christie didn't *know* that killing was wrong; rather he didn't *care*. Dr Matheson (the Principal Medical Officer at Brixton Prison where Christie had been held on remand) was called first for the Crown. He told the court that Christie was not suffering from the disease of hysteria but rather that he had an hysterical personality, which meant that he sometimes *acted* as a man who suffered from hysteria would act. In modern language we would say that Christie was a neurotic man suffering from anxiety. And an anxious person is far from an insane one. In Dr Matheson's opinion:

> the history does not reveal evidence of disease of the mind but it is the history, in my opinion, of a man with an inadequate personality who, under stress, is liable to behave abnormally. The history suggests that he possesses a weak sex instinct which, to satisfy, he has to adopt abnormal and exaggerated practices.

Lust was the real reason for the murders. Christie's 'weak sex instinct' and his fear of impotence meant that in order to obtain sexual satisfaction he needed to 'adopt perverse practices': to ensure that the woman was unconscious, or dead. Soon this was the only way that Christie could achieve satisfaction: lifeless bodies were what excited him. Dr Matheson concluded that 'he knew the nature and quality of his acts and he knew they were wrong', thus his behaviour did not fall within the McNaughten Rules.

Dr Curran, also for the Crown, when asked by the judge what, in his opinion, had been the motive for the killings, said, 'I presume sex', adding, 'I can only think that he wanted to have relations with unconscious people'. Christie was not, Dr Curran said, suffering from gross hysteria, and the supposed 'falsification of memory' was neither more nor less than a deliberate attempt to hide the truth. He remembered things perfectly when it was beneficial for him to do so, but when it was not he 'forgot': Christie's memory loss was 'purposive, if not convenient'. In his prepared statement Dr Curran said that Christie was 'an egocentric and conceited man' who kept photographs of himself in his cell and compared himself to John Haigh (the acid-bath murderer). He was 'alert and attentive ... [and] played for time when ... asked awkward questions.' 'He is certainly not a mental defective', Dr Curran continued, 'he is above average intelligence. He is a very highly abnormal character rather than a victim of mental disorder' with 'no delusions, hallucinations or misinterpretations'. As his report had said, Christie was 'a pathological liar [with] an unparalleled facility for self-deception' who 'always [found it] difficult to sort out fact from fiction'. This was not because he was suffering from any mental disease, but because he was 'full of snivelling hypocrisy' and couldn't bear it to be known that his murders were sexually motivated as he was of outwardly prudish character. It was the Crown's contention that Christie was a sexually deviant, cunning and violent man; not a legally insane one.

The defence's position was weak. Christie's behaviour after Ethel's death seemed entirely deliberate and calculated, not the work of a madman. And if the defence had a psychiatrist that said Christie was insane, well, the Crown had two that said he was not. The defence did, however, have common sense on their side, which Mr Curtis-Bennett used to his utmost advantage when he colourfully summed up for the defence by suggesting that 'there is no other conclusion but that Christie was as mad as a March hare when he killed these people', 'hopelessly and truly mad'. Even putting aside the medical evidence, said Mr Curtis-Bennett, the killing of Ethel Christie was obviously madness, the most insane of all the murders as it was the fundamentally motiveless killing of the woman Christie loved most in the world: 'I suggest that is maniacal behaviour', 'This man's crazy, isn't he?' Furthermore, Mr Curtis-Bennett continued, in an emotive speech:

> You may think that a man who has intercourse with a dead or dying body is mad, and that I submit has been proved here on one occasion at least. Here is this man, living from day to day with these dead people in the garden, slowly rotting away to skeletons, the bodies in the cupboard becoming more and more rotten, and it is said that he is sane within the meaning of the law.

And if common sense was not good enough to recommend that Christie was mad (which it is not within the law) then consider the expert opinion of Dr Hobson who testified that Christie was suffering from the mental disease of hysteria to a 'gross degree'. If he was right in his diagnosis, said Mr Curtis-Bennett, then there was no option but to deliver a verdict of 'guilty but insane'. 'I submit that we have shown that on 14 December he was legally mad within the McNaughten Rules. However distasteful, however much you think he ought to be out of this world, on a fair view the proper verdict is one of insanity.' The murder of Ethel Christie was, Mr Curtis-Bennett said, 'absolutely motiveless. What is the clue to it? Insanity.'

But the murder was not without motive. Although it was not the job of the prosecution to offer a motive, one had arisen through the testimony of the psychiatrists for the Crown. The series of murders was committed out of lust, and the murder of Ethel Christie was committed, in a sense, as a by-product of this same lust: the lust to continue the series of murders that he had started. Ethel was simply in the way; she knew, or at least suspected, too much. Introducing evidence concerning the other murders was intended to aid the defence in a finding of insanity. But ultimately it assisted the prosecution, as it showed that

Christie was a sex murderer who was prepared to kill his wife in order to continue to indulge his lust for killing.

On 25 June the jury took just eighty-four minutes to agree with the Crown. Christie was found guilty as charged: he had killed his wife, Ethel Christie, and when he had done so he knew both what he was doing and that it was wrong. After the verdict had been announced, the judge's clerk placed the black cap on Justice Finnemore's head as he told Christie:

> You have been found guilty of murder by the jury and for that crime there is only one sentence known to our law, and that is that you be taken from this place to a lawful prison and thence to a place of execution and there suffer death by hanging and that your body be buried in the precincts of the prison.

Crowds had gathered outside the Old Bailey waiting for the verdict. When one woman was asked by a reporter why she and her friend were there, she replied that 'we wanted to see if he was really human'. Many thought not. On 15 July 1953 Christie was hanged at Pentonville prison. He was the last serial killer to be hanged in Britain, in the very place in which Timothy Evans had been executed three years earlier, for a murder that he did not commit. Ironically, the case of Christie can be used to justify the use of capital punishment (surely such a man deserves to die) while at the same time providing a terrible example of what happens when a miscarriage of justice occurs. It is not possible to recall Timothy Evans from the dead.

4

IAN BRADY AND MYRA HINDLEY

yra Hindley was, by all accounts, a normal and reasonably happy little girl. Born in Gorton, an industrial district of Manchester, on 23 July 1942, Myra was the first child of Nellie (or Hettie, as she was known) and Bob Hindley. Hettie, who worked as a machinist, raised Myra for the first three years of her life without the help of her husband, as Bob was serving in a parachute regiment. Hettie had support from her mother, Ellen Maybury, in whose house she and Myra lived until Bob returned, when they bought a place of their own just around the corner. Bob had some trouble readjusting to civilian life, and though he got a job as a labourer, he seemed to spend most of his time at the local pub. Never having been a particularly affectionate man, and having missed the first few vital years of his daughter's development – when parent and child bond – Bob and Myra were never to be close.

Indeed, Myra Hindley claimed years later – in the *Guardian* in 1995 – that her father was 'taciturn' and 'bad tempered', with a reputation locally as a 'hard man' who drank every night, invariably getting himself into fights and coming home bruised and battered. If Hettie had the cheek to complain she would be beaten; if Myra tried to stop him, she would be his next target. She recalled:

I disliked him intensely for his violence and the tyrannical way he dominated the household. We were in almost constant conflict, and with hindsight I can see that my sense of family values and relationships were seriously undermined by his influence upon me as a child ... Through witnessing and being on the receiving end of so much violence within my own family, I was given many lessons in dominance and control.

One might think that such memories are unusually clear for a child of four, for this is the age at which Myra moved out of the family house. In August 1946 the arrival of a second child, Maureen, inevitably generated more work and it was decided that it would be best for all concerned if Myra moved in with her grandmother, Ellen. Most commentators on Myra's life agree that the move was not at all traumatic for the child. She loved her grandmother, who lived just round the corner, and had always spent a lot of time with her. Thus, her move was convenient and happy for everyone as it meant that Ellen was no longer lonely, Maureen and Myra did not have to share a bedroom, and the strain on Hettie and Bob (who were both working) was lessened. But we must remember that Myra was only four years old. Although she did have a close relationship with her grandmother, it wouldn't have been natural if she hadn't felt a little perplexed and rejected at being usurped by the new arrival in her parents' home.

At the age of five Myra started at Peacock Street Primary School, where she is remembered as a mature and sensible little girl, although she could act rather spoilt at times. Her grandmother doted upon her, letting her stay home from school on the slightest pretence, so Myra developed a bossy streak with the other children, as she was so accustomed to getting her own way at home. She is also remembered as a bit of a tom-boy, who was out with her friends every night, getting into some mischief or other. It was a surprise when Myra failed her 11+, for she had an IQ of slightly better than average (109), but her bad attendance went against her and she was not accepted at the local grammar school, instead going to Ryder Brow Secondary Modern. Although her attendance record continued to be bad at Ryder Brow, she was consistently in the 'A' stream in all her subjects; her headmaster, Lloyd Jones, remembers that she had some talent for creative writing and poetry, where her efforts were used as examples to her classmates. She also loved sports, played netball and rounders, was a good swimmer and enjoyed athletics. In appearance and personality she was never very feminine, which is perhaps why she never had any boyfriends at school; when the boys referred to Myra at all it was often by her nickname of 'Square Arse' – due to her big hips – and she was also teased about her unsightly nose.

In her letter to the *Guardian* in 1995 Myra Hindley claimed that when she was growing up she was 'never cruel to animals or children', contrary to the stereotype of the childhood of the serial killer, and indeed it seems as if she was genuinely fond of both. Her love of children, and the fact that she was a mature and responsible girl, meant that she and her friends were frequently trusted to baby-sit for neighbours' children. One of these neighbours, Joan Phillips, remembers that her husband, 'used to say he liked Myra to baby-sit because we could go out in peace, knowing everything would be all right if she was there. My boys loved her because she would spoil them.' Myra's love of animals was manifest in her devastation when her grandmother's dog, Duke, was run over by a car and killed. Only a few years later Myra was again heart-broken when her own dog, Puppet, died while she, and it, were in police custody. 'Murderers!' she screamed at the police, with no sense of irony.

At the age of fifteen one of her best friends, thirteen-year-old Michael Higgins, drowned, which was to have a profound effect on Myra. Given their age difference, she and Michael were an unlikely partnership, but she looked after the timid and fragile boy as if he were a younger brother. Myra and Michael's initials were the same, which she felt pre-destined them to everlasting friendship. On a hot day in July Michael had asked Myra if she would like to go swimming with him in the disused reservoir that the local children played in, but she had declined as she already had something planned. Later, when she learned that Michael had got cramp while swimming and drowned, she was inconsolable. She was a strong swimmer and thought that if she had been there she might have saved him.

In the ensuing weeks she vacillated between hysteria and depression. She cried, dressed in black, went to church every night to light a candle in his memory, and collected money from the neighbours for a wreath. Her best friend, Pat, remembered years later that it was the only time she had ever seen Myra cry. Myra herself later recalled that she was soon told that her grieving was excessive and that she was to pull herself together as she had become 'soft in the head'. This, Hindley said, was a classic example of what she had been taught throughout her childhood, that any real feelings were to be repressed lest they overwhelmed you. Later, she claimed that she was able to play her part in the murders because she had learnt this lesson too well. She knew the murders were wrong, she cared that they were wrong, but to please her partner, Ian Brady, she rendered these feelings inaccessible.

There were two immediate consequences of Michael's death for Myra. Firstly, she converted to Roman Catholicism, which was Michael's religion; secondly, her school work began to deteriorate, under the strain of grief, indifference, and missed time. She left school at fifteen, not considered bright or motivated enough to stay on to do her O-levels, and got a job as a junior clerk at the electrical engineering firm of Lawrence Scott and Electrometers. As a teenager, having just left school, Myra was in most respects like the other Gorton girls. She liked going out dancing and to cafés, listening to rock 'n' roll (she loved Elvis Presley), maybe flirting with the local boys and having a surreptitious cigarette. She began to take more of an interest in her appearance and began bleaching her hair – sometimes rinsing it pink or blue – and wearing thick make-up to make herself look older. On her seventeenth birthday she became engaged to Ronnie Sinclair, a local boy who worked as a tea-blender at the Co-op.

Underlying this ordinary and tolerably contented exterior, however, dissatisfaction was brewing: Myra Hindley was beginning to feel the tedium and the constraints of the life to which she was expected to conform. Getting married, buying a nice little semi, having a few children, and trying to make ends meet while your husband spent the housekeeping money on beer, seemed to be about all her friends could envisage. When she realized that this wasn't what she wanted, she broke off her engagement after six months. She was, she said, fed up with Ronnie's immaturity, his heavy drinking and smoking, and his limited outlook on life. Unlike most of the girls she knew, Myra wanted something more exciting, she didn't want to be 'living a kitchen-sink drama'. She wanted, in her own words, 'a career, to better myself, to travel and to break free of the confines of what was expected from me'. Eventually she applied for entrance forms for the navy and the army, thought about working as a nanny in America, and went off to London in search of a job. The forms were never sent, however, the job in London never located. But a chance of something exciting and new arrived in Gorton itself, in the form of Ian Brady.

Christened Ian Duncan Stewart, Ian Brady was born in Glasgow on 2 January 1938, making him four years older than Myra Hindley. Ian's mother was Margaret (known as Peggy) Stewart, who worked as a tea-room waitress in a hotel. His father, Peggy has always insisted, was a journalist for a Glasgow paper who died a few months before Ian was born. Despite her single status, for official records Peggy always signed herself as Mrs Stewart, as having an illegitimate child in 1938 was still viewed with disfavour. When her son was born, having no husband to support her, Peggy needed to keep her waitressing job, at least part-time. This sometimes meant leaving baby Ian at home by himself when Peggy couldn't afford a baby-sitter. But leaving a small baby alone in a rented room in Caledonia Road in the Gorbals, then one of the roughest slums in Glasgow, was far from ideal. When it became apparent to her that she simply couldn't manage, she advertised for a permanent child-minder, somebody who could take Ian into their home and give him the care that she was unable to provide.

Her advertisement was answered by Mary and John Sloane, a couple who already had four children of their own and seemed trustworthy and caring. Peggy unofficially turned over four-month-old Ian's welfare to them, and from this point Ian became known as 'Sloany'. Initially Peggy would go to visit her son every Sunday bearing gifts, and as he grew up he knew her as 'Peggy', while Mary Sloane was 'auntie' or 'ma'. It must have been confusing for the small boy: who was 'mum'? Nobody ever told Ian that Peggy was his natural mother, and he was left slowly to realize it for himself. As time passed Peggy's visits became increasingly infrequent, and when she married Patrick Brady when Ian was twelve, she and her new husband moved to Manchester. There was to be no contact between Peggy and Ian for four years.

Although in retrospect Ian Brady recalled his early childhood with the Sloanes as the happiest time of his life, as a child there was always the niggling feeling that he didn't rightfully belong in the family, that he was imposing. His ambiguous relationship with 'Peggy' didn't help to clarify matters, nor did the discovery, when he was thirteen, that he was illegitimate. Despite the Sloanes' best efforts to provide a loving environment, Ian seemed resolutely determined not to respond to their care and attention. As a child he was lonely, difficult and angry, banging his head on the floor and having frequent temper tantrums.

As he grew older, it is often said – although the truth of these stories has been questioned – that he began to be cruel to other children and to animals. A childhood friend, John Cameron, remembers Brady's cruelty: 'He once tied me to a steel washing post in the backyard, heaped newspapers round my legs and set fire to them. I can still remember feeling dizzy with the smoke before I was rescued.' Cameron also remembers how Brady would throw cats off the top of three-storey tenement buildings, ostensibly to see if they would really fall on their feet. At other times he would dig holes at the cemetery and trap cats in the home-made graves to see how long they could live without food and water. 'The cats weren't worth bothering with after he'd finished with them,' Cameron said. Brady apparently also took pleasure in killing birds and once, shortly before his tenth birthday, he allegedly cut the heads off four white rabbits. Yet, on another occasion, when he saw a horse fall in the street and break a bone, he ran off crying; and when his dog got ill he prayed that it wouldn't die. When it expired anyway, he firmly decided that there was no God.

At Camden Street Primary School, Ian Brady is remembered as a rather bright boy who didn't try as hard as he might have. To the other boys and girls he seemed different, secretive, an outsider. He was not interested in sports, unlike most young boys, and the others used to call him 'Big Lanky Sloany' or a 'big lassie' because he was useless at football. He seemed to identify more with nature than he did with his peers. When he was nine the Sloanes took the family on an outing to the moors where, Ian later recalled, the wide open spaces and surrounding country-side fascinated him. The winds, the sky, and the water were awe-inspiring and engaged his imagination, evoking for him a deeper power than he had ever encountered. This feeling was to re-emerge in adulthood when he took his victims out onto the moors. He had internalized the numinous quality of these brute natural surroundings, identifying with their bleakness and intro-jecting their monumental power. They became an objective correlative of his unconscious life.

At the age of eleven Ian passed his exams to Shawlands Academy, a school for pupils with above-average intelligence. But he was lazy, never applied himself, and began to misbehave: he took up smoking, all but gave up his school work, and started to get into trouble with the police. He also developed an interest in the Second World War and began to collect Nazi war memo-rabilia. Frank Fraser, a school-mate, remembers that,

> He read all kinds of books about the Nazis and never stopped talking about them. Even when we were playing war games he made a great point of being a German. My brother was stationed in Germany and Ian was always badgering him for Nazi souvenirs. When Ian used to shout 'Sieg Heil!' and give the Nazi salute, people would laugh.

At the age of thirteen he was charged with housebreaking and bound over by the juvenile courts. Nine months later he was bound over again for burglary. When, at sixteen, he was again found guilty of similar charges, the court decided that Ian would not be given a custodial sentence on the condition that he made a new start, in Manchester, with Peggy (whom he had not seen in four years), and Patrick Brady, the step-father he had never met.

At the end of 1954 Ian set off to his new home in Moss Side. Here he became more socially withdrawn than ever, his pronounced Scottish accent instantly distancing him from the community. He had never formed a real identity: his illegitimacy, ambiguous relationship with his mother, and the feeling of being an outsider in his foster family had all made for an unsure and uncentred youth. In an attempt to establish himself within some kind of familial and social context, Ian changed his name to Brady, although he and his step-father apparently didn't get on very well, and took the job that Patrick got him as a porter at the local market. But it wasn't enough. He needed something else, a direction, something to believe in. He began visiting the library, and there he found literature that excited him, and that he could relate to: books such as Dostoyevsky's *Crime and Punishment*, the works of Marquis de Sade, and sadistic literature in general – *Justine*, *The Kiss of the Whip* and *The Torture Chamber*. Books on fascism and Nazism also continued to stimulate him greatly.

Dr Robert Brittain, in his study of the sadistic murderer (published in 1970), which is based on more than twenty years of dealing with such people in his career as a forensic pathologist and psychiatrist, makes an observation that fits Brady exactly: 'These people ... commonly relate to some of the following: De Sade and his works, sadism, torture, cruelty, Nazism ... atrocities, brutalities ... sexual perversions, obscenities, erotica generally, guns and other weapons, or uniforms.' A psychiatrist later postulated that the young and unformed Brady, already with an anti-social and aggressive streak, was enticed by the literature's 'loss of feeling'. It seemed freeing to him. He was enthralled by stories of people who weren't bound by convention, who invented their own realities, and grasped whatever it was they wanted, without compunction. Increasingly, he himself became estranged from other people's feelings, and he began to think of them as objects.

It was inevitable that he would return to his criminal ways. Just over a year after his move, Ian was arrested for aiding and abetting. He had left his job at the market and had been working in a brewery where his employers discovered that he was stealing lead seals. This time the courts weren't so lenient and Ian was given two years in borstal. After sentencing, and while awaiting a place to become free at a borstal, Ian was placed in

Strangeways Prison in Manchester for three months. At the age of seventeen Strangeways must have been a daunting place, and Ian Brady was forced to toughen up quickly. After three months he was moved to Hatfield, Yorkshire, an institution for young offenders who are brighter than most and being punished for relatively minor offences. Instead of appreciating the light regime, however, Ian took advantage of it, and he was soon brewing, and drinking, his own alcohol, and running gambling books. After a drunken scuffle with a warder, it was decided that he should be sent to a tougher borstal in Hull Prison. It is widely believed that this is where Ian actively set out to learn more criminal ways, seeking to make as many 'contacts' as he could among his fellow inmates. He even took courses to learn how to handle the money that he intended to make upon his release, by whatever means possible. But Colin Wilson's claim that, 'Three months in Strangeways and two years in borstal had turned a youth with a minor criminal record and a tendency to bookishness into an antisocial rebel', perhaps overestimates the effects of his incarceration. Brady was heading for trouble long before he was imprisoned.

On his release in November 1957, Ian went home to Peggy and Patrick and, after several months of unemployment, found a labouring job which he kept for six months. His family noticed that after his release he was even more silent and brooding. He continued avidly to read sadistic and fascist literature, retained his criminal contacts, and dreamt of money-making scams. But until he was ready with a plan he decided to put some of his newly acquired book-keeping skills to some legitimate use. In 1959 Brady got a job as a stock clerk with Millwards Merchandising, a chemical distribution company. Just over a year later, in January 1961, a new secretary arrived.

Even before she started at Millwards Myra Hindley had been intrigued by Ian Brady. A friend had described him to her as shy, good-looking, well-dressed and, above all, different. Hindley couldn't have agreed more, and she felt, she later claimed, 'an immediate and fatal attraction'. She found his silent and aloof demeanour (which others interpreted, rightly, as morose and sullen), enigmatic, worldly, and a sign of intelligence. She had never met anybody like him before. The boys she had gone out with previously – like Ronnie Sinclair – were, in contrast to Brady, dull, naive, and unambitious. To Hindley's intense disappointment, however, the attraction seemed to be one-sided. Every night she wrote in her diary of her longing for him: 'Ian looked at me today', 'I pray to God Ian will come to love me', 'He is cruel and selfish, and I love him'. But Brady remained steadfastly uninterested for the first year that they worked together, a year Hindley later described as a time of 'emotional torture' as she fluctuated from 'loving him to hating him'. Eventually, fuelled by a few drinks at the office Christmas party, Brady asked Hindley to go out with him that evening: 'Eureka', she wrote in her diary, 'today we have our first date'.

Hindley's initiation into Brady's secret life began immediately. That very first date he took her to see *The Nuremberg Trials.* As their relationship progressed he played her records of Hitler's marching songs, and encouraged her to read books like *Mein Kampf* and works by de Sade, as well as *Crime and Punishment*, which she did happily. Brady had been an unformed personality when he moved to Manchester, before borstal and the start of his avid reading, and now Hindley was in a similar position. She wanted something different, that would distinguish and brighten her life, and she had neither the training nor the inclination to distinguish between the substantial and the spurious, the healthy and the dangerous. She quickly became 'totally besotted with him, always trying to fathom out the mystery he'd become to me, the aura which emanated from him'; and Brady, who realized this, was ready to exploit it. Eager to please the man who quickly became her first lover, Hindley conscientiously soaked up Brady's ideas, for which he cited sources such as Dostoyevsky, and bolstered with misinterpreted philosophical theories involving the Nietzschian superman. He was the worst and most dangerous kind of autodidact: he learned only in order to justify himself, and interpreted material only in the light of his own nature.

Hindley even began to dress to please him, in Germanic style, with long boots and mini skirts, and bleached hair. And she allowed him to take pornographic photographs of her, and of the two of them having sex. Soon Brady – whose ideas were becoming increasingly paranoid and outrageous – was telling Hindley that Jews and black people deserved to die, that there was no God, that people were maggots to be trodden upon, and that rape and murder were not wrong, indeed murder was 'a supreme pleasure'. Hindley later said that, 'Within months he had convinced me there was no God at all; he could have told me the earth was flat, the moon was made of green cheese and the sun rose in the west, I would have believed him.' To Hindley's family, friends and colleagues the change in her was obvious. The foreman at Millwards said that she started to 'become overbearing and wear kinky clothes'; the manager said she was 'surly at the best of times and aggressive if you spoke to her in the wrong way'. Most tellingly, Hindley's sister Maureen testified in court that her sister,

> Used to go to church, liked dancing ... she liked the normal way of life and had many girlfriends. She liked children. She also liked swimming and reading. She stopped going to church. She said she didn't believe in marriage. She said she hated babies and children and hated people. She never used to keep things under lock and key, but she started after she met Brady.

As Hindley herself later acknowledged, 'my whole self became almost totally subsumed'.

What began with ideas – of the merits of sadism, atheism, fascism – began to move towards reality. Hindley had accepted her lover's theories, but would she put them into practice? In early 1963 Brady began to talk of robbing a bank together, and Hindley responded by starting driving lessons so that she could fulfil her role as get-away driver, and by joining the Cheadle Rifle Club and purchasing two guns. The robbery was never carried out. But Hindley had shown willing, that was enough, it was now time, Brady felt, to cement their relationship.

For Brady, murder could be justified by the literature he read. Raskolnikov, in *Crime and Punishment*, had rationalized his murders to his friend Sonia, by claiming that, 'Power is given only to him who dares to stoop and take it. There is only one thing that matters here: one must have the courage to dare ... I wanted to dare and – and I committed a murder. I only wanted to dare, Sonia, that was my only motive.' If only Hindley could have reacted to Brady as Sonia did to Raskolnikov: ' "Oh, be quiet, be quiet!" Sonia exclaimed deeply shocked. "You have turned away from God, and God has struck you down and handed you over to Satan".' But Hindley had lost all interest in what was right, and at this point in their relationship they were, in Brady's words, 'one mind'. Brady later told journalist Fred Harrison that in the period before the murders began he felt as Raskolnikov did, he had 'reached the stage where, whatever came to mind, get out and do it ... I led the life that other people could only think about.' This is not to say, of course, that Dostoyevsky created a murderer – just as sadistic pornography does not create a rapist: 'The seed was already there ... Raskolnikov's situation was a sort of synopsis of precisely how I was.' Had Brady bothered to finish the book, he might have known the consequences of Raskolnikov's actions. But readers like Brady do not want to understand, but to use, to justify, to misapply. And so a novel written as a critique of unrestrained egoism became, in Brady's mind, the justification for it.

On the evening of 12 July 1963, sixteen-year-old Pauline Reade was going to a dance at the Railway Workers' Social Club. Her friends Linda, Barbara and Pat were meant to be going too, but their parents had discovered at the last minute that there was to be alcohol available, and decided not to allow their daughters to attend. Pauline had called on them all, and her mum, Joan, had even been round to one of the girls' parents to try to persuade them to change their minds. But it was no good. Disappointed, but not deterred, Pauline decided to go alone; after all, it wasn't as if she wouldn't know people there. So at eight o'clock, dressed in her pink party dress, Pauline set out. Pat, Pauline's friend who was not allowed to go to the dance, and Pat's friend, Dorothy, were watching as Pauline made her way to the dance. They wanted to see if she really would dare to go by herself.

Unnoticed by Pauline the girls followed her most of the way to the Railway Club, right past Bannock Street where Myra Hindley lived with her grandmother, and past Westmoreland Road where Brady lived with his mother and step-father. When they were nearly there, Pat and Dorothy took a short cut which would get them to the club before Pauline. There, on the street outside the club, they waited. Pauline never arrived.

When midnight came and went and Pauline was still not home her mother and father, Joan and Amos, went out to look for her. They searched all night but could find no trace of their daughter. The police were contacted and they too began to search for Pauline. It seemed as if she had simply vanished.

Nearly six months later, on 11 November 1963, twelve-year-old John Kilbride and his friend John Ryan had gone to the afternoon showing of *The Mongols* at the local cinema. Leaving the cinema at five o'clock, the boys decided to go to the market in Ashton-Under-Lyne. They often helped the stall-holders, to earn some extra pocket money, and to help their parents out. Not long after they arrived John Ryan got talking to some classmates, while John Kilbride went off to do some other errands. John Ryan remembered two years later in court that 'When I set off to catch the bus, John Kilbride was not with me. I last saw him beside one of the big salvage bins on the open market near the carpet dealer's stall. There was no one with him.'

At some point after this, John disappeared from the market. When he didn't return that evening his mother and father, Sheila and Patrick, called the police. Once again a search began, with police and thousands of volunteers combing the surrounding land for any clue as to John's disappearance. But, like Pauline, there was no sign of where he might have gone. Danny Kilbride, John's brother, remembers: 'He just went missing. All we know is he didn't come home at tea-time. After a week went past, then a month, a year, we knew he weren't coming back.' At the week-ends Myra Hindley frequently shopped at Ashton market, and that particular weekend she had hired a car.

Six months elapsed and another child went missing. On the evening of 16 June 1964, twelve-year-old Keith Bennett was on his way to his grandmother's house, less than a mile away from his home. It was a Tuesday, and on every other Tuesday Keith would go to stay the night with his grandmother. His mother, Winnie, who was on her way to the bingo on the other side of the road, watched her son over the crossing to make sure he was safe, as he had broken his glasses the day before, and then continued in the other direction towards the bingo hall. At some point during the remainder of the short walk to his grandmother's house, Keith disappeared. That day Myra Hindley had picked up Ian Brady from his mother's house on Westmoreland Road. Their return route took the couple down the Stockport Road, where Winnie had lost sight of her son.

Nobody realized that Keith was gone until the next day. Winnie assumed he was with her mother; his grandmother, Gertrude, thought that for some reason Winnie had decided not to send Keith to her that week. Winnie remembers:

> The next morning my mam came up to our house and I said, 'Where's Keith?' because normally she brought him up with her on her way to her job ... She said he hadn't come to her last night. She said she'd been expecting him, but then she thought I must have made some other arrangements. We both started to panic.

Again, the police were contacted and an investigation began; again no sign of the child was located.

Another six months passed. On the afternoon of 26 December 1964 ten-year-old Lesley Ann Downey went to the local fair with her two brothers, and some of their friends. Setting off at about half past four, the children walked, unaccompanied by an adult, to Hulme Hall Lane just ten minutes away. It didn't take them long to spend the bit of money their parents had given them and soon all the children except Lesley Ann were bored and wanted to go home. Lesley Ann decided to stay on by herself for a little while. After her companions had left she was seen for the last time by a classmate, at just after half past five, standing by herself next to one of the rides.

When Lesley Ann didn't return home, her mother, Ann, and Ann's future husband, Alan, began to search for her. Finding no trace of the girl they quickly rang the police. Again the wheels of a missing-child investigation were set into motion. The country-side was searched, people at the fair were questioned, and missing posters were issued. There were no clues as to what had happened.

On the day of Lesley Ann's disappearance, Myra Hindley's grandmother, Ellen Maybury, had spent the day with her son, Jim. Hindley was due to pick her up at half past nine that evening, but she arrived two hours late, only to tell Ellen that she could not take her back to the house they now shared in Wardle Brook Avenue (in which Brady usually resided as well). She blamed the state of the roads, claiming that there was snow on them, but Jim remembers that they were clear.

Four children had disappeared, one every six months: summer, winter, summer, winter. There were several points of similarity which suggested that the same person – or persons, in this case – were responsible for the disappearances. The victims were all aged between ten and sixteen, they had all vanished from a public place without a trace, and they had all disappeared from a similar geographical area, east of Manchester. But after careful investigation, no bodies had been found, and there were no significant leads. In the 1960s the possibility of a serial killer would not have sprung to mind as readily as it does nowadays. And even today the difference in the victimology – two boys, two girls, aged from between ten (prepubescent) and sixteen (almost a woman) – does not exhibit the consistency of pattern that we regularly encounter in serial killers. No local man-hunt was staged, no national search ensued.

There might have been many more 'disappearances' had it not been for David Smith. When David Smith married Myra Hindley's sister, Maureen, in August 1964, Ian Brady actively set out to recruit him into his world of crime, sadism and murder. Hindley had assisted her lover in four murders, and her loyalty was unquestionable, but the thrill was wearing off, and another partner in crime might, Brady felt, add a new dimension. David Smith was certainly no stranger to violence: at the age of eleven he had been convicted of wounding with intent, and at both fourteen and sixteen he was convicted of assault occasioning actual bodily harm. Brady gave the seventeen-year-old Smith books to read and lectured him on his 'theories', as he had done with Hindley. Smith concurred with some of these: he later remembered that Brady's 'philosophy on Jews and pornography seemed right'. The older man seemed 'all grown up and worldly' compared to him, and Smith was flattered by his attentions. He even went so far as to 'case' the bank for the robbery that Brady was forever planning. Together they went to the moors, with Myra and Maureen too, and drank and practised shooting. When their friendship was firm, Brady told Smith that he had murdered several people and buried their bodies on the moors, and that he and Maureen had sat right by the graves on their visits to Saddleworth. But Smith dismissed this as fantasy. In retrospect, he recalled that 'the violence was still around, but at the time I probably didn't realize what shape it was taking.'

Brady and Hindley chose 6 October 1965 as the day for Smith's initiation. The couple drove to Manchester Central Station, where Brady encountered Edward Evans, a seventeen-year-old young man whom Brady later claimed to have met on a previous occasion. Brady believed that Edward was homosexual and asked him if he would like to go home with him, the implication being that some sexual activity would take place. For this reason, he introduced Hindley as his sister. On their return to Wardle Brook Avenue Hindley left Brady and Edward alone while she slipped out to David and Maureen's house with a trivial message for her mother. When she asked Smith to walk her home, claiming to be scared to walk back in the dark, he agreed. On returning to Wardle Brook Avenue, where grandma Maybury was tucked up safely in bed, Hindley invited Smith to come inside, where she left him in the kitchen, saying that Brady had some miniature bottles of wine to give to him.

The evidence later suggested that while Hindley had been away Brady and Edward Evans had engaged in some kind of sexual activity, although whether this was consensual or not we do not know. At the post-mortem examination of Edward's body, dog hairs were found, as Mr Justice Fenton Ashton later put it, 'round his anus – actually round the back passage', which matched the dog hairs on the couch at Wardle Brook Avenue.

The inference from this bizarre bit of evidence clearly suggested that the boy had sat naked on the couch.

In court Smith testified about what happened when he was standing in the kitchen of Wardle Brook Avenue:

> I was reading this label [on a wine bottle] and then all of a sudden I heard a scream, very loud, and it sort of went on ... then I heard Myra shout out: 'Dave, help him' ... I ran out of the kitchen into the living room, and I just froze ... My first thoughts were that Ian had got hold of a life-size rag doll and was just waving it about ... Then it dawned on me that it was not a rag doll. It fell against the couch not more than two feet away from me. My stomach turned over. It was half screaming and groaning. The lad was laid out on his front and Ian stood over him with his legs apart with an axe in his right hand ... The lad groaned and Ian just lifted the axe over his head and brought it down upon the lad's head. There were a couple of seconds' silence and the lad groaned again, only much lower. Ian lifted the axe way above his head and brought it down. The lad stopped groaning then. He was making gurgling noises like when you brush your teeth and gargle with water. Ian placed a cover over his head ... He had a piece of electric wire, and he wrapped it round the lad's neck and began to pull it, and kept on pulling it, and pulling it; and he was saying 'You fucking dirty bastard' over and over again. The lad just stopped making this noise and Ian looked up and said to Myra 'That's it, it's the messiest yet.

Hindley then made tea, and she and Brady joked about the look on Edward's face when Brady struck him ('Did you see it? The terror registered in his eyes.'), and laughed about an earlier occasion when a policeman had confronted Hindley while Brady was off burying one of their other victims on the moors. Horrified, and frightened for his own safety, Smith decided that the best course of action was to keep calm, help them to clean up the mess, tie up the body, put it in the spare bedroom upstairs, and promise to return the next day to dispose of it. When he

John Reginald Halliday Christie. (PA NEWS)

10 Rillington Place, where John Christie rented the ground-floor flat and where his victims were found. (POPPERFOTO)

Timothy Evans, who was hanged for the murder of his wife, Beryl; Christie later confessed to the crime. (POPPERFOTO)

The queue for seats in the public gallery before Christie's trial at the Old Bailey. (PA NEWS)

John Christie being led away by police after having been found guilty of the murder of his wife, Ethel. (POPPERFOTO)

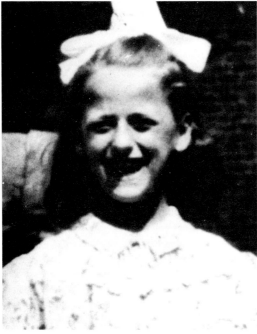

Myra Hindley on Saddleworth Moor in 1987, where she was taken by police in an attempt to locate the graves of Pauline Reade and Keith Bennett.
(REX FEATURES)

Myra Hindley as a girl.
(POPPERFOTO)

Ian Brady at the time of his arrest. (REX FEATURES)

The famous mug shot of Myra Hindley at the time of her arrest.
(REX FEATURES)

16 Wardle Brook Avenue, where Myra Hindley and Ian Brady lived with Hindley's grandmother, and where Edward Evans was murdered. (POPPERFOTO)

The moorland grave of John Kilbride was found in October 1965. (POPPERFOTO)

Peter Sutcliffe, aged four (front left), with family members including his mother (back left), his grandmother (second right) and his great aunt (right).
(NEVILLE PYNE)

Peter Sutcliffe and his wife Sonia on their wedding day.
(NEVILLE PYNE)

The Sheffield street where Peter Sutcliffe was arrested in January 1981. (NEVILLE PYNE)

The crowd outside Dewsbury Crown Court, where Peter Sutcliffe was charged with murder. (NEVILLE PYNE)

finally got home in the early hours of the morning, he was violently sick and told Maureen everything. Together they went to a phone box to call the police at Stalybridge. Smith carried a carving knife and screwdriver with him, afraid that Brady might come after him.

The rest is straightforward: Superintendent Talbot and Detective Sergeant Carr, assisted by other officers, went over to 16 Wardle Brook Avenue and, after some initial resistance from Hindley, were given the key to the spare bedroom where they found the body of Edward Evans which was, one of the officers remembers, 'trussed up like a turkey'. The axe which had killed him was also there, as were Hindley's two guns, each loaded with five bullets. Brady was arrested (Hindley was not arrested until four days later) and his explanation at the police station, as it was at their trial, was that there'd been 'a row' between himself and David Smith, and Edward Evans, and a fight had broken out which had got out of control. He lied further by implicating Smith in the murder and by totally exonerating Hindley: 'David hit him with a stick and kicked him about three times ... There was a hatchet on the floor and I hit Eddie with it ... Then we tied up the body, Dave and I. Nobody else helped.'

On questioning, Hindley's story was the same, and she further claimed to have been crying, horrified, frightened and 'sick through seeing the blood'. But the written 'murder plan' found in Hindley's car told a different story. The three-page document detailed – often in abbreviated form – how their victim's bloodstained clothing should be disposed of, how the house should be cleaned after the murder, what alibis would be offered should the police ever identify them as suspects, and where on the moors the body would be buried.

In spite of this evidence, Hindley might conceivably only have been charged as an accessory, and Brady charged only with the murder of Edward Evans, had it not been for Smith telling the police that Brady had told him on several occasions that he had committed other murders and buried the bodies on Saddleworth Moor. Furthermore, a local girl, twelve-year-old Pat Hodge, told the police how Hindley and Brady used to take her up to the moors for picnics. (Presumably she was never harmed as her parents knew who she was with.) Additionally, during their search of Wardle Brook Avenue the police had found numerous photographs that Brady had taken at the moors. There were too many references to Saddleworth moor to be ignored. Between the photographs, and the testimony of David Smith and Pat Hodge, the police were able to pinpoint the areas of the moors that Brady and Hindley frequented, and the digging began. The police had four particular unsolved disappearances in mind.

On 10 October 1965 the first body was found: that of ten-year-old Lesley Ann Downey. Her body was naked, buried in a shallow grave, her clothes at her feet. But the police needed evidence beyond hearsay and the circumstantial to connect Brady and Hindley to the murder of Lesley Ann. Detective Chief Inspector John Tyrell decided to carry out a more thorough search of Wardle Brook Avenue. On 15 October, he found a left-luggage ticket, tucked in a prayer book, which led the police to a locker at Manchester Central which housed two suitcases. Inside them, amongst other pornographic and sadistic paraphernalia, were semi-pornographic photographs of Lesley Ann Downey. She was captured by the camera in several different poses, naked, bound and gagged. But there was worse to come – a harrowing tape recording of the girl screaming, crying, and begging for her life. A man could be heard threatening Lesley Ann: 'If you don't keep that hand down I will slit your neck'; a woman said 'Shut up or I will forget myself and hit you one'. The voices on the tape were those of Myra Hindley and Ian Brady, the prosecution contended at their trial. Ann Downey – now Ann West – was obliged to listen to the tape in order to identify her daughter's voice. 'I couldn't believe what I was hearing,' she later said.

Ann was also asked to look at two of the nine photographs which had been taken of her daughter. Police officers told her they had picked the two which they hoped would be the least distressing to her. Ann remembers, 'I nearly died. I can see them now. They had Lesley naked, tied over a chair, gagged and her hands bound behind her back, naked. And the next one was on Hindley's bed and she had her mouth stuffed and gagged and she was bound. Her hands together as though she was in prayer, on Hindley's bed.' If these, she wondered, were the 'best' photographs, what did that say about the worst? To this day, Ann West says, she recites the Lord's Prayer every night, but there is one line she simply cannot bring herself to say. She will never forgive.

Even in the face of such comprehensive evidence of guilt, both Hindley and Brady denied murdering Lesley Ann. Their implausible story was that the girl had been brought to the house by David Smith, who wanted Brady to photograph her, and the recording was of their voices as they tried to subdue her for the pictures to be taken. The tape was saved, and copied, according to Brady, as it was an 'unusual' piece. Hindley explained that she had adopted a harsh tone with Lesley Ann because she had panicked when the girl started to cry: 'The front door was wide open, and the bedroom door was open, and I was frightened someone would hear me ... I was worried. That's why I was so brusque and cruel in my attitude to her. I just wanted her to be quiet.' After the photographs were taken, according to this improbable account, Lesley Ann had left unharmed, with Smith. The implication was that if she was dead then Smith had killed her.

But the evidence left little room for doubt, and Brady and Hindley were jointly charged with Lesley Ann's murder. Without the evidence relating to Lesley Ann – with Hindley's voice on the tape, her fingerprints on the photographs, the photographs taken on her bed with a camera she had purchased – it was still conceivable that Hindley could have emerged from the other murders as a naive and unwilling accomplice of the monstrous Brady. But the evidence in relation to this charge shattered any doubt that Hindley's role in the murders was an active one.

Eleven days after Lesley Ann's body was discovered, a second body was found. Sheila Kilbride vividly remembers that her son's body was found 'not in a grave' but 'in a hole, head-first, with his feet nine inches from the top', his trousers and underpants around his knees. As it had been in the ground for over two years, John's body was badly decomposed, and it was identified by Sheila when she recognized one of his shoes. She remembers the moment clearly, 'I was just stunned, I didn't cry, I just sat there feeling very sick.' But there was, at least, some palpable sense of relief: it was over. 'It was devastating but it was the end of the waiting, at least I knew.'

The evidence which implicated Brady and Hindley in John Kilbride's murder was not overwhelming – there was no tape, no pornographic photographs – but it was incriminating enough. At Wardle Brook Avenue police found the name 'John Kilbride' written in Brady's hand in his notebook; a photograph was found, which had been taken by Brady, of Hindley actually posing on John's grave at the moors; Hindley had hired a car for the very day that John was abducted and it was returned in a muddy state. Finally, Maureen Hindley testified that her sister and Brady shopped every week at Ashton market, from which John had disappeared. The evidence was sufficient to charge them.

When Brady and Hindley were questioned about this evidence their replies were unconvincing. In answer to why he had written the name 'John Kilbride' in his notebook, Brady claimed that he knew a 'lad in Hull' with the same name. And, according to Brady, the photograph of Hindley at John's grave was just a snap-shot of Hindley looking at the dog. Hindley, of course, claimed that she had no idea she was being photographed at a grave. She had hired the car, she claimed, as she had just passed her test and wanted, on that very day, to 'go for a run so I could keep my hand in at driving', and she denied the car was dirty when she returned it.

The search of the moors continued, the police still convinced that the bodies of Pauline Reade and Keith Bennett, who had disappeared in similar circumstances to the other children, were also buried there. They didn't, however, have any further evidence to connect Brady and Hindley to these disappearances, as they did with Lesley Ann, Edward and John. When the search had lasted some months, and no more bodies had been discovered, the police had little choice but to call off the search.

On 27 April 1966, Hindley and Brady were brought to trial at Chester Assizes for the murders of Edward Evans, Lesley Ann

Downey and John Kilbride. They pleaded not guilty to all charges. As if the crimes themselves were not enough to ensure that Hindley and Brady would be universally detested, their cowardly and steadfast attempt at their trial to blame another man for the murders only reinforced public hatred of them. Because they did not confess, neither could they express any remorse for their crimes, nor any sorrow for the families of their victims. Throughout the trial, Sheila Kilbride remembers them as 'very cold', they showed 'no heart', manifested no remorse. However, despite their unwavering refusal to admit any knowledge of the crimes, the evidence was overwhelming and Brady was found guilty of the murders of Lesley Ann Downey, John Kilbride and Edward Evans; Hindley of the murder of Lesley Ann Downey and Edward Evans, and for harbouring Brady with the knowledge that he had killed John Kilbride. They escaped death by a matter of months. The Murder (Abolition of the Death Penalty) Act 1965 had come into effect just four weeks after their arrests.

The case of the 'Moors Murderers' has arguably become the most notorious case in the history of modern British crime. Murders in the 1990s, like those committed by Robert Black, though every bit as horrific, simply haven't generated such a phenomenal amount of media and public attention. But in 1965 the case was unique. This was the first time in Britain that a woman, and a woman in her early twenties at that, had been involved in a killing partnership which involved serial sex murders committed against children. It simply wasn't something the public could comprehend. How could a woman – the archetypal figure of mothering, nurturing and caring – take a part in the killing and sexual assault of young boys and girls? Ann West encapsulated the nation's feelings when she said, 'It is because she is a woman that her crime is so evil and so unforgivable.'

For their first few years of incarceration Hindley and Brady wrote to each other constantly, even applying for permission to be allowed to marry, on the grounds that they were already common-law man and wife. Hindley enlisted Lord Longford's help in their application. But gradually a rift opened between them. Brady settled down into prison life, quietly accepting his sentence and, by implication, his guilt; Hindley vehemently continued to assert her innocence, insisting that the murders had been carried out by Brady and Smith. She appealed against her sentence immediately after the trial in 1966, on the grounds that she and Brady should have been tried separately. But after carefully considering her case, the court of appeal was satisfied that no miscarriage of justice had occurred.

Hindley's determination to win back her freedom, and the knowledge that she would never see Brady again, gradually dispelled his hold over her, and in the early 1970s she decided to break contact with him. She would consider any tactics which might bring her freedom, but she had to be patient. In 1977, after more than ten years' imprisonment (which is the average time spent in prison by a murderer in Britain), Hindley began work on a 20,000 word apologia in which she portrayed herself as an innocent victim of Brady's manipulative personality: 'He became my god, my idol, my object of worship and I worshipped him blindly.' She blamed the crimes squarely on Brady, with Smith as his accomplice. She claimed to have no knowledge of the bodies and graves. The document was finished in 1979 and sent to the then Home Secretary, Merlyn Rees. A committee comprised of Home Office and parole board officials decided, however, that Hindley's case for parole would not be heard for another three years.

Brady, meanwhile, released his first public statement in 1978, in response to Lord Longford's unrelenting campaigning for Hindley's freedom:

Lord Longford is well aware, as is the Home Office, that I have never applied for parole and have no intention of applying, and that I have always accepted that the weight of the crimes both Myra and I were convicted of justifies permanent imprisonment, regardless of expressed personal remorse and verifiable change.

Over the next few years Brady's mental state started to deteriorate. He began to suffer from visual and auditory hallucinations and, labouring under the delusion that the Home Office was trying to kill him, he all but disappeared from public view. Hindley, on the other hand, was never far from her next headline in the tabloid press.

In 1982, the next Home Secretary, William Whitelaw, also declined to act: Hindley would not be considered for parole for a further three years. In 1985, twenty years after the crimes, her case was finally considered by the parole board, and rejected. Home Secretary Leon Brittan announced the parole board's decision that her case should not be heard again for at least five years. Unofficially, Brittan was quoted as saying that he personally believed she should serve at least another fifteen years in prison. When her case was rejected as 'inadmissible' by the European Court of Human Rights in 1986, Hindley must have realized that her story of the naive girl who had no involvement in the murders was totally implausible.

At the end of 1986 an opportunity arose for Hindley to change her tactics. She received a letter from Winnie Johnson, mother of Keith Bennett, imploring Hindley to tell her what had happened to her son, whose body had never been found.

> Please, I beg of you, tell me what happened to Keith. My heart tells me that you know and I am on bended knees begging you to finally end this torture and finally put my mind at rest ... By telling me what happened to Keith you would be announcing loudly to the world that you really have turned into the caring warm person that Lord Longford speaks of.

'WORLD EXCLUSIVE, COMPULSIVE, STUNNING, FRIGHTENING: CONFESSIONS OF MYRA HINDLEY. "I'M A DISGRACE TO WOMANKIND". FULL AMAZING ADMISSION' the *Daily Mirror* screamed. The letter had obtained its desired results. During 1987 Hindley made a confession first to the Reverend Timms – her prison confidant – and then formally to Detective Chief Inspector Peter Topping. She now admitted both knowledge of, and involvement in, all five murders, including those of Pauline Reade and Keith Bennett. She claimed that she had driven the car, helped to kidnap the children and helped to 'clean up' afterwards. She still maintained, however, that she had not killed anybody, that was Brady's doing. Her statement to the press read:

> When I was arrested, tried and convicted I was still obsessed and infatuated with Ian Brady. I could not bring myself to admit the truth about our crimes ... Throughout my sentence I have been haunted by the continued suffering of the relatives of the two children who were missing at the time of my arrest, and until recently I have been utterly overwhelmed by the numerous difficulties of revealing the truth.

After taking religious direction however, and after receiving the letter from Winnie Johnson, she told the press that she had made a confession in which she:

> admitted my role in these awful events and said I considered myself to be as guilty as my former lover, Ian Brady, although our roles were different ... I know that the parents of the missing children may never be able to forgive me and that words of mine can NEVER express the remorse I feel ... To those who believe that I am seeking some narrow advantage I would stress that I am in my 24th year of imprisonment ... I have informed the Home Office that I do not wish to be considered for release on parole in 1990 [when her next review was due] and for as far ahead as I can see I know I will be kept in prison.

After Hindley's confession, Brady too spoke to Peter Topping, officially confessing to the Moors Murders. He did not choose publicly to express the remorse that his partner had, telling journalist Fred Harrison that he was not:

> interested in verbal hairshirts ... I'm not interested in people expressing remorse because they don't know where the line stops between remorse for being caught or remorse for the act. They don't know, they just play a role. They play that

role for so many years that they become that role. M's a good case.

Actions, he thought, spoke louder than words, and he chose to show his remorse through the Braille work that he undertook for the blind, and in his acceptance that in his case life meant life.

Hindley's and Brady's confessions confirmed suspicions that the remains of Pauline Reade and Keith Bennett were still buried somewhere on the moors. Hindley's confession was made public in April 1987, and the digging began that month. Hindley was taken to the moors to see if she could recognize the area in which they had buried Pauline and Keith, but she could not. Brady, too, was taken onto the moors, but by this time his mental state had deteriorated so irrevocably that he could provide no useful information.

Meanwhile, more information was finally surfacing. Hindley relived with Topping the day that Pauline Reade disappeared. On Pauline's short walk to the dance at the Railway Club, Hindley had stopped to offer her a lift in the van she had hired. Pauline had no reason to be suspicious: Hindley was only a few years older than herself, and she was alone. Hindley and Brady had gone on their first murder hunt in separate vehicles, Hindley in the van and Brady following behind on a motorbike. Once Pauline was inside the van Hindley told her that she had lost a glove at Saddleworth Moor and asked if she would help her find it. In return for the favour Hindley offered to give her some records. Pauline accepted.

According to Hindley's account, when they arrived at Saddleworth moor, Brady pulled up on his bike and Hindley introduced him as her boyfriend. While Hindley waited at the car, Brady and Pauline set off to look for the fictitious lost glove. Brady returned after dark alone and led his partner to Pauline's body. He had raped her and cut her throat. Hindley helped him to bury the body.

We must not, however, accept Hindley's version of events unquestioningly. It is in direct contradiction to the account that Brady gave in an open letter to the press in 1990. In this statement he claimed that Hindley was not only instrumental in luring Pauline to the moors and burying her body, but that she had also played an active role in Pauline's murder, helping him to assault the girl both physically and sexually.

The remains of Pauline Reade were found three months after Hindley's confession on 1 July 1987. Her body was identified by her pink party dress. Tranquillized, her mother Joan Reade was taken to the funeral by two hospital nurses. Thirty years on she says, 'Even now I think about her every day.' Despite Hindley's and Brady's confessions – whichever version was the truth – it was felt that it wasn't in the public interest to prosecute them after so much time had elapsed.

Although the body of John Kilbride had been found in 1965, his family still needed to know what had happened to him that day. According to Hindley's account, she and Brady had met John at Ashton market and asked him if he would help them find a lost glove, promising him a bottle of sherry for his time. On arriving at the moors, Brady and the boy went off to look for the fictitious glove, and Brady alone returned some time later. He had, he told Hindley, killed John and buried his body, adding that as his knife had been too blunt to cut his throat, he had strangled him instead. Hindley told DCI Topping that she believed that Brady had raped John, although he had told her that he had just taken down John's trousers and given him 'a slap'. John's body had been found with his underwear and trousers rolled down around his knees.

Keith Bennett's grave has never been found. His mother has been unable to bury her son properly, but she has been told something of how he died. In her confession Hindley said that she had encountered Keith on his way to his grandmother's and lured him into her Mini by asking him if he could help her load some boxes from an off-licence. Again, the presence of a solitary young woman must have seemed unthreatening, and the child was taken to the moors. Walking on the moors years later, Winnie pieced together her son's last minutes, 'Brady walked down through the gully, he took him down the stream, and Keith said "it's nice up here, me mam would like it if she came up here", and he said, "I'll have to go now because me mam will be looking for me". And I think that was when he actually killed him.' Keith was strangled and buried. Brady admitted to raping him. 'What,' he added, 'does it matter?'

Lesley Ann Downey was not brought to Wardle Brook Avenue by David Smith, Hindley told DCI Topping. She and Brady had snatched her from the fair and taken her back home, where Brady began to photograph her, while Hindley went off to run a bath. According to her account, when she returned, Brady had strangled Lesley Ann, and the blood on her thighs suggested that he had also raped her. In his open letter to the press in 1990, however, Brady had a different story to tell. He claimed that Hindley had not only played an active part in Lesley Ann's murder, but executed it herself, strangling Lesley Ann 'with her own hands, using a two-foot length of silk cord, which she later used to enjoy toying with in public, in the secret knowledge of what it had been used for'.

What was the truth? Was Hindley directly involved in the murders, as Brady claimed? And why did Hindley decide to confess? Was she genuinely remorseful? Or was she thinking long-term? Initially the horror would resurface, but after a time, would people come to respect that she had finally admitted to her crimes? If she could convince them that she was genuinely remorseful and rehabilitated, would that lead to her eventual parole? Her solicitor, Michael Fisher, said, 'I myself actually believe in light of the confessions, she may eventually be released: but not for at least another ten years.' Reverend Timms, Hindley's confidant, takes a more charitable view of her confession: 'It didn't suit her purposes ... to face the possibility of a new trial for murder: why? ... She wanted to do what she hoped she'd have done twenty years earlier. She made that difficult step into facing the truthfulness of what happened.'

But telling 'nothing but the truth' is not necessarily telling the 'whole truth'. As DCI Topping says, in Hindley's 'confession':

> She was very careful in what she said, particularly in respect of her own role in these murders. She was always, if you like, in the car, over the brow of the hill, in the bathroom. She was never there when it happened, according to her. This moor is quiet... the silence you can almost hear on

occasions. She was but a few yards away but could never give any details of sounds that she heard.

Any admission of having played a more direct role in the murders would, of course, ensure that Hindley would never be released.

In 1987 Hindley claimed to have abandoned her fight for parole; eight years later, on 18 December 1995, the fight for release recommenced. The *Guardian* published 'MYRA HINDLEY: MY LIFE, MY GUILT, MY WEAKNESS', a 5,000-word essay which she had written (but for which she had not been paid) in answer to an article the *Guardian* had run referring to her as a psychopath. Her response was an attempt to convince the public that she was both repentant and rehabilitated, but was actually little more than an exercise in passing the buck: to her violent and control-ling father, to Brady for brain-washing her, to Home Secretaries, the Prison Service and the government for using her to further their own political agendas, and to the press for unfairly demon-izing her as 'a symbol of the nation's revulsion at all those who prey on innocent children'. She spoke – and we hear Lord Longford's voice here – of repentance, which she feels is a better term than remorse, even though she admits that this is what 'the media, the public, the penal and criminal justice system, hold so much store by'. She claimed that she had, 'become a political prisoner serving the interests of successive Home Secretaries who have placed political expediency and effectively, a lynch-mob mentality before the dictates of basic human rights'.

This bit of unconvincing special pleading did nothing to improve public opinion, and in 1996 Hindley was told by former Home Secretary Michael Howard that she was to be one of twenty-three prisoners incarcerated in Britain who would never be released. Among the others were her partner, Ian Brady, and serial killers Peter Sutcliffe, Dennis Nilsen, Robert Black and Colin Ireland.

Having said in her 'confessions' that she had resigned herself to the fact that she would be in prison for 'as far ahead' as she could see, ten years later – the period mentioned by Michael Fisher – her battle resumed. In 1997 Hindley was given leave to challenge the former Home Secretary Michael Howard's decision, in a judicial review by the High Court. Both Lord Astor, ex-editor of the *Observer*, and Lord Longford were behind her. Lord Astor said, 'I simply object that this woman is not being given British justice like other prisoners ... that's the whole story and that needs to be said.' Lord Longford appealed for Hindley's release on similar grounds: 'The public should be reminded that her original tariff was thirty years. That is the seriousness that was attached to the crime at the time. No one seriously suggests that her crime has got worse over the years ... no humane person can fail to set a limit to the amount of cruelty inflicted on a fellow human being.'

In January 1998, Hindley's council, Mr Edward Fitzgerald QC, argued in the High Court that Hindley had been 'singled out' for a tougher stance on crime because of her notoriety, as her case (and Brady's) have been the only ones in which the original tariffs for the crimes have been extended. In addition, Hindley's was the only case where the 'secondary party' was given natural life. Furthermore, said Fitzgerald, Home Secretary Jack Straw – while publicly maintaining that cases such as Hindley's would be subject to review in the case of 'exceptional progress' – was quoted privately as saying, 'I will not be the Home Secretary who sets her free.' Such statements, said Fitzgerald, created the 'expectation' that Hindley would never be freed and thus made it impossible for any future Home Secretary to do so.

Again, Hindley was unsuccessful. It is hard to envisage any future Home Secretary risking his career by releasing her. In 1996 Michael Howard appealed to the weight of public opinion as a final factor in making his decision about her freedom. When the Opinion Research Centre conducted a poll to gauge the public view of her release when she applied for parole in 1978, an overwhelming 93 per cent were opposed; when the *Sun* and *The Times* conducted similar polls some years later, the former found 86 per cent of the public opposed to her release, and the latter 83 per cent. In 1997, Channel 4's poll, which covered 2,000 people nation-wide, found that ten per cent were for her release, while 80 per cent were against it. But, Hindley's lawyers asked, just which members of the public were consulted, and how? Was the Home Secretary simply bowing to the demands of the readers of the tabloid press?

The parents of the victims, and their supporters, have vowed to continue their campaign to oppose Myra Hindley's release. Ann West, particularly, has been relentless in her fight to keep Hindley in prison. She told the *Sun* that, 'I was sentenced to a life of heartache and misery because of Myra Hindley … I have lost my health. I have had no life since I lost Lesley Ann. There is no parole for me. My sentence will only come to an end when I die … Life should mean life for Hindley.' Winnie Johnson, the mother of Keith Bennett, says that 'The Government should listen to what the people are saying and never let her go.' John Kilbride's brother, Danny, has presented petitions with hundreds of thousands of signatures on them opposing Hindley's release. And he has recently made a promise: 'Without any doubt if I ever got the chance I would do her, and the rest of my family would. If I ever came face to face with Myra Hindley she's just dead.'

While the supporters of Myra Hindley's release continue to argue largely from judicial criteria, and those that oppose it from emotive, there can be no resolution. A 'right-minded person' might well find both arguments compelling, and the process of mediating between them well-nigh impossible. When considering the crimes in themselves it seems understandable that people will feel that the sort of person who commits them should never be released. But they are. In our society, where a 'life sentence' usually means an average of ten years in prison, child murderers are regularly released. At the beginning of 1998, for instance, Robert Oliver and Sidney Cooke, who were part of the paedophile gang who raped and killed fourteen-year-old Jason Swift, were paroled. The gang is believed to have been involved in numerous other cases of child abuse and murder, and Oliver and Cooke are still considered to be extremely dangerous, whereas Hindley is not. Yet they have been released. Why should Hindley be treated any differently?

The answer to this question is complex, and involves several factors. Myra Hindley was the first woman to be accused and convicted of multiple child-murders, and the initial public shock

– indeed astonishment – that a woman could act so appallingly seems hardly to have abated. It has been kept alive, too, by the unrelenting campaigns by the victim's families to keep her incarcerated. In some way the Moors Murders marked the end of an era of innocence. After 1965 the streets were considered an unsafe place for children to play; parents began to walk their children to and from school, and were reluctant to let them out of their sight in the evenings, or at the weekends. Their children were safe nowhere, and with no one. But perhaps the most telling reason that Myra Hindley may never be released lies in the public image of her; not so much in their ideas about her, but through their perception of what she looked like: the incarnation of evil. To release Myra Hindley would be to unleash a demon back into the world.

Most surviving pictures of Myra Hindley as a child show a bright-eyed girl, a little plain perhaps, but contented-looking. No one could imagine that the prevailing image of this unexceptional youngster would be transformed, not so many years later, not merely by an unspeakable set of acts, but by a single, unforgettable photograph. Selected with an editor's eye for the archetypal image, the picture shows a peroxided, dark-eyed and glowering Hindley, mouth set in a poisonous grimace, her face somehow infiltrated by shadow, staring brazen and direct into the camera. The face of a murderer. The image still has such potency that when it was reproduced on gigantic scale (in the 1997 Royal Academy *Sensations* show), having been produced by an artist using the handprints of children, a member of the public actually attacked the painting, and Ann West, dying of cancer, stood outside in the street to protest her outrage.

Myra Hindley committed, with Ian Brady, five gruesome and horrific murders of children. But while details of these crimes, along with the face of Ian Brady, have faded from memory over the years, that single image remains, and it might be argued that it is the public response to that picture of her face that keeps her in prison beyond the dictates of her original sentence.

How did that little girl turn into that apparent monster? At an impressionable age Myra Hindley had fallen victim to the condition known as *folie à deux*. As the submissive member of the

partnership, she began to take on her lover's dominant character. Brady shaped the impressionable Hindley as he wanted her,
her unformed and receptive personality eagerly embracing all
that he wished her to be. There was nothing in Myra Hindley's
personality or behaviour patterns that, up to her association
with Brady, would have labelled her as potentially lethal. She
had been a little lazy, easily led perhaps, something of an under-
achiever. Her family life had been disrupted in ways that might
have been upsetting to her, and were unlikely to have led to an
increase in her belief that she was lovable and worthy. Unlike
Brady, and other offenders we will look at, none of the fundamental indicators of a later disposition to violence or psychosis
were present: no history of childhood abuse, either physical or
sexual, no neglect, no sign of childhood sexual dysfunction, no
broken family, no sadistic treatment of animals or children, no
unhealthy fixations on themes associated with death or dying.
She was generally liked and trusted, and no-one in her community would have picked her out as a future killer.

It seems unlikely that, without the presence of Brady, she
would have become a murderer. Having said that, he was hardly
irresistible. His relations with women had been negligible, he
was a miserable, crimped, sullen young man, and most people
avoided him. But Myra found him fascinating. Though he
quickly revealed the nature of his interests to her, in the full
range of their nastiness and perversity, she did not back away. It
was as if she were a void waiting to be filled. Local men had
seemed to her jejune and uninteresting; she had wanted something larger and fuller, more exciting. With Brady she got it, in
the darkest possible version, and she had neither the sense nor
the courage to back away. He didn't merely dominate her, he
imprinted himself upon her very being.

In this sense, one may see Hindley as more an accessory than
a principal in the Moors Murders. Accessories are equally guilty
under the law, but they may be more sympathetic in character,
easier to find excuses for, fundamentally more forgivable.
Hindley has had her share of sympathetic adherents over the
years: people of good-will who have been convinced of her reha-
bilitation. But perhaps she has been badly served by those who

have sought to protect her interests. Whatever one makes of the role of Lord Longford in counselling her and arguing her case, in retrospect it is clear that his intervention happened too quickly, before the public was emotionally ready to hear, much less to consider, the case for her release. If such arguments had been made only as the initial thirty-year recommended sentence was ending, they may have been given a more sympathetic hearing.

5

PETER SUTCLIFFE

A puny baby, and an immediate disappointment to his father, Peter William Sutcliffe was born in Bingley, a town six miles south of Bradford, on 2 June 1946. John and Kathleen had been married the year before, after a long engagement, when Kathleen was twenty-five and John twenty-three. Although he was the first of six children, Peter displayed none of the characteristics traditionally, if not always accurately, associated with first-born males. He certainly didn't resemble the child that John, his overtly masculine and domineering father, was eagerly expecting. A tiny baby, Peter spent his first ten days in the world in an incubator, as he weighed just five pounds at birth, and was to stay small for his age throughout his childhood, which became a dominating determinant of his later development and self-image.

Withdrawn and socially without self-confidence, Peter was sent to school when he was just four years old, as John and Kathleen hoped that mixing with other small children would bring Peter out of himself. A pupil at St Joseph's, his former class-mates and teachers – if they remember him at all – recall him as a shy, withdrawn boy, a loner who preferred his own company to that of his peers. In the school playground he was usually to be found standing meekly in the corner by himself, rather than joining in with the loud, and often brutally physical, games of the other children.

On returning home from school in the afternoons, and at the weekends, Peter steadfastly refused to go outdoors and play, either by himself or with the local children, preferring to sit inside on his own quietly reading or following his mother around. John Sutcliffe, who was a keen outdoors and sporting man, encouraged his son to go out like the other children, and was frustrated and dismayed when Peter refused. Like the other fathers, John took Peter to watch him play cricket, and bought him a footballkit, but Peter remained resolutely uninterested. To John's profound disappointment, Peter was the complete antithesis of himself, a man who both worked (first as a baker and then at the mill) and played hard. He sung in the local choir, was a member of both the football and cricket teams, and was also involved in amateur dramatics. He was well-known in town, a man who wasn't afraid of a bit of hard work and who liked his sport and his beer. Given all his interests outside of the home, John was rarely in, but his family all agree that when he was present what he said went undisputed.

According to later accounts by his children John could be a bully. He had a terrible temper and sometimes beat them – the girls as well as the boys – particularly after a heavy night drinking at the pub. Peter's brother Carl, who was similar to Peter in many ways, and the child that seems to have been particularly affected by their father's violent temper, told Gordon Burn, writer of the book *Somebody's Husband, Somebody's Son*,

> We were all frightened to death of me dad, he were like a monster. He were never in the house, but when he was he ruled the roost. When he came in drunk we'd all sit there in fear; you didn't move ... Nobody dared say owt. Oh Christ, he had a foul temper. I seen Maureen [his sister] get a beating off him when she was about fifteen, an' he once beat me black and blue when I were a kid.

Carl says that his hatred for his father was so strong at times that he even thought about killing him. Yet, while all of the children were scared of his violent temper, John also had another, softer, side to him. He would often slip chocolate bars into his children's pockets at night so they would find them at school the next day, and he would visit Peter at his school at playtime to ensure that he was all right. He once said that to live and not to have children would be a meaningless existence.

Another of John's sporting interests seems to have been the local ladies. His own father, Arthur, was a something of a ladies' man, and John took after him. John's sons remember that their father used to boast crudely about his exploits to them, telling them of the 'cracker he'd had last night'. On one occasion he even moved in with one of their neighbours for a time. His family remember, too, how he used to touch and flatter his sister's friends – indeed, virtually every woman or girl he ever came across. Years later Carl described his father's behaviour towards women: 'He mauls 'em ... If he's in a pub an' any woman comes anywhere near, he'll always grab hold an' touch them, pretending to be joking and messing around.'

Kathleen knew of her husband's affairs, but such things were to be both expected and tolerated. Men like John Sutcliffe need a passive woman who will look after their children, clean their house and cook their meals without complaint or criticism. Kathleen fitted the bill. Her daughter Maureen later described her as, 'an honest, ordinary, motherly type of person who, all she ever did all her bloody married life, was work and bring up kids. She didn't have any pleasure or any hobbies or anything because she had too much to do ... she had a miserable bloody existence.'

Kathleen has been described as a devoted and loving mother and a hard worker, who never complained about her husband's constant absences, their relative poverty, and the burden of both going to work and looking after the home and children single-handedly. As she got older Kathleen's health started to fail – she had a bad heart – yet she still had a job cleaning offices while, Carl remembers, John 'went to the pub wi' sixty quid in his pocket'. Friends and neighbours remember Kathleen as: 'the kindest lady in the world', the 'backbone of the street' and the 'sweetest person alive'. She was devoted to all her children, but particularly to Peter who was undoubtedly her favourite, partly due to his weakness compared to the other children, and partly because he was her first born. (Fortunately Kathleen's death in 1978 preceded Peter's arrest.)

As Peter grew up, his closest relationship was with his mother, as he felt increasingly estranged from his father's overtly masculine and aggressive character. Throughout his childhood Peter was inordinately attached to, and identified with, Kathleen, which earned him the reputation of being a 'mummy's boy' at school. When he began to walk, at rather a late age, it was by hanging on to his mother's skirts – something he was still doing when he was seven. In response to Peter's neediness and vulnerability, Kathleen became over-protective, which sadly served only to encourage his timidity. As John observed about his son to Gordon Burn years later, 'he was always on his mum's side as well as being at her side'.

If Peter was opposite in almost every way to his father, the same was true of himself and his younger brother, Mick, who took after John. As a teenager Mick used to boast that he could knock anybody in Bingley out in less than a minute and would drink until his bad stomach made him sick, and then carry on. To him, women were 'for frying bacon and for screwin' '. By the age of thirten Mick already had a criminal record, since which time he has been imprisoned four times on various charges of assault, robbery, actual bodily harm and grievous bodily harm. As John told Gordon Burn, 'Mick's always been a hard lad ... the very antithesis of Peter, who was always the shivering wall-flower ... who would always avoid confrontations.'

If those who knew the Sutcliffes had to speculate about which brother would be the one to commit murder, there would have been no contest. Nobody thought Peter capable of any violent act. Even Mick told the *Evening Standard* after his brother's arrest: 'The police have had me in several times for the Ripper murders because I've got form for grievous bodily harm, actual bodily harm and a bit of burglary. But I didn't know they suspected Peter. I can't imagine he's guilty.' We will find that this is often the case with serial killers: they usually have no record of violence and seem the least likely people to commit murder in the eyes of those who know them. Their aggression is of a far more dangerous type, repressed, simmering under the surface.

Despite John's controlling personality and violent temper, the Sutcliffe household is remembered as friendly and welcoming. Billy Emery, a childhood friend of Peter's, says he used to call round practically every night, as there was always something going on and he invariably received a warm welcome. Friends and neighbours were constantly coming in and out, and there was plenty of chatter, tea and fun. Peter, however, did not join in the merriment. Sometimes he would be so quiet that his family wouldn't even know whether he was there or not. They recall that he used regularly to sit in a trance-like state, staring into space, perfectly still. Another odd habit his family remember is that Peter spent hours locked in the bathroom. His brothers and sisters would sometimes spy on him through a small hole in the bathroom door, and find him standing in front of the mirror staring at his reflection.

Not having done well enough in his 11+ to go to the local grammar school, Peter went instead to Cottingley Manor, the Secondary Modern, in 1957. His school years were spent in a cloud of academic and social anonymity. Many of his teachers and fellow-pupils cannot remember him at all, and those that do, recall, as his headmaster did, 'a very ordinary boy', 'the sort of boy a teacher could easily overlook'. Years later, after Peter Sutcliffe's arrest, one of his former teachers told a BBC reporter, 'All I can remember is that he was a very quiet, obedient, respectful boy. He never shone in any way and I would simply say that he was of average intelligence but very quiet and reserved.'

Peter's introspection and loneliness were intensified by the larger school, where he found himself once again amongst the youngest and smallest. His size and meek demeanour made him an ideal target for the school bullies, who picked on him mercilessly. Eventually the bullying became unendurable and Peter took to pretending to go to school, instead hiding in the loft of his house, where lying alone in the dark all day or reading by torch-light was preferable to going to school. He carried on like this for two weeks, until a letter was sent to his parents from the school and the issue had to be addressed. Despite Peter's protests he was sent back to school by his father, who visited the headmaster to try to sort matters out. Peter never played truant again, although whether or not he continued to be bullied is unknown.

As a child and an adolescent Peter was simply an outcast from his culture: he was physically frail, did not enjoy sport, had no interest in girls, nor in getting drunk, and he preferred his own company to that of his peers. All this began to change at around the time Peter left school at the age of fifteen, having done adequately, but failing to take any of his exams before going to work in an engineering company. Peter's confidence started to build: he began to go out more, and took up weight-lifting to build up his small body. Eventually, when he and his brother Mick competed with Peter's gym equipment, it was Peter who won. Another interest that emerged was a passion for motorbikes, and he bought his first machine in 1962. At night he could usually be found outside the house taking bikes apart and putting them back together. He even kept an engine underneath his bed. However, having failed his test once, Peter didn't get a licence for some years and also drove without the benefit of tax or insurance. In his mid-teens he earned himself the reputation of being a bit of a dare-devil and years later his friends remember that he used to drive 'like a maniac'. The inevitable happened: in 1966 he had an accident, running into a telegraph pole on his bike. Years later, after his arrest, Sutcliffe claimed that he was rendered unconscious by this knock, perhaps hoping to convince somebody that he had been brain damaged, yet there is no official record of his having lost consciousness.

Another significant change in Peter's life occurred in 1964 when he encountered death for the first time. At the age of eighteen he got a job in Bingley cemetery as a gravedigger. He seemed to enjoy the work: he was always eager to volunteer for overtime, and he also used to help out at the local morgue, where he would prepare the bodies for burial. The corpses held a peculiar fascination for Peter. His workmates recall that he used to stare at the bodies for a long time, sometimes even jumping into the graves and opening the coffins to have a better look. Gleefully, he would tell his friends and family highly imaginative tales of bodies sitting upright in their graves, along with vivid descriptions of how they looked. Peter also enjoyed playing morbid and inappropriate practical jokes at work. On several occasions he went in early and laid himself on a slab, jumping up and scaring the others when they arrived; another time he chased some schoolgirls with a skull. He also thought nothing of stealing jewellery from the bodies, some items of which he offered to his sister, who was horrified. This morbid interest in death didn't stop at his job. Peter also regularly visited Nicholson's 'Museum of Anatomy' in Morecambe, a pastime which Dr Robert Brittain describes as popular with sadistic killers. Nicholson's contained wax models of infamous murderers as well as an anatomy section with models of female torsos with cross sections removed to show diseased sex organs and different stages of pregnancy.

Due to the unusual nature of their job, the men who worked in the cemetery tended to form friendships with one another, and Peter began socializing with his workmates in the evenings, when they would go to the pubs in Bingley and Bradford. Peter, who had a low tolerance for alcohol, was moderate in his consumption compared to the others, tending not to join in with their raucous drunken behaviour, preferring simply to sit and take everything in. Although he was considered good-looking and he dressed with care, Peter never had a girlfriend until he met the girl who was later to become his wife. In the company of women he seemed to revert to his old self. He was shy and tongue-tied, just as he had been as a child, when one of his early female companions at nursery school recalls that 'you only had to look at him and he would colour up and turn away'. He never approached girls himself, appearing to view such activity with distaste, and when any initiated contact with him he remained uninterested. Not that they did this often, however, as most of the local girls thought that there was something 'not quite right' or 'weird' about Peter, with his brooding silences, awkward demeanour and protracted stares. The men acknowledged that he was a bit different from the rest of them, but didn't find this threatening as the girls did. In fact, they thought that his quirky sense of humour and sometimes mildly dangerous and inappropriate behaviour could be amusing: in a pub one night he called out the fire service just for fun; another time he kicked a rather large woman when her back was turned and then just laughed at her; on a different occasion he was sitting having a drink and smashed the glass on the table for no apparent reason; and once he simply picked up a friend's sister and threw her down the stairs, laughing as she fell.

Peter met Sonia Szurma, his first real girlfriend, and future wife, in 1966 when she was just sixteen and he was twenty-one. Of Czechoslovakian descent, she was different from the Bingley girls; she dressed more conservatively, and didn't join in with their gossip, drinking and talk about boys. In many ways Sonia and Peter were very much alike, both marginal to the prevailing culture, and both what can be variously interpreted as shy or aloof. While John Sutcliffe described Sonia as 'very quiet', Maureen, Peter's sister, described her as a 'prim little miss'. Both happy to have found somebody they could relate to, Peter and Sonia quickly grew very close, to the point of excluding all others from their conversations at the pub and in the house, preferring to be in each other's company.

Despite their closeness, however, one day Mick spotted Sonia with another man, whom it seems she'd been seeing, although she later denied to a psychiatrist that she had been sleeping with him. Peter was furious, but got nowhere when he confronted her. Revenge seemed the best option, and he went out to pick up a prostitute. But Peter's opinion of women plummeted further when the prostitute conned him. On arrival at the woman's flat in Bradford Sutcliffe asked her for his change from the £10 note he had given her earlier. As she didn't have it, she suggested going back to the place where they had met, in order that she could get his £5. When they arrived, however, the woman went into a garage and refused to come out; two men appeared and drove Sutcliffe away. To make matters worse, Sutcliffe encountered the prostitute in a pub some weeks later where she taunted him, humiliating him in public.

That same year, in 1969, another woman proved to be untrustworthy: his mother. When John Sutcliffe found out that Kathleen was having an affair with a policeman who lived locally, rather than simply confronting her with this knowledge, he set her up to be humiliated in front of her family. Pretending to be her lover on the phone, John organized a date at the nearby Bankfield Hotel, telling her to 'bring something nice to wear in bed'. When he went to meet her, he brought the children along with him. Peter was deeply shocked. He had always idolized his mother, believing that it was his father who was the disloyal one; after all, that's what he'd been bought up to think that men were like. Now the two most important women in his life, the women that he had regarded as loving, gentle and faithful, had betrayed him. His madonnas, he thought, had turned out to be whores.

Peter Sutcliffe was no saint himself, however. Those who suggest that it was purely Sonia, his mother and the prostitute who irrevocably changed his character and behaviour are wrong. These events might well have been triggers, but the seeds had been sown long before. Research studies by the FBI have shown that a person does not suddenly, as a result of an adverse event in his or her life, become a lust-murderer. They have been building up to it in their fantasies for years. From the time of his late teens Peter Sutcliffe had been leading a kind of Jekyll and Hyde existence. With his family and Sonia he was quiet, polite and respectable: he didn't drink, swear or get into trouble with the law like many of the other local lads. As Mick told writer Roger Cross, 'As far as our family is concerned Peter is faultless, ten times better than me. I would swop places with him, you know. Peter's been so good all his life. He has been so good to everybody who has met him, apart from his victims.'

However he revealed another side to some of his friends, boasting of experiences with prostitutes and driving around red-light areas shouting abuse at the 'filthy slags' who walked the streets. Robin Holland, Maureen's boyfriend, said, 'The rest of the family seemed to think Peter was a saint, sort of the perfect son. But I know he wasn't. I had regularly gone out with him drinking to pubs in the red-light districts and his main topic of conversation had been sex and prostitutes.' Well before the episodes with Sonia, Kathleen or the woman who conned him, Peter Sutcliffe had an unhealthy interest in prostitutes and red-light districts. Coupled with his interest in death, the combination was to prove explosive.

On 5 July 1975, thirty-four-year-old Anna Rogulskyj had gone into Bradford for a night out with her friends. When she arrived home in Keighley at about one in the morning, she was annoyed to find that her boyfriend wasn't waiting for her as she had expected, so she decided to walk round to his house to see if he was there. Discovering that he wasn't, Anna became angry and broke his window. When she had calmed down, she decided to walk home. It was just as she was leaving her boyfriend's house that she encountered Peter Sutcliffe.

Sutcliffe smashed Anna over the head three times with a hammer. When she became unconscious he lifted her skirt, pulled down her pants and slashed her across the abdomen. At that moment a neighbour came out to see what the noise was, yet in the darkness he failed to see Anna lying on the ground. The interruption was enough to scare Sutcliffe off, and probably to save Anna's life. Not long afterwards, at twenty past two, Anna was found. She was alive, but only just. She was rushed to hospital where surgeons performed a twelve-hour operation on her brain which saved her life. Over twenty years later Anna is still haunted by the memories of that night, living her life, often sedated, under the constant fear of another attack.

Just over a month later, on 15 August, Sutcliffe struck again, this time in Halifax. His victim was forty-six-year-old Olive Smelt who, like Anna Rogulskyj, was alone late at night after an evening out. Sutcliffe had also been out that night, drinking in Halifax with his friend Trevor Birdsall. Trevor later testified that he and Sutcliffe had been on their way back home through Boothtown, when Sutcliffe spotted Olive, whom they had seen in a pub earlier that evening. Sutcliffe stopped the car and got out, telling Trevor to wait for him. Out of Trevor's sight, Sutcliffe approached Olive as she went to buy some take-away fish and chips, and after making a banal comment about the weather, he hit her on the head twice with a hammer to render her unconscious, then slashed her twice with a hacksaw across her back. Luckily for Olive, Sutcliffe was disturbed by a car and fled. Six years later, after his arrest, he told police: 'I was going to kill her but I did not get the chance.' After ten days in hospital, Olive was on the road to recovery and provided the police with a good description of her attacker. She said he was quite a good-looking man, about thirty years old, around 5' 10", with dark slightly wavy hair, facial hair and long sideburns. He spoke with a clear Yorkshire accent.

Three months later, on 10 October 1975, Sutcliffe committed his first murder. His victim was Wilma McCann, a twenty-eight-year-old prostitute and a mother of four, who lived in Leeds. Like Anna Rogulskyj and Olive Smelt, Wilma McCann had been returning home from a night out when she encountered Sutcliffe some time in the early hours of the morning. Sutcliffe later claimed in his statement to the police that Wilma had been thumbing a lift and when he picked her up she asked him if he 'wanted business'. He accepted, and drove her to some playing-fields. But he was unable to obtain an erection inside the car, which made Wilma impatient, and she told him that he was 'fucking useless'. She got out of the car and walked into the field, telling him to 'Come on, get it over with'. He did: he hit her twice on the head with a hammer. Returning to his car, Sutcliffe looked back and saw that Wilma was still moving. He returned to her writhing body, ripped open her jacket and blouse, pulled her bra up, took her trousers and pants down and stabbed her in the neck, chest and abdomen fifteen times, in a 'blind panic'. 'I didn't want intercourse with her,' Sutcliffe later said, 'I just wanted to get rid of her.'

When Wilma's children awoke at about four o'clock in the morning to find that their mother wasn't home yet they went out to search for her. It was not them, but the milkman who found Wilma's body a few hours later, at 7.40. The Yorkshire Ripper had claimed his first victim.

Although Sutcliffe may have hated prostitutes, Wilma McCann was not killed primarily for this reason. When he assaulted Anna and Olive, Sutcliffe had no reason to suppose that they were prostitutes. He attacked, and fully intended to kill them, because violence, mutilation and ultimately murder, excited Sutcliffe. In 1949 J. Paul de River could have been talking specifically about Sutcliffe when he said that, 'The lust-murderer, usually after killing his victim, tortures, cuts, maims, or slashes the victim in the regions in or about the genitalia, rectum, breast in the female, and about the neck, throat and buttocks, and usually these parts contain strong sexual significance to him, and serve as sexual stimulus.' Sutcliffe later told police that after his first murder the urge to kill 'grew and grew until I became the beast that I am'. After Wilma's murder he felt some satisfaction, but the memory of the killing soon faded, his lust regenerated, and the need for another killing intensified. He continued, 'After that time I developed and *played up* a hatred of prostitutes in order to justify within myself why I had attacked and killed Wilma McCann' (my emphasis). If Sutcliffe could reason that his murders were committed out of a loathing of prostitutes he could go some way towards justifying his behaviour, initially to himself, and later to others.

Three weeks later, on 20 November 1975, a woman was murdered on the other side of the Pennines, in Preston. Twenty-six-year-old Joan Harrison, an alcoholic and prostitute, was found in a garage on 23 November; her trousers, tights and pants had been pulled down, and her bra pulled up. Both her handbag and purse were missing. The post-mortem determined that she had been struck viciously on the back of the head, probably with the heel of a shoe, and kicked and stamped upon. Her left breast had a pronounced bite mark upon it, and she had had vaginal and anal sex just before her murder. It was determined from the semen that her murderer had the rare blood group B, which only six per cent of the male population share.

Because of the resemblance between the murder of Joan Harrison and that of Wilma McCann three weeks earlier, the Lancashire police contacted the Yorkshire police to see if the same man might be responsible for both killings. The most obvious similarities were that both women were prostitutes who seemed to have been killed by a client late at night. Furthermore, both women's trousers and pants had been pulled down and their bras pulled up. Yet there were also glaring differences. Wilma McCann had been stabbed and hit with a hammer, suggesting that somebody had come prepared for her murder, whereas Joan Harrison had been hit over the head with a shoe and kicked to death, which almost certainly pointed to an unpremeditated act of violence. Joan Harrison had also had both vaginal and anal intercourse before her death, whereas Wilma McCann's body showed signs of neither. The police remained undecided as to whether there was a link between the murders.

The case of forty-two-year-old Emily Jackson, on 20 January 1976, was more clear-cut. Emily and her husband had gone to the Gaity, a pub in Leeds, the arrangement being that he would go for a drink, while she would go off to make some money, as times were hard. Outside the pub, Emily was picked up by Peter Sutcliffe who took her to a derelict building, where her lifeless body was found the next morning. Sutcliffe had hit her over the head with a hammer repeatedly, then stabbed her in the neck, chest, abdomen and back. There were fifty-two stab wounds in all. His confidence and his lust were increasing, his fantasies growing more elaborate. However in his frenzy Sutcliffe made his first mistake, leaving his size seven boot-print on Emily's thigh. Emily's murder was linked to the case of Wilma McCann as the method of attack (with the hammer and subsequent stabbing) was identical. The police began to suspect that they had a serial killer on their hands.

Over the next five years eleven more women were to die in this way, and at least five more were attacked. Less than a hundred years after the Whitechapel murders, England had another Ripper on the loose, whose killings were just as horrendous and who was to be active for far longer. The similarity of the murders to those performed in 1888 by Jack the Ripper was inescapable. The first four of the Yorkshire Ripper's murder victims (and eight altogether) were prostitutes and, like the Whitechapel murders, the victims were subjected to mutilations centred around their abdomens after death. Neither Ripper raped his victims, deriving sexual pleasure instead from the act of killing and mutilation. To the police the similarities were so striking that it must have seemed as if Jack the Ripper were back: the Devil had been reincarnated.

On 8 May 1976, twenty-year-old prostitute Marcella Claxton survived an attack by Sutcliffe, and supplied the police with a description of her attacker which was very similar to the one given by Olive Smelt. Both accurately described Sutcliffe's distinctive beard, moustache and black crinkly hair. There were no more attacks that year, but in 1977 the rate of Sutcliffe's murders began to accelerate, as we would expect of a serial killer whose fantasies are escalating and control decreasing. After the murder of Emily Jackson, Sutcliffe recalled that he felt 'satisfaction and justification' but it was short-lived. On 6 February he killed twenty-eight-year-old prostitute Irene Richardson, who had left her room in Chapeltown, Leeds, late at night to go to a club. Her body was found the next morning on Soldier's Field, where Marcella Claxton had been attacked. According to Sutcliffe's statement, as Irene crouched down to urinate before sex he hit her on the head three times with a hammer; when she was unconscious he then stabbed her in the neck, throat and abdomen. The stabbing of her abdomen was so vicious that it caused her intestines to come out of her body. 'By this time,' Sutcliffe later told police, 'I couldn't stop myself. It was some sort of drug.'

By 23 April Peter Sutcliffe was ready for another victim. Stripper, erotic dancer and prostitute Patricia Atkinson encountered Sutcliffe after she had left her friends following a night out, and they went back to her flat for a bit of 'business'. Her body was found the following evening by a friend. Sutcliffe had hit Patricia over the head four times as they entered her flat. He then pulled her jeans and pants down, pulled her bra above her breasts and stabbed her six times in the abdomen, back, and side. He later recalled to police the 'horrible gurgling noises' she had made and his shock at seeing red blood for the first time, as his previous murders had always been committed in the dark. On her bed he left a size seven boot-print.

Two months later, on 26 June, Sutcliffe claimed his fifth official victim. Sixteen-year-old Jayne MacDonald left her house in Leeds in the evening to go dancing, and was last seen alive at about half past ten that night. Her body was found just before ten o'clock the following morning, lying face down, in an adventure playground in Chapeltown. She had been hit on the head with a hammer three times, stabbed in the chest – numerous times in the one wound – and stabbed in the back. At the postmortem a broken bottle was found embedded in her chest. In this attack Sutcliffe claimed not one but two victims, as the trauma of identifying his daughter's body left Jayne's father paralysed, and he was soon to die.

After this murder, the inquiry took on a different complexion as Jayne was not a prostitute, but, as the press dubbed her, 'an innocent sixteen-year-old lass, a happy, respectable, working-class girl from a decent Leeds family'. Detective Chief

Superintendent Jim Hobson made an extraordinary statement at a press conference:

> He [the Ripper] has made it clear that he hates prostitutes. Many people do. We, as a police force, will continue to arrest prostitutes. But the Ripper is now killing innocent girls. [To the Ripper:] That indicates your mental state and that you are in urgent need of medical attention. You have made your point. Give yourself up before another innocent woman dies.

Now any woman, even the most 'innocent' and 'pure', was at risk. People now cared.

A month later, on 9 July, when prostitute Maureen Long survived an attack by the Ripper in Bradford, the police were given another lead, as a nightwatchman saw a white Ford Cortina Mark II saloon with a black roof, speeding away from the scene. Unfortunately it was a common car, and the guard had not seen the number plate. In Manchester, three months later, on 1 October, Jean Jordan was the next woman to die at the hands of the Yorkshire Ripper. Some time before half past nine that night Sutcliffe picked up Jean in Moss Side and gave her £5 in advance. He took her to a piece of deserted land and hit her with a hammer thirteen times, until 'the moaning stopped'. On returning home, however, Sutcliffe realized that he had left Jean's handbag with the £5 note he had given to her in it. When Jean's body had still not been discovered over a week later, on 9 October, he returned to recover the note, but the bag seemed to have disappeared. Seeing the body again brought back the memory of the murder and rekindled Sutcliffe's lust: he could not resist taking the clothes off Jean's body and stabbing the chest, abdomen and vagina some eighteen times. He also made an unsuccessful attempt at decapitation. This was not, as it was later thought, to try to hinder identification, but to satisfy Sutcliffe's increasing appetite for violence and mutilation.

Jean's body was found three days later, on 12 October, though her bag was not discovered until some days later. Inside it the police found their best clue yet – the new £5 note. The bank traced the £5 note to a batch of £50,000 and gave the police a list of firms to whom the notes had been issued for them to pay their workers. Some of the money was untraceable but, as it happened, one of the firms that the police checked out – T. and H. W. Clark – was where Sutcliffe was employed and, indeed, where he had received the £5 note in his wages. Police began the painstaking process of interviewing every employee of every possible firm, which amounted to over 8,000 interviews. The possible suspects were eventually narrowed down to just 300 but Sutcliffe's alibi seemed strong. On the night of Jean Jordan's murder he had been at the house-warming party that he and Sonia had given for friends and family. The party guests were happy to confirm this, but nobody mentioned that Sutcliffe had given lifts home to various members of his family after the party, leaving him plenty of time to then drive to Manchester, where Jean Jordan met her death.

Two months later, on 12 December, prostitute Marilyn Moore survived an attack in Leeds. Marilyn's description of the Ripper corresponded closely to previous ones: a stocky thirty-ish man with dark wavy hair and a beard. Later the police said that although the descriptions of Sutcliffe were good in hindsight, it was impossible for them to place too much reliance upon the recollections of women who had been subjected to such severe head trauma. In 1978 Sutcliffe killed a further three times. On 23 January 1978, prostitute Yvonne Pearson was reported missing, yet her body remained undiscovered for over two months. While the police were searching for Yvonne, eighteen-year-old Helen Rytka was murdered in Huddersfield on 31 January. By this time Sutcliffe said his urge to kill was 'practically unendurable'.

That night, Helen had been working on the streets with her twin sister, Rita. Because they were frightened of the Ripper, the sisters had arranged a system whereby they took the number plates of each other's clients. Tragically, that day the system went wrong and Helen ended up with Sutcliffe in a secluded timber yard, where he hit her over the head five times. Sutcliffe remembered that 'she just crumpled, making loud moaning noises'. He then repeatedly stabbed her in the chest and abdomen. When she was found, three days later, she was wearing only her bra, jumper and socks. She was also the first victim to have been raped. Sutcliffe claimed that as the area was a regular beat for prostitutes, the curiosity of two taxi-drivers parked nearby would not be aroused if he was performing a sexual act.

On 10 March a letter signed from 'Jack the Ripper' arrived for Assistant Chief Constable George Oldfield, who was co-ordinating the Ripper inquiry. It told Oldfield that 'My purpose [is] to rid the streets of them sluts. My one regret is that young lassie MacDonald, did not know cause changed routine that night. Up to number 8 now you say 7 but remember Preston 75.' The police had, of course, received various crank letters and calls purporting to be from the murderer. Yet the reference to Joan Harrison made them take this one more seriously than the rest, as the possibility of her being a Ripper victim had not been widely publicized in the media. Four days later the *Daily Mirror* also received a letter, which was also signed 'Jack the Ripper'. Again there were references to Joan Harrison, apologies for the murder of Jayne MacDonald, and derogatory references to prostitutes.

On 26 March, the disappearance of Yvonne Pearson was finally solved when her body was found under an abandoned sofa on waste ground in Bradford, where she had lain since 21 January. Sutcliffe had returned to Yvonne's body, as he had to Jean Jordan's. He had deliberately placed a copy of the *Daily Mirror*, dated 21 February (exactly one month after Yvonne's murder) under her arm. Studies by the FBI have shown that serial killers often return to their murder sites, particularly if the body is still there, to relive the killing, perhaps masturbating over the memories, as David Berkowitz – the 'Son of Sam' – told the FBI that he did.

The police should now have realized that the letters they had received from 'Jack the Ripper' were fakes. The letters had arrived in early March; Yvonne Pearson was murdered in January, but her body was not discovered until late March, after the letter was posted. The real Ripper would obviously have known of her death, but it was never mentioned in the letters, although the killer was keen to taunt the police with the murder of Joan Harrison. The conclusion should have been obvious: the sender was not the Yorkshire Ripper.

On 5 May, Vera Millward became Sutcliffe's ninth official victim. Vera, a prostitute who lived in Moss Side with her boyfriend and seven children, was picked up by Sutcliffe and taken to the grounds of the Manchester Royal Infirmary. Her body was found the next morning on a rubbish heap in the corner of the car park. She had been hit three times with a hammer, and her back and abdomen stabbed until her intestines protruded. She had also been stabbed in the eye. Tyre tracks were found at the scene. Sutcliffe later told police that at the time of this murder, 'The feelings I had [to kill] came welling up and each time they were more random and indiscriminate. I realized I now had an urge to kill any woman.'

In March 1979, a year after the last letters from 'Jack the Ripper', another letter arrived for George Oldfield, claiming responsibility for the murder of Vera Millward. The letter mentioned that some time before her murder Vera had received treatment in Manchester Royal Infirmary, where her body had been found, a fact that not many people knew (or so the police thought). This piece of information reinforced their earlier suspicions that the letters were genuine, and tests – which had been inconclusive on the last two letters – were immediately done on the flap of the envelope to test the saliva of the sender. The results showed that the sender of the letters had blood group B. Joan Harrison's murderer also had the rare blood group B. In light of this the police now believed both that the Ripper was responsible for the murder of Joan Harrison and that he was the sender of the letters, which was clearly faulty logic.

The next month the real Yorkshire Ripper claimed his tenth victim, building-society worker Josephine Whittaker. 'No woman was safe while I was in this frame of mind,' he admitted in his later statement; 'I realized Josephine was not a prostitute but at that time I wasn't bothered. I just wanted to kill a woman.' On 4 April, as Josephine walked back through the park from her grandparents' house in Halifax to her home, she was approached by Sutcliffe who asked her the time. As she looked at her watch he hit her over the head with a hammer. As he did so he told her, 'You can trust nobody these days.' In a frenzied attack Sutcliffe then stabbed her a total of thirty-five times in the abdomen, breasts, thighs and vagina with a sharpened screw-driver. After her body was discovered the next morning, Assistant Chief Constable George Oldfield said:

> If this is connected with the previous Ripper killings, then he has made a terrible mistake. As with Jayne MacDonald, the dead girl is perfectly respectable ... It appears he has changed his method of attack and this is concerning me, i.e. now in a non-red light area and attacking innocents. All women are at risk, even in areas not recognized as Ripper territory.

In June 1979 the Ripper investigation suffered an irrevocable setback, due to an ill-considered practical joke and some bad judgement, which the *Daily Mirror* referred to as the '£1m blunder'. When a tape arrived from the sender of the three 'Jack the Ripper' letters, addressed to George Oldfield, he was immediately convinced of its veracity. The tape taunted the police – 'I see you are still having no luck catching me' – and warned them that he would strike again that year, maybe in Manchester where 'there's plenty of them knocking about', bragging that 'At the rate I'm going I should be in the book of records. I think it's *eleven* up to now isn't it?' (my emphasis). Actually, the official number of victims was ten, but the sender of the tape was still including Joan Harrison. The voice on the recording had a distinctive Wearside accent. From that moment it was official: the Ripper was a Geordie. But Sutcliffe had a strong Yorkshire accent, as had been described by Olive Smelt, one of his surviving victims.

With this new impetus, the investigation was stepped up and Project R was launched. The tape was taken around pubs, clubs and bingo halls; it was played over loudspeakers at sports grounds; it was repeatedly aired on the television and radio; and 878,796 calls were made to the free number which could be rung to hear the message. Over one million free newspapers were produced and delivered, which gave samples of the handwriting on the letters and details of the murders. Billboards were put up all over the North of England. One read:

HELP US STOP THE RIPPER FROM KILLING AGAIN. LOOK AT HIS HANDWRITING [and there was a sample of the handwriting from the letters]. LISTEN TO HIS VOICE [and a phone number was given]. IF YOU RECOGNISE EITHER, REPORT IT TO YOUR LOCAL POLICE.

George Oldfield – who was '99 per cent certain' of the letters' and tape's authenticity – established five criteria by which to eliminate suspects:

    1) Was the man born between 1924 and 1959?
    2) Is he white?
    3) Does he have a shoe size under nine?
    4) Is his blood group B?
    5) Does he have a Geordie accent?

The police interviewed people from 1,600 households in the mining village of Castletown, near Sunderland, to which the accent had been traced; a further 11,000 houses were visited in the surrounding areas. Sutcliffe's friend Trevor Birdsall, who was with Sutcliffe the night that he attacked Olive Smelt, suspected that Sutcliffe might be the Ripper, but he justified his silence by the fact that his friend did not have a Geordie accent.

But the police had been hasty. The 'evidence' of the letters' and the tape's authenticity was flimsy. The information contained in them could easily have come from a detailed reading of newspaper reports. There had been no allusion to the murder of Yvonne Pearson; and there was no evidence that the rare blood group B (which was the blood group both of the author of the letters and the murderer of Joan Harrison), was the blood group of the killer of any of the official victims of the Yorkshire Ripper. Furthermore, a comparison of the MO and signature in the murder of Joan Harrison with those in the other murders, should clearly have shown that the perpetrators were two different people. Joan Harrison's breast had been bitten, and she had been subjected to vaginal and anal intercourse before being killed in a spontaneous outburst of rage. Her purse had been stolen afterwards. The other victims were not sexually assaulted, were killed quickly, and were mutilated after death. What we see when we compare the murders, are two entirely different means of achieving sexual gratification. Joan Harrison was not a victim of Peter Sutcliffe: he later admitted to all his other attacks, but emphatically denied this one.

While the police were scouring the country for a Geordie, the Yorkshire Ripper struck again in September 1979. Barbara Leach was another 'innocent', a student studying social sciences at Bradford. But as Sutcliffe's 'urge to kill remained strong', it only mattered to him that she was a woman and vulnerable to attack. Barbara had been out with her friends to their local pub and decided, afterwards, not to go with them for a curry but to go for a walk. Just two hundred yards along the way she was attacked by Sutcliffe. She was found two days later in a yard under an old carpet. Her shirt had been pulled up, her jeans pulled down; she had been hit with a hammer and then stabbed in the abdomen and shoulder blade eight times with a sharpened screwdriver.

There then followed a year's lull, and it was hoped that the attacks had ceased just as suddenly as had Jack the Ripper's. But Sutcliffe had not stopped, he couldn't stop. On 8 August 1980, civil servant Marguerite Walls was returning home from work at about 9.30 in Pudsey, a genteel suburb of Leeds. Sutcliffe hit her on the head twice and then tore off her clothes, repeatedly hitting her body with the hammer, and finally strangling her with rope. For this murder Sutcliffe had changed his MO in the hope that police would not attribute Marguerite's murder to the Ripper. He hated the name given to him by the police, preferring to refer to himself as the Headbanger. Like Jayne MacDonald's father, Marguerite's father died four months after his daughter's death, his grief too much to bear.

In October and November, both Dr Upadhya Bandara and Teresa Sykes, neither of whom were mistakable for prostitutes, survived attacks by the Ripper. On 17 November Sutcliffe struck again. Jacqueline Hill, a language student at Leeds University, had been to a seminar in the evening and was returning home when Sutcliffe attacked her. He hit her on the head with a hammer, then stabbed her body. He also stabbed her in one eye: 'Her eye was wide open and she seemed to be looking at me with an accusing stare. This shook me up a bit so I jabbed a screwdriver into her eye.' Jacqueline was Sutcliffe's thirteenth, and last, victim.

The Yorkshire Ripper was eventually caught, not as a result of the huge police inquiry, but thanks to a large dose of good luck coupled with some conscientious routine police work. In Sheffield, on the evening of 2 January 1981, twenty-four-year-old prostitute Olivia Reivers almost became the Ripper's fourteenth victim. Olivia was walking down Broomhall Street, having just finished with a client, when she was stopped by a man in a Rover who asked her if she was doing business. It was the first time that Sutcliffe had been trawling for a victim in Sheffield, and the prostitutes were less wary than those on the streets of Bradford and Leeds. They quickly negotiated: £10 for sex with a condom in his car. Olivia got in the car and Sutcliffe – calling himself Dave – drove them to the secluded headquarters of the British Iron and Steel Producers Association. Once they had parked Sutcliffe asked Olivia if they could talk for a while before having sex, and went on to tell her that he had had an argument with his wife. When he asked her a few minutes later if she would like to get into the back seat, Olivia replied that she was fine where she was. Her answer probably saved her life: if she had agreed to get into the back seat Sutcliffe would have hit her on the back of the head with a hammer when she got out of the car. Conscious that time was ticking on, Olivia undid Sutcliffe's trousers and (unsuccessfully) tried to arouse him, eventually telling him that she didn't think they would be able to have sex.

While Sutcliffe's trousers were still undone, Police Constable Robert Hydes and Sergeant Bob Ring pulled up in a squad car behind them. As the area was known for its high incidence of prostitution, and Sergeant Ring was sure that he recognized Olivia, they questioned Sutcliffe about her identity, to which he replied that she was his girlfriend. He did not, however, know her name. 'Who are you trying to kid. I haven't fallen off a Christmas tree,' Sergeant Ring told him (the judge later commented that 'we are very grateful that he had not'). The officers routinely radioed the station for a check on the car and its owner and found that the number plates on the car were false – they actually belonged to a Skoda – as was the tax disc, and the name that the driver had given them (Peter Williams). Sutcliffe and Olivia Reivers were taken down to the station for further questioning.

Yorkshire police officers had been instructed to be particularly vigilant with arrests of men with prostitutes. If there were any unusual circumstances at all the Ripper squad was to be called with the details. In this case, the false name and number plates alerted the officers' suspicions. As more incriminating facts emerged about Sutcliffe the Ripper Squad were again notified. Then there was a vital breakthrough. Sergeant Ring remembered that while he was taking Olivia to the police car, Sutcliffe had slipped away on the pretext of going to urinate. Ring returned to the spot, and there lay a hammer and knife: the Ripper's instruments of murder. Sutcliffe was interviewed by Detective Inspector Boyle, Detective Sergeant O'Boyle and Detective Sergeant Peter Smith, who told him that they had found the tools, and started to question him about some of the Ripper attacks. The breakthrough came as they were asking him about the night of 5 November 1980, when Teresa Sykes was attacked. Out of the blue, Sutcliffe said, 'I think you are leading up to the Yorkshire Ripper', and when DI Boyle asked him what he meant, he replied, 'Well, it is me. I'm glad it's all over. I would have killed that girl in Sheffield if I hadn't been caught'; 'I just want to unburden myself'. This he did, in a confession admitting full responsibility for the murders and attempted murders, which took nearly sixteen hours to record and filled thirty-four pages.

The fact that Peter Sutcliffe had been able to kill thirteen women and attack a further seven without being caught was perplexing. He hadn't even tried to hide his victims' bodies as John Christie, or Brady and Hindley had. It did not reflect well upon the police that they had been investigating a series of murders for over five years without coming any closer to finding their man. Sutcliffe had not even been on the '1,000 most likely suspects' list, although he had been interviewed on nine separate occasions.

That the Ripper had eluded the police was not through inertia on their part, in fact their extreme thoroughness was part of the problem. The investigation generated such an immense amount of data that the sheer volume of it often hindered, rather than helped, them. The Yorkshire Ripper inquiry was the biggest to date in the history of British crime: around 32,000 statements were taken; more than 260,000 people were interviewed; 5.4 million car registrations were recorded; 250 detectives worked full time for three years, some 5 million hours; and the cost of the investigation amounted to over £6 million. At one point the paper records weighed twenty-four tons, so heavy that there were anxieties over the stress to the building where they were stored.

This amount of data today would not pose the problem that it did in the 1970s, when it was uncommon to use a computer for investigations. None of the information was computerized. Chief Constable Ronald Gregory of the West Yorkshire police later said, 'If we had known this investigation was going to reach such proportions we would have used a computer from the beginning.' But of course they didn't know. Who would have thought that the murder of Wilma McCann – a 'fish and chips job', the murder of a prostitute after the pubs turn out – would be followed by twelve more? As the investigation went on, the police became literally swamped with information, making cross-referencing a nightmare, if not an impossibility. As Gregory further admitted, 'Our filing system was chaos. At times there was a nine-month back-log of reports waiting to be cross-indexed.' Thorough they were; organized they were not.

This cross-referencing breakdown was the major reason that allowed Sutcliffe to be interviewed on *nine* separate occasions during the course of the investigation, and still not be added to the lists of strong suspects; his name was put in the 'not happy' file. Yet Sutcliffe had the same (small) boot size as found at two of the murder scenes; he had a previous conviction for being found in a woman's garden with a hammer and screwdriver; he closely matched photofit pictures created by surviving victims; he was one man out of only 300 who could have received the £5 note found in the handbag of Jean Jordan; his car had been logged almost fifty times in red-light areas; his only alibis were provided (unwittingly) by a close relative, his wife; and he had previously been questioned concerning an attack on a woman in a red-light area. Evidence enough, one would have thought, to make Sutcliffe a very strong suspect indeed.

Even Sutcliffe himself later said, 'It was just a miracle they did not apprehend me earlier. They had all the facts.' All the facts were indeed there, but they remained unconnected. As Gregory later said, in four out of the nine times that Sutcliffe was questioned, the police believed that they were interviewing him for the first time. They were not, therefore, in full possession of 'all the facts': each officer had one piece of the jigsaw, but they were never put together to form an entire puzzle. Finally, in the summer of 1979, Police Constable Andrew Laptew realized while interviewing Sutcliffe that there seemed to be one too many coincidences and he submitted a report saying that he thought Sutcliffe should be investigated further. 'He stuck in my mind,' Laptew later said; 'I was not 99 per cent certain otherwise I would have pulled him in. But he was the best I had seen so far and I had seen hundreds.' Tragically, the report was filed, and never acted upon. Why? Because Sutcliffe did not have a Wearside accent.

The hoax 'Jack the Ripper' letters and tape had disastrously diverted the investigation, but we have to wonder why the police were so convinced of their veracity on the basis of such insubstantial evidence. It has been argued that because the police already unofficially believed that Joan Harrison was a victim of the Ripper, as she was a prostitute, they were looking for evidence to justify that conviction. When they glimpsed such evidence, they grabbed it, and the spurious conclusions to which it led. They wanted Joan to be a Ripper victim, as it would confirm their preconceived idea of what the Yorkshire Ripper was like, how he thought and operated. He was inevitably identified with Jack the Ripper, England's most famous prostitute killer and mutilator. The problem with this, of course, was that 'Jack' was never caught. Thus the image of him, and so of the Yorkshire Ripper, as a knife-wielding fiend on a mission to eradicate prostitutes was the one which was adopted, however unconsciously, from the beginning of the investigation.

Thus Joan Harrison was unofficially included on the list of suspected victims as she was a prostitute, and Tracey Browne (who, it later transpired, had survived an attack by the Ripper in 1975) was excluded, because she was a fourteen-year-old school-girl, and not the Ripper 'type'. When the police received the letters, their image of the Ripper as primarily a prostitute-killer was reinforced. The first letter said that his purpose was 'to rid the streets of them sluts'; a letter sent to the police in 1888 supposedly from Jack the Ripper similarly claimed: 'I am down on whores and I shan't quit ripping them till I do get buckled.' This is what the police wanted to hear, for it was what they already believed. They could understand, although obviously not condone, these motives. So convinced were they by their own image of the killer that George Oldfield confidently predicted, 'If we had twenty or thirty suspects in one room we would know very quickly which one was the Ripper.'

Presumably he would have been the one with the blood-stained clothes, the mad glint in his eye, raving about his hatred for 'whores' and 'sluts'. As Carl Sutcliffe later said, 'I imagined him to be an ugly hunchback wi' boils all over his face.' The police were not looking for a man, they were looking for a monster. But Sutcliffe did not stand out as being different or abnormal in any way, as his nine interviews attested. He was a quiet thirty-four-year-old lorry driver, with a local Yorkshire accent, a wife who was a teacher, and a nice house in a good part of Bradford. As Joan Smith, journalist and writer, puts it:

> One of the chief ironies of the whole Yorkshire Ripper case is that the police spent millions of pounds fruitlessly searching for an outsider when the culprit was an ordinary bloke, a local man who shared their background and atti-tudes to a remarkable degree. Sutcliffe was not a needle in a haystack: he was neither as conspicuous nor as alien as that image suggests.

Of course, it is all too easy with the advantage of hindsight to catalogue the mistakes made, and to forget the hard work put in, under immense pressure, and without adequate tools of detection.

Computers, psychologists and offender profilers were not readily available to the police in the 1970s. As one detective said,

> Our critics should remember that they never came forward to help solve these crimes during the five years. The way some people are talking it looks as though we did not want to catch him. No other force in the country, even Scotland Yard, could have done more. With hindsight we now know which blind alleys we went up. But at the time we were walking in the dark.

The investigation may well have been, as *The Times* put it, 'an embarrassing amalgam of occasional misfortune, misadventure and some bad judgement', but with the methods of detection available to the police in the 1970s the search for the Ripper was rather like trying to build a table without proper tools. But at least the police can learn from these errors, to provide, as *The Times* further suggested, 'a useful framework should an operation of similar scope and magnitude ever arise again'.

After Sutcliffe's trial, Lawrence Byford – at that time Her Majesty's Inspector of Constabulary for the region that encompassed West Yorkshire – led a review of the case. His report concluded that lessons needed to be learnt in the following areas:

- the computerization of records
- the standardization of procedures
- the training of senior investigating officers
- the appointment of advisory teams
- the use of specialist and scientific support

The use of computers was a priority, and as a result of what was fast becoming known as the Sutcliffe 'fiasco', the Home Office developed a system to assist police in major investigations: in 1984 the Home Office Large Major Enquiry System was born. The purpose of HOLMES is to simplify the collation and comparison of large amounts of data generated by an investigation. The computer can be 'asked', for instance, whether a suspect's car has featured in the investigation so far. In the Sutcliffe inquiry the investigating officers would have quickly been able to establish, when going to question him, that Sutcliffe had been interviewed on numerous other occasions, thus making him a higher priority suspect. As a result of lessons learnt in the Sutcliffe investigation, when Hector Clark was put in charge of the investigation into the murders by Robert Black in the mid-1980s, one of his aims was to see how the use of computer technology could help the police in their search, and he thus utilized HOLMES in his inquiry.

They may have taken a rather long time about it, but at last the police had their man. However, although Sutcliffe had given the police a full confession, he now decided to change the details of his story, maintaining that he had previously lied to the police when he told them of his overwhelming and indiscriminate urge to kill. In fact, he said, he had been on a 'divine mission' from God who had instructed him to kill prostitutes. On the basis of this, he was diagnosed by psychiatrists as a paranoid schizo-phrenic. Sutcliffe informed his defending counsel, Mr Chadwin, that he wished to plead not guilty to murder, but guilty to manslaughter on the grounds of diminished responsibility. In turn, Chadwin approached the prosecution, and Attorney General Sir Michael Havers – who had decided to prosecute the case himself, due to the serious nature of the charges – decided to accept the plea. This would mean, both Chadwin and the Attorney General hoped, a short and unsensational trial involv-ing the Attorney General presenting the case, uncontested, for diminished responsibility and the judge passing his sentence. They came before Judge Boreham on 29 April 1981, to present the plea.

To everyone's surprise and chagrin, Judge Boreham had other ideas about how the case would proceed. Where, he asked, was the *factual basis* for the assertion that Sutcliffe's responsibility for his acts was diminished through an abnormality of mind? The psychiatrists who had interviewed Sutcliffe may have diagnosed him as suffering from paranoid schizophrenia, but on what did they base their conclusions? Was it merely on Sutcliffe's own claims to have heard the voice of God commanding him to kill? It would appear so, the Attorney General had to concede. That was simply not good enough for Judge Boreham, who maintained that there needed to be more concrete and objective evidence for Sutcliffe's supposed condition if such a plea were to be accepted at this stage. He ordered a trial by jury. The prosecution was to uphold the charge of murder, and the burden was upon the defence to prove a case of diminished responsibility. This made for a nice irony: the Attorney General, who was initially convinced of Sutcliffe's diminished responsibility, now had to argue against it.

Sutcliffe's trial by jury – six men and six women – began on 5 May 1981, at the Old Bailey. The crux of the case was quite simple: was Sutcliffe, as the defence claimed, suffering from paranoid schizophrenia which diminished his responsibility; or was he simply, as the prosecution contended, 'a sadistic, calculated, cold-blooded murderer who loved his job', feigning mental disorder as a means to avoid a life sentence in prison? Was Sutcliffe's sixteen-hour statement to the police, which claimed in several places that he had an unendurable urge to kill any woman the truth; or was it, as he later claimed to psychiatrists, all lies designed to hide his 'divine mission' from God?

The prosecution began by asking why it was that Sutcliffe had not mentioned his 'divine mission' until 5 March, two months after his arrest, and after he had been interviewed eight times at Armley jail, where he was being held? Why had he not previously told his friends and family about the miraculous thing that was happening to him? If these voices had been with him for fourteen or fifteen years, as he claimed, surely he would have confided in someone? But he had not.

Furthermore, Sutcliffe had been overheard by prison-guard John Leach telling Sonia that: 'I am going to do a long time in prison, thirty years or more, unless I can convince people in here that I am mad and maybe then ten years in the loony bin.' Another officer, Frederick Edwards, testified that Sutcliffe had told him that the doctors thought that he was mentally disturbed, which he found ridiculous. 'He was quite amazed by this', said Edwards, adding that Sutcliffe was 'smiling broadly, rocking back in his chair and he said, "I'm as normal as anyone."' If the officers were to be believed, Sutcliffe was a calculating murderer, not a schizophrenic.

Sutcliffe had good knowledge of the symptoms of paranoid schizophrenia, as Sonia had been diagnosed as suffering from the very same disorder when she spent twenty-two days in a psychiatric hospital after a nervous breakdown in 1972. She had experienced religious delusions, thinking that she was the second Christ. The likelihood of both man and wife suffering from the same relatively uncommon mental disorder, manifesting itself in the same manner, is highly improbable. Furthermore, the results of several recent research projects have shown that if you know the major symptoms, schizophrenia is not a difficult illness to feign. For example, in a controlled experiment in America, eight researchers went to nineteen different psychiatric institutions claiming that they were experiencing aural hallucinations, hearing voices. All of the doctors diagnosed them as schizophrenic purely on the basis of this. (It was only the other patients who were not fooled: they thought the researchers were journalists.)

The major arguments of the prosecution's case emerged in the cross-examination of Sutcliffe and of the psychiatrists who had assessed him. If the prosecution could show the jury that: (1) Sutcliffe knew that some of his victims were not prostitutes, and (2) that he had gained sexual pleasure from their killings, then the case for the defence would effectively collapse. The prosecution asked why, if Sutcliffe had a divine mission to kill prostitutes, were five of his victims obviously not prostitutes? Contrary to his statement to the police, Sutcliffe now claimed that he had believed at the time that all of his victims were prostitutes. But Josephine Whittaker hardly looked like a prostitute as she walked across a park in a nice area of Halifax; neither did Barbara Leach nor Jacqueline Hill, who were dressed like students and attacked near their university campuses; nor did Marguerite Walls or Jayne MacDonald. None of these women was dressed 'provocatively', or out very late at night, drunk, in red-light areas, as his initial victims had been. There was nothing to indicate that they were prostitutes and thus no reason for

Sutcliffe to have murdered them, if his divine mission story was to be believed. As Mr Ognall for the prosecution said, 'I suggest that the circumstances of these last five killings show this man ... to be a liar and a fake.'

Furthermore, if Sutcliffe's victims were attacked as part of a mission prescribed by God to exterminate prostitutes, why were the murders quite clearly sexual in nature? If the idea was simply to *eradicate* them, why mutilate them at all, let alone in ways which were obviously sexual? Why place a piece of wood against Emily Jackson's vagina? Why stab Josephine Whittaker in her breast and vagina? Why scratch Olive Smelt's buttocks with the blade of a hacksaw? Why scratch Marguerite Walls at the entrance of her vagina? If, as Sutcliffe now claimed, the murders were purely functional, in order to satisfy the voices, and he did not want to commit them, then why do any more than necessary? Why return to Jean Jordan's body days after the murder to mutilate her? What other purpose could Sutcliffe's mutilation of his victims' sex organs and his display of their bodies serve, if not sexual gratification?

Dr MacCulloch, forensic psychiatrist for the defence, testified: 'I have considered the alternative diagnosis [to paranoid schizophrenia] of personality disorder involving sexual abnormality, but there appears to me to be no evidence of it.' No evidence of sexual abnormality when a woman's clothes are pulled up and she is stabbed twenty-two times in her breasts, stomach and thighs, and three times in her vagina? Dr Milne, also a forensic psychiatrist for the defence, similarly testified that, 'There is no suggestion that he had a sadistic, sexual deviation.' Dr Terence Kay, the third expert witness for the defence, agreed, testifying that Sutcliffe was not a sexual sadist as he killed quickly, whereas sadists draw out the killing in order to enjoy their victim's suffering. The psychiatrists were right here, Sutcliffe was not a sadist. But sexually deviant? He was certainly that. A sexually deviant killer, a lust-murderer, is not necessarily also a sadist. Perhaps, Dr Milne suggested – the psychiatrists appearing more stupid by the minute – he'd stabbed Josephine three times in her vagina *by accident*. Realizing that this diagnosis was ridiculous Milne eventually conceded under cross-examination that six of Sutcliffe's attacks – on Josephine Whittaker, Helen Rytka, Emily Jackson, Marguerite Walls, Jacqueline Hill and Olive Smelt – had sexual elements. He further conceded that the attacks having sexual elements seriously undermined the story of Sutcliffe's divine mission.

If Sutcliffe didn't have a divine mission, if he wasn't suffering from paranoid schizophrenia, why had he murdered thirteen women? This wasn't, of course, a question that the prosecution were compelled to provide an answer to – as the burden of proof was on the defence – but their case would be even more plausible if they could. Presenting the crimes as lust-murders was not a viable option, as the concept was insufficiently developed at the time. So the prosecution referred back to Sutcliffe's story of picking up a prostitute to 'pay Sonia back' for being unfaithful to him in 1969. The prostitute had conned him out of £10 and he had got nothing for it; a few weeks later, when he had seen her in a pub, she had jeered at him in front of his friends. Sutcliffe had told Dr Milne that from this time on: 'I had a hatred of prostitutes ... It was a pathological hatred. I was seized in a grip, difficult to explain, occasionally getting depressed, deeply depressed at times with splitting headaches. Sometimes I didn't want to go on living.'

Sutcliffe further claimed that it was after this incident that the voices began to tell him that prostitutes were the cause of all his problems and that they should all be killed. But his contention that he began to hate prostitutes after having been cheated by one undermined his 'divine mission' story. The Attorney General summed it up: God had simply 'jumped on the bandwagon' after Sutcliffe had already developed a hatred for prostitutes. As Ognall put it to the court, after this incident Sutcliffe had 'a perfectly sensible reason for harbouring a grudge against prostitutes'; the Attorney General reiterated the point:

Was this not a classic case of provocation? ... God hasn't told him to hate prostitutes or kill them. It was a reaction which ... was not altogether surprising. The reaction of a man who has been fleeced and humiliated ... The sort of loss of control which you don't have to be mad for a moment to suffer.

The Attorney General was not saying, as some outraged feminists have suggested, that the murders were justifiable and rational, merely that in Sutcliffe's mind he had a reason, a reason that however reprehensible was nonetheless not necessarily the reason of a madman. His murders had begun from a hatred of prostitutes, but soon enough – after he had got a taste, a lust, for killing – any women would do and he began to kill indiscriminately.

The stage was now given to the defence who would have to show, if it was to prove their contention that Sutcliffe was mad, not bad, that:

1) At the time of the murders Sutcliffe was suffering from an abnormality of mind.
2) This abnormality was caused by inherent causes, mental disease or illness.
3) This abnormality was of such proportions as to substantially diminish Sutcliffe's mental responsibility for his acts.

The defence's case rested upon the expert testimony of the three psychiatrists who had examined Sutcliffe while he was on remand, all of whom agreed that Sutcliffe was indeed suffering from paranoid schizophrenia, an abnormality of mind that substantially diminished his responsibility for his acts. For their diagnoses they relied exclusively upon what Sutcliffe had told them, which was that his murders were part of a 'divine mission' from God to kill all prostitutes. Sutcliffe had told them that about fifteen years earlier he had been digging a grave in Bingley cemetery, when he heard 'an echoing voice, vague and distant' which seemed to be coming from the top of a gravestone. 'I decided', Sutcliffe said, that 'it was some kind of message from God'. This, the psychiatrists testified, was Sutcliffe's primary schizophrenic experience. Over the years the voice repeatedly came back to him, giving him different messages such as, 'God giveth and taketh away life' and 'God works in mysterious ways'.

Claiming that he had been chosen to carry out God's work, when the voice told him that prostitutes were 'the scum of the earth' and to 'kill, kill, kill', Sutcliffe reported that he had no choice but to comply. The voice told him that 'God knew best'. When the voices commanded him to kill Wilma McCann, he claimed 'I could not stop myself – it was God who was controlling me'; similarly, when the voices told him to kill the 'filthy prostitute' Marguerite Walls he 'killed her with no doubt'. In return for doing God's work, God had protected Sutcliffe from capture, engineering the hoax letters and the tape in order that he could continue his mission. 'Everything was in God's hands', Sutcliffe testified, 'the way I escaped, the way they [the police] went away satisfied [after interviewing him], everything else, there was no chance of catching me'.

Sutcliffe explained to the doctors and the court that because of the voices he truly believed that each one of his victims was a prostitute and therefore deserved to die. When he found out that Jayne MacDonald was a 'decent lass' he said: 'I felt absolutely shattered mentally. I could not accept it. I felt terrible and full of remorse. Because the headlines seemed to be screaming at me I could not see how I could have been wrong.' The voice of God was also wrong when it commanded him to kill student Jacqueline Hill, whose 'adjusting of her skirt or stocking' suggested that she was a prostitute and therefore deserved to die. God also told him that Josephine Whittaker and Barbara Leach were prostitutes, and 'God knew best', 'God couldn't make a mistake'. After Sutcliffe realized that these two women were actually a building-society worker and a student, he claimed to have been filled with anguish, which is why he didn't kill again for another year after Barbara's murder. But when he did, his next victim, Marguerite Walls, was again not a prostitute.

I was on my way to Leeds primed with weapons for the mission. She lifted her leg up, put it down again and then lifted it up again. She looked like a prostitute and was

walking slowly at a snail's pace. I killed her with no doubt.
The voice shouted 'filthy prostitute'. It wasn't like my voice
it was filthy and angry.

Sutcliffe certainly presented an impressive catalogue of schizophrenic symptoms: aural hallucinations; bodily hallucinations
(such as sensations of being touched inside the body, like
Sutciffe's description of a tingling all over and a hand gripping
his heart); influence of thought (Sutcliffe claimed both that his
own thoughts were being interfered with and also that he could
read other people's thoughts); passivity (Sutcliffe told doctors
that his will was being usurped by a higher power and that his
actions were not controllable by himself); and delusional perception (seeing things that are not really present). He also displayed
an inordinate calm when talking about his hideous crimes,
which is characteristic of a paranoid schizophrenic. Dr
MacCulloch testified that there were eight primary symptoms of
schizophrenia, any one of which would be sufficient for a diagnosis. Sutcliffe displayed four.

Nobody disputed that all of the above symptoms are
displayed in paranoid schizophrenia, and a man who really
believes that God is telling him to murder prostitutes may well
be suffering from the disorder. But did Sutcliffe truly hear these
voices or not? Had he faked the symptoms, and duped the
doctors, or were they genuine? Dr Milne declared, when asked
whether he might have been misled by Sutcliffe: 'I do not
believe the accused is, in fact, simulating mental illness. He is
suffering from schizophrenia of the paranoid type ... As far as I
can see ... either he is a competent actor or I am an inefficient
psychiatrist ... Perhaps I have been duped. It is for the jury to
decide.' Both Dr MacCulloch and Dr Kay agreed with the diagnoses. Dr MacCulloch had apparently decided within half an
hour that Sutcliffe was a paranoid schizophrenic; Dr Kay said he
had 'no doubts'. Mr Chadwin concluded for the defence that
Sutcliffe had: 'a sick mind, a diseased mind, and a diseased mind
which had the effect that it substantially impaired his responsibility for what he did ... a known disease of mind called
paranoid schizophrenia'.

The jury disagreed. The evidence for Sutcliffe's supposed paranoid schizophrenia was simply not strong enough, as the prosecution had shown. On 22 May the jury returned a verdict of guilty on all counts, by a majority of ten to two, and Sutcliffe was sentenced to life imprisonment with the recommendation that he serve at least thirty years. Outside the Old Bailey the crowds gave the jury three cheers.

Many papers commented the next day that it was not just Sutcliffe who had been on trial, but also the psychiatrists. The problem with the case had been the age-old one of scientific fact versus opinion. Forensic psychiatry falls uneasily between these two categories. When a forensic scientist is called to court to testify about a bloodstain, fingerprints or fibres, there is little room left for doubt, as the processes used to identify a fingerprint are purely objective, and other forensic experts' conclusions will concur, with very rare exceptions. Psychiatry is not like this: not a verifiable, or *a priori*, science. It is the study of the human mind and human behaviour, subjects about which we still know relatively little. And the mind, we must remember, is an intrinsically private domain. One cannot know another person's mental state. The inherent privacy that shrouds the inner life of persons means that psychiatry is necessarily a science which relies upon self-reporting, not on objective fact.

As Mr Ognall rightly pointed out to the psychiatrists at Sutcliffe's trial: 'Your diagnosis stands or falls by what this man has told you. That is the beginning and the end of it.' When a person claims to have experienced visual or auditory hallucinations, we have only his word that this is true. And when this word, as in Sutcliffe's case, stands directly opposed to what he had previously said, its veracity is even more doubtful. The difficulty is that psychiatrists often have no evidence to use aside from these self-reports, and tend to place too much faith in them. Yet when it comes to serial killers, a healthy dose of scepticism goes a long way.

6

DENNIS NILSEN

Olav and Betty Nilsen's marriage was a typical war-time union, producing a lifetime of unhappy consequences from a few hours of pleasure snatched from the stress of war. Olav, a Norwegian soldier, and Betty, a local Fraserburgh girl, had met, fallen in love and married all too hastily, in May of 1942, caught up in a whirlwind romance during Olav's posting to the Scottish coast. Being in love had seemed good enough reason to get married, but reality soon set in, and while Olav's postings took him round the world, Betty was left in Fraserburgh living with her parents. Under the strain of Olav's unavoidable absences the marriage began to suffer. During his infrequent visits home their children – Olav, Dennis (born on 23 November 1945) and Sylvia – were conceived. None of the children had any sort of relationship with their father, he was simply a man who occasionally called round. Betty later told journalists that Olav 'did nothing for me. I had to bring up the children virtually single-handed. When he did come home he was as good as useless'. After seven years, Olav and Betty were divorced.

Their parents' divorce made little difference to the children. Dennis was four when the separation occurred and has no memories of his father, save those elicited by a photograph of him in uniform that his mother kept. As Betty later said, Dennis would not have recognized his father if he had walked past him in the street. There was thus no unsettling emotional separation for the children, and their living arrangements remained the same. Betty, Olav, Dennis and Sylvia continued to share one room at 47 Academy Road, which was Betty's parents', Andrew and Lily Whytes', home. The council flat was certainly overcrowded, but Dennis remembers it as a happy time. Betty, still young and with three children to look after, relied heavily upon

Andrew and Lily, who became like surrogate parents to the children.

Dennis and his grandfather were particularly close, and Andrew became Dennis's role-model, the only stable, strong, male influence in his life – 'my great hero and protector' as Nilsen said years later. Andrew Whyte was a typical Fraserburgh man: strong-minded to the point of rigidity, unwavering in his religious and moral beliefs, but loving and gruffly kind-hearted. In common with most of the other male villagers, Andrew's life was one of relentless harshness and toil. He was a fisherman, and his job necessarily involved him going out to sea in all conditions to bring home the fish which the women of the village would then prepare for sale. Consequently Andrew was often away, and at those times Dennis would be listless and morose. When he returned, Dennis was invariably at his grandfather's side, going for long walks, watching football and chatting endlessly.

Unfortunately, this emotional warmth, which Dennis had always shunned from his mother, was cruelly snatched from him when he was just five. Andrew Whyte went out to sea and died in his bunk from a heart attack. The last image Dennis had of his grandfather was of his body, laid out in a coffin in the lounge of Academy Road. But he was only five, he didn't understand. If his grandfather was just asleep, as his mother had told him, why was everybody crying? Nobody explained to him or his siblings that his grandfather was dead, and that it meant he was never coming back. So Dennis kept waiting for him. It was not until some time later that he realized that his grandfather, like his father, was gone. Nilsen later wrote to his biographer, Brian Masters, 'My troubles started there ... I have spent all my emotional life searching for my grandfather and in my formative years no one was there to take his place ... Father and grandfather had walked out on me, probably to a better place, leaving me behind in this not so good place, alone.'

From this time, in Dennis's mind – in a little boy's imperfect logic – death became a desirable state. He loved his grandfather, who always knew best, and his grandfather was dead. But he was not gone. He was constantly alive in the grieving boy's mind, the best and most loving presence of his experience. If his grandfather was dead then, in some inexplicable way, death must be a desirable state: it preserved the one image of love to which he had responded.

Betty certainly did her best to provide her son with love and affection, but Dennis would never let her close, physically or emotionally. In the years after Andrew's death the boy became increasingly distant, uncommunicative and sullen. He spent much of his time wandering, going for long walks by himself, often to the shore or to other places where his grandfather had taken him. He also loved animals, and was distraught when boys killed the pigeons that he and some friends had lovingly reared. Years later, after her son's arrest, Betty remembers him as a soft-hearted and kind boy. 'He was so gentle as a young lad. He'd come home with injured birds and say, "Mam, fetch me a shoe box." Then he'd make a nest with cotton wool and care for the bird until it was better.'

Although he made a few friends at school Dennis was always something of an outsider, his small body and congenitally weak spine and curved shoulders making him reluctant to join in boyish sports and games. Always self-conscious as a boy, he is remembered as shy and withdrawn. He later described himself as 'a very lonely and turbulent child' who lived in a 'secret world full of ideal and imaginary friends'. Dr Bowden, psychiatrist for the prosecution at Nilsen's trial, described him as a well-adjusted and normal boy on the surface: 'Although at first fatherless, he was part of a close family and was intelligent, artistic and did develop close relationships with other boys his age'. He continued, however, by noting that 'somehow one was left with the impression of someone who always felt something of an outsider'.

After years of relying upon her parents, Betty and the children were finally allocated their own council flat. They had not been at their new home long, however, when she decided to remarry. Adam Scott, a local labourer, was a positive replacement for her first husband, and soon moved his family to a new house in nearby Strichen. Over the next few years four more children were born and the family was forced to move again to accommodate the new additions. Sadly, the larger family meant that the bond between Betty and Dennis weakened further, and the boy came to resent his new step-father for diverting his mother's attentions. Nevertheless as he matured Dennis came to realize that Adam wasn't a bad man: he worked hard to provide for his family and was at home – and sober – every night, which was more than could have been said for Olav.

Betty remembers that, as an adolescent, Dennis was 'not one for the girls' and that if there was ever an occasion that required him to take a 'date' he would invariably take Sylvia, his sister. His first crush was when he found himself drawn to an illustration of a boy which adorned the cover of his French text book. This infatuation with the sexually stimulating image of the male figure progressed until Dennis found that he was attracted to some of the other boys at school, but he never experimented sexually with friends, as some children do. The only actual sexual contact that Dennis experienced was when he and Olav shared a bed and, curious, he reached out to touch his brother, stopping when Olav became aroused.

Nilsen told Brian Masters that he has no idea whether Olav was even awake, as the episode was never mentioned, much less repeated. Literally or figuratively, his crushes were always distanced and safe. His image of a sexual partner was that of an imaginary figure or an unconscious body which was unaware of his desires. His sexual attachments were directed at figures who could neither know about them nor reciprocate them. Thus they were safe, for while they could not return love, neither could they reject it. Dennis was free to offer without fear of denial. In a sad and isolated way, he was wholly in control.

When he began to fantasize sexually, the passivity of the loved object – whether sleeping, imagined, or dead – became a recurring theme for Dennis. The image of his grandfather's dead body retained its power as an object of love. In some way the illustration of the boy, or the particular schoolmate he had a crush on but never approached, became images of the desirability of a body which is unavailable and ignorant of his desire. In the process fantasy and reality begin to merge: the grandfather was not really dead, and the boy in the illustration was not really imaginary and lifeless. As an adult Dennis recalled an 'event' as a boy where the (clearly imagined) themes of sexuality and unconsciousness were conflated. He remembers wandering out to sea in a daze, and being rescued from near drowning by another boy. While this is perfectly plausible, his contention that this boy then carried him back up to the beach and masturbated over his unconscious body, leaving a peculiar stickiness on his stomach, is surely fantastical. An inextricable union between unconsciousness, death and sexuality was beginning to form in Dennis's mind, a union in which it was not clear where reality ended and fantasy began, and which would later have tragic consequences.

At school Dennis was unremarkable, his grades mediocre at best. He later said that his self-image was so poor that in his own eyes he felt 'dim, slow-witted, and unintelligent' and therefore the effort he put into his subjects was minimal. His old head-mistress, Melita Lee, remembers him as 'an average boy, a willing pupil. He just got on with anything you gave him'. Although not particularly academic, Dennis did apparently have a flair for art. His mother remembers that 'As he got older, he used to draw and paint... He was always first in his class.' She continues, 'He was a sensitive lad, not at all sporty like the rest of my children. He loved classical music and reading history'. Melita Lee confirms that 'he was always better at art than scientific subjects and I always thought he would take up a career with an artistic bias'. Betty thought so too. But Dennis surprised them all when he was ready to leave school at fifteen. He wanted to get out of Fraserburgh, broaden his horizons, get some qualifications, see the world. He decided to enlist in the army.

Dennis Nilsen was to stay in the army for the next eleven years. Under the harsh discipline he toughened up, and soon began to relish the unity, the sense of purpose and the all-male camaraderie. At eighteen Nilsen passed his catering exam, having decided that he wanted to be a chef. He also passed five subjects in his senior education test, the army's equivalent to GCSEs, and completed full arms, foot and weapons training. He then began a series of different postings, working as a chef in

Germany, Aden, the Persian Gulf, Cyprus, Berlin and Bavaria. A soldier who knew Nilsen at the time, Michael Procopis, remembers that Nilsen 'wanted to be the best chef he could be, the best in the Army'. And he was very good; apparently when there was a party the other officers 'insisted that he should prepare the food'. Procopis also recalls that Nilsen 'had a very odd thing about knives', about which he talked obsessively: the sharpest, the most reliable, the best knives for different meats. Even more prophetic, and more sinister in its implications, is the fact that part of Nilsen's catering training inevitably involved the best way to cut up a carcass.

Now more sure of himself, Nilsen gradually began to explore his sexuality. He liked to think of himself as bisexual although his clear preference was for males. He had to keep this quiet of course, as such an admission in the army would have had serious repercussions for his career and isolated Nilsen from the other men. With this in mind Nilsen echoed his comrades' homophobic attitudes, and even had intercourse with a prostitute, an experience which he found 'overrated and depressing'. He infinitely preferred the Arab boy with whom he had his first homosexual sex on one of his postings. Most satisfying however, was the sex he had while alone in his room masturbating in front of a mirror. The image he found most arousing was that of himself lying in front of the mirror, his face whitened with talc, his eyes blackened with charcoal, his body smeared with fake blood: the corpse as an object of desire. All his adult life Nilsen strove to recreate the last image of his grandfather: in effect trying to expunge the terrible finality of death, and the permanence of loss, by converting the image of the dead body into an object of recurring delight. He later told Brian Masters that 'My sexual and emotional aspirations became entrenched in creating and enhancing the "dead" image. I became dead in my fantasies. In the mirror I became dead.'

In the army, images of death were infrequent but exciting to him, the occasional sight of the maimed, the mutilated and the dead, fuelling his fantasies. His masturbatory practices were also enhanced through filming his own fantasies, where he used to 'direct' a fellow soldier to pretend to have been wounded and

153

killed in battle. When alone later, Nilsen would replay the films and masturbate over the image of the 'dead' man. After his arrest, Nilsen remembered an incident which occurred while he was posted in Aden (another recollection which is surely part reality, part fantasy). He claims that having fallen asleep in a taxi, the Arab driver hit him over the head and the next thing he was aware of was being naked in the boot of the car. When the driver opened the boot, Nilsen decided to play dead to buy himself some time. As the Arab stroked his hands over Nilsen's buttocks, Nilsen claims that he hit him over the head and put him in the boot. While the event may have had some grounding in reality, the fusion of sexuality and unconsciousness is surely pure fantasy.

By 1972, at the age of twenty-six, Nilsen had served eleven years and his service record was exemplary, although he had only risen to the rank of corporal during this time. Having been distressed by a case of unrequited love, and disillusioned with the British Army's attitude to the Irish situation, Nilsen decided it was time to move on. While deciding what to do with his life he returned home to Strichen. But the insularity of village life soon reminded him of why he had left in the first place, and after an argument about homosexuality with Olav, Nilsen decided to leave one month later. The army had suggested that he might join the police force, so Nilsen headed for London where he became a Metropolitan Police officer, posted to Willesden Green. Former Police Constable Roger Huth clearly remembered Nilsen during his time as a police officer:

> He first struck me as a remote sort of guy. He was never interested in socializing. And if we were ever off-duty and I suggested going out for a drink and perhaps looking for some female company, he would not acknowledge what I was saying ... He seemed to have a big chip on his shoulder. He had a big personality problem. He felt people were against him.

He was 'definitely a misfit', but a misfit who was a 'good, all-round copper' with a decent record.

Both of Nilsen's careers thus far involved occasional exposure to the presence of violent death, which was becoming increasingly stimulating to him. He later admitted that the first time he and the other new recruits were shown a mortuary with corpses in various stages of post-mortem examination, 'I felt a bit fascinated'. And Roger Huth's memory (no doubt nudged by tabloids like the *Sun* which headlined the 'WEIRD WORLD OF PC ODDBALL') is particularly vivid in recalling the first time that he and Nilsen were sent to investigate a case of sudden death. 'I was standing over the body taking notes. I suddenly became conscious of Des at my side taking a morbid interest in the body. He was riveted.'

After serving in the police for only a year Nilsen found that he was becoming increasingly left-wing in his political and social attitudes, and the life-style which he had begun to lead in London was at odds with his role as a police officer. Lonely and still sexually curious, Nilsen had started going to gay pubs and bars. He was searching for some sort of meaningful relationship, but he was looking in the wrong places, and found only a long series of one-night stands which he later described as 'soul-destroying'. Both practically and morally, this promiscuous gay life-style was difficult to maintain for Nilsen while he was still in the police force, so he decided to leave. As Dr Bowden later said, 'He found it difficult to equate his work as a police officer with his wish to entertain men in his room – which was Metropolitan Police property.'

Nilsen was now faced with a serious predicament: he had no job, nowhere to live, and little money. Unaccustomed to being out of work, Nilsen took a position as a security guard with P.S.A. Security, and a room in Manstone Road in north London. However the work was unsatisfying and Nilsen soon left, and was forced to claim unemployment benefit in order to pay his rent and bills. His unemployment was short-lived, however, and he was soon interviewed for, and subsequently offered, a job as a clerical officer in the Civil Service in May 1974. He stayed at the Denmark Street Job Centre in Soho for eight years until he was promoted to the position of executive officer at the Job Centre in Kentish Town in 1982, where he was still working at the time of his arrest.

Nilsen was a reliable and dedicated worker, always the first to volunteer to work late or to help his colleagues when they had taken on more than they could handle. On occasions he displayed considerable – if cutting – wit, although his tendency was for sarcasm. He also became increasingly passionate about Civil Service union issues (he later wrote that, 'You must instinctively distrust all organized power') and eventually became branch secretary of the union. But his fierce and radical opinions won him few friends. He became a bore to his colleagues and a difficult employee to his superiors.

In a letter to his mother, written at the beginning of his Civil Service career, Nilsen told her that 'I have acquired a very intimate circle of friends in town and feel that any other place would be a poor substitute for good old LONDON', but nothing could have been further from the truth. He was still the loner he always had been, and the anonymity of the big city only intensified this. During his time as a civil servant Nilsen became increasingly isolated, cruising the gay bars and having casual encounters with men, which soon led to his being evicted from his room in Manstone Road, forcing him to relocate to Teignmouth Road in Willesden. However, in 1975 Nilsen met David Gallichan, a homeless young man who had been living in a hostel, and after one night together they, somewhat precipitously, decided to set up home at 195 Melrose Avenue in Cricklewood. For months Nilsen and Gallichan maintained a façade of happiness and normality: they refurbished their flat (with Nilsen's money), bought pets, gave each other affectionate nicknames, gardened, and met each other's friends and colleagues. But there was tension beneath the surface.

Although Nilsen had initially stopped looking for other partners, Gallichan never had, and in the last stages of their relationship both men began to bring home strangers. Sexual relations between the two of them had never been good, and they slept in separate beds. Gallichan later told journalists that although Nilsen had propositioned him on a couple of occasions, 'I don't think he was very interested in sex, or very good at it.' The relationship finally broke down, and after a huge row Gallichan left in 1977.

Dennis Nilsen

By 1978 Nilsen was at his lowest ebb; 'I felt defeated on all fronts' he later wrote in prison. To compensate, his participation in union issues became more fervent than ever, and he was involved in several industrial disputes, where he marched, picketed, and staged walk-outs. This in turn only made him unpopular with the management and in 1978 he was turned down for promotion due to his 'personality and attitude' rather than his ability to do his job. He also felt disappointed and betrayed by the workers' indifferent attitudes to what he was trying to achieve on their behalf. His professional life may have been frustrating, but his personal life was reaching crisis point: he was drinking heavily and having unsatisfying and meaningless sexual encounters with strangers.

Nilsen's auto-erotic practices were becoming increasingly involved and disturbing at this time. His long-standing mirror-fantasy was still prominent, but he had refined it, made it more elaborate, and assigned a situation and a narrative to go with the image. In addition to the talcum powder, the charcoal, the bullet holes and the blood stains utilized to simulate a corpse, Nilsen had woven an intricate fantasy surrounding the image.

I have been executed and left there by the SS ... an old hermit ... drags my dead body back into his old shack. He is wearing rags and he decides that I have no further use for clothes and begins to strip my limp body. He is speaking to me as though I were still alive. He pulls my now naked body off the bed to the floor. He washes me. He ties my penis and puts wadding in my anus ... he ... carries me back into the woods and buries me. Later he returns and digs me up and takes me back to the shack. He masturbates me and my penis comes to life and I ejaculate.

By now the images of death and sex were indelibly fused in Nilsen's consciousness. Dead was sexy. As Brian Masters writes in his account of Nilsen's life, *Killing For Company*, the serial killer becomes a danger to others 'when the boundaries between fantasy and reality break down, when fantasy life is cherished so lovingly that the subject's hold on reality evaporates.' For Nilsen

157

the boundaries were about to collapse. His fantasies had become too overpowering to remain inside his head. On 30 December 1978 he went out to find someone, anyone, to combat his post-Christmas loneliness and depression. It was the 'night things began to go terribly and horribly wrong'.

As in the case of John Christie, the police were unaware that a serial killer had been operating until the remains of the victims were found, quite by chance. It all started innocuously enough on 3 February 1983, when the downstairs tenants of 23 Cranley Gardens in Muswell Hill found that their toilets wouldn't flush. The rental agents were called and a local plumber, Mike Welch, arrived at Cranley Gardens the next morning. Welch went through the usual procedures for unblocking domestic drains, but the problem stubbornly remained and the pans were close to overflowing. Welch told them that it was a job for Dyno-Rod, who were called, but as the rental agents were unable to authorize the work until the beginning of the following week, the tenants were left without any working toilets for the weekend.

When the occupant of the attic flat returned home on Friday evening he was told of the problem and asked not to flush his toilet as it would cause the others to overflow. As Dennis Nilsen walked away he began to wonder if his recent activities might be the cause of the problem.

On Tuesday morning when nothing had yet been done about the drainage, Nilsen himself wrote to the letting agents, telling them that 'the drains are blocked and unpleasant odours permeate the building'. Perhaps he thought that the letter would have a catalytic effect, speeding up events to their inevitable conclusion. He later told psychiatrist Dr McKeith that 'In a strange way I think the risky dismembering and disposal of bodies became part of the wish to be caught. I was at a time of breaking point, willing to be caught so that I could be released from guilt.'

That evening Dyno-Rod were finally given the go ahead and Mike Cattran was sent round. Having established that the source of the problem would be located under the ground, Cattran opened the manhole. Both he and Jim Allcock, the ground-floor tenant, were instantly hit with a terrible stench. Not surprising one might think, after all sewers aren't supposed to smell sweet. But this was different: 'I may not have been in the game for long, but I know that isn't shit,' Cattran told Allcock. He climbed down the manhole and what he saw confirmed his suspicions: 'It was a white mass, blotched with red. It wasn't human waste. It wasn't anything like I'd seen before. It was something from one of those television shows that carry a warning that is unsuitable for children. What I saw wasn't fit for adults.' He later remembered in court that what he saw looked like 'White, meat-like pieces similar to Kentucky Fried Chicken', but he thought at the time that it wasn't chicken: 'There is flesh, fat, gristle, slivers of skin with flesh attached. And it looks bruised.' He decided to inform his manager straight away.

Cattran's supervisor, Gary Wheeler, told him that the best thing to do was to wait until morning when the contents of the drain could be seen more clearly. The meat was probably from an animal of some description. Although Cattran was convinced that what he'd seen was human, he agreed to wait for Wheeler to see the drain before going to the police. When Cattran returned with Wheeler the next morning and lifted the manhole lid, the mess from the night before had gone. Angry and confused, Cattran rang the doorbell of the house and spoke to the downstairs tenants. They told him that the night before they had heard somebody leaving the house and removing the manhole. When Jim Allcock had gone to investigate he had caught Dennis Nilsen, the quiet civil servant from the attic flat, coming back into the house with a torch, claiming that he had nipped out to relieve himself.

Cattran climbed down into the drain again, hoping to find something that had been missed by the late night visitor. When he finally re-emerged he was holding some bruised flesh attached to three pieces of bone: it looked disturbingly like a human hand. The police were called and the flesh was promptly sent to Professor David Bowen, a forensic pathologist, who confirmed that it was human.

Initially the investigation looked clear-cut: the remains of a body had been found in a house, and a man who lived there had done his best to clear away the evidence before it was found.

Although Nilsen had gone to work as usual that morning, he knew it was over. In his eyes, 9 February was 'the day help arrived'. He later wrote from prison, 'I was sure that I would probably be arrested when I came home or some time that evening. I was through running. I was totally resigned to this inevitability.' Leaving a note for his colleagues at work telling them of his possible arrest, Nilsen went home as usual. Detective Chief Inspector Peter Jay, Detective Inspector Steve McCusker and Detective Constable Geoffrey Butler were waiting. The following conversation ensued:

DCI Jay: Mr Nilsen?

Nilsen: Yes?

DCI Jay: I have come about your drains.

Nilsen: Since when have police officers been interested in blocked drains?

DCI Jay: Come upstairs to your flat and I will tell you. [They go upstairs.]

Nilsen: Are they health inspectors [nodding at McCusker and Butler]?

DCI Jay: No, they're police officers. [They enter Nilsen's flat.]

DCI Jay: The reason why I'm interested in your drains is that they were blocked with human remains.

Nilsen: Oh, good grief, how awful.

DCI Jay: Don't mess about. Where's the rest of the body?

Nilsen: In two plastic bags in the wardrobe next door. I'll show you.

DCI Jay: I thought so. What's been going on here?

Nilsen: It's a long story. It goes back a long time. I'll tell you everything. I want to get it off my chest, not here but at the police station.

As the officers took their suspect to Hornsey police station the investigation metamorphosed into the biggest case of serial murder in British legal history. When they asked Nilsen: 'Are we talking about one body or two?' he replied, 'Neither, it's fifteen or sixteen, since 1978.' Nilsen's case was the first of four in which

160

homosexual men were to become the targets of serial killers: Italian-born Michael Lupo followed him in 1986, Colin Ireland in 1993 and Peter Moore in 1996.

That night DCI Jay returned to Cranley Gardens accompanied by DS Chambers and Professor Bowen. Although prepared, they could not have imagined the horror of what they were to find. In various plastic bags they discovered the left side of a man's chest with the arm still attached; the right side of a man's chest and arm; two torsos, one with both arms still attached; some internal organs, including a heart, two lungs, a spleen, liver, gall bladder, kidneys, and intestines; and a head and skull.

Horrific as this was, when the body pieces were assembled in the mortuary – like ghastly human jigsaw puzzles – there were only three bodies. Nilsen had claimed there were fifteen or sixteen. And there were, Nilsen assured them; he had only lived at Cranley Gardens for just over a year, and most of his murders had occurred at his previous flat at 195 Melrose Avenue. Over the ensuing days Nilsen accompanied the police to Melrose Avenue where in the garden they found more than a thousand fragments of charred human bones that had not been entirely obliterated by Nilsen's bonfires. It began to look as if his boasts of being 'the murderer of the century' were not unfounded.

As the days passed and Cranley Gardens and Melrose Avenue were excavated the headlines changed from the noteworthy – 'A CUT UP CORPSE FOUND IN DRAIN' (in the *Daily Mirror*) – to the sensational: 'I MIGHT HAVE KILLED THOUSANDS' (in the *Daily Star*). Nilsen was questioned by the police for thirty hours in the eleven days after his arrest. Ralph Haeems, Nilsen's solicitor, told the press that his client 'is anxious to help. He is willing for police to show him pictures of any young men in unsolved murder or suspicious death cases that might fit the pattern – and if he remembers being with them, he will say so.' The notion that Nilsen was doing the police a favour by 'helping' them in their inquiries, is deeply ironic. He described in minute detail how he had murdered and dismembered his victims in a cold and emotionless tone, prompting DS Chambers to describe him as 'an evil man with no moral conscience'. Nilsen himself claimed that he simply wanted to relay the events as clearly as possible –

he had been a policeman himself, and he knew that displays of emotion could cloud the hard facts. Furthermore he told police, 'I have no tears for my victims'; 'I don't lose sleep over what I have done'. Dr Brittain notes that this is often the case with such killers: 'Intellectually he *knows* that it is wrong to kill but emotionally he does not *feel* this to apply in his case.'

With Nilsen's recollections and some, albeit limited, forensic evidence – in the form of dental records, fingerprints, clothes and jewellery – the identities of eight of his victims were established and the police began to piece together the events of the past four years. It all began on that lonely night on the penultimate day of 1978. Nilsen had gone to the Cricklewood Arms, a familiar haunt where he had been on other lonely occasions in search of somebody to talk to, perhaps even spend the night with. He told the police that on arriving at the pub he began drinking heavily and talked to many different people. 'But,' said Allan Green, prosecuting council at Nilsen's trial in 1983, 'everyone else seemed to be with someone or in a group. Then he got in conversation with a young Irishman.'

Nilsen and the man with the southern Irish accent talked and drank together until closing time, at which point Nilsen suggested that they go back to his flat for a late drink. Whether the man was homeless, homosexual, lonely or just fancied a few more drinks, we shall never know, but he accepted the invitation. At Melrose Avenue the two men listened to music, talked, and – in Nilsen's words – had 'a damned good old drink'. In the early hours of the morning they collapsed into bed together, too drunk and exhausted to contemplate sexual activity.

In Nilsen's confession to the police he said only that 'In the morning, he was lying on the bed fully clothed. I was on the other bed. He was dead. I came to the conclusion that I had killed him.' Nilsen gave a more candid account to Brian Masters:

I snuggled up to him and put my arm around him. He was still fast asleep ... I ran my hand over him exploring him. I remember thinking that because it was morning he would wake and leave me. I became extremely aroused and I could feel my heart pounding and I began to sweat ... I looked down on the floor where our clothes lay and my eyes fixed on my tie. I remember thinking that I wanted him to stay with me over the New Year whether he wanted to or not. I reached out and got my neck tie. I raised myself and slipped it on under his neck. I quickly straddled him and pulled tight for all I was worth. His body came alive immediately.

The young man fought for his life but Nilsen's hold on him was too strong and his victim finally succumbed to unconsciousness. While he lay immobile on the floor Nilsen filled a bucket and then held the man's head under the water until 'the bubbles stopped coming'. He sat down and had a cup of coffee and a cigarette, staring at the body of the man he had just killed. He later wrote, 'I had started down the avenue of death and possession of a new kind of flat-mate.' Death was experienced not as an end but a beginning: the deceased entered Nilsen's world as a person only post-mortem, as a friend and live-in companion. He would be constant, and available. He would not leave.

So rather than turning himself in or quickly disposing of the body, Nilsen began a ritual that he would continue to enact with the rest of his victims. He bathed, caressed and talked to the body that, in his own mind, was never quite to become a mere corpse. Just because it was lifeless that didn't mean that it had no place in his affections. Quite the reverse. First he ran a bath and put the Irishman's body in it. He told Brian Masters that, 'With washing-up liquid I washed him and his hair. Getting him out of the bath wasn't easy as his wet skin made it difficult to hold him. I pulled him out by the wrists and sat him on the lavatory seat. I towelled him dry ... and laid him on the bed ... and pulled the bedclothes up to his chin.' Later he dressed the body in underwear and got into bed with it. 'I began to remove his pants and explore his body under the blankets. (I had an erection all this time.) When I tried to enter him my erection automatically subsided.' This was Nilsen's first and last attempt to penetrate any of his victims after death. Almost proudly he claimed that 'with every single victim in this case, I never engaged in sexual intercourse'.

Nilsen then went to sleep next to his companion. The next

day he decided to put the body under the floorboards. A week later he retrieved it from its resting place and masturbated over it. It then remained under the floorboards for the next seven months until he finally burnt it in a bonfire in August 1979. No remains were ever recovered of Nilsen's first victim and no identification ever made.

The necrophilic desires that Nilsen had been elaborating in his fantasies for years had now been consummated in reality. The word necrophilia literally means 'love of the dead'. A necrophile is not just someone, like John Christie, who has sex with dead bodies, as is commonly thought. Indeed, some necrophilia is inherently harmless, and may be displayed in acts of mourning, when a man is so devastated by his wife's death, for example, that he cannot bear to let her go, and keeps her body for a time after death. This type of behaviour is referred to as non-sexual necrophila. The necrophilic sex murderer, however, kills in order to produce a corpse. It is not the act of killing *per se*, but the result of that act, the production of a dead body, that is the purpose of murder. After killing, the necrophilic sex murderer may then penetrate the body, masturbate over it, simply fondle it, or perform the type of ritual that Nilsen developed – all these behaviours are forms of worshipping and relating to the beloved corpse. Eric Fromm, author of *The Anatomy of Human Destructiveness*, defines necrophilia, broadly speaking, as the desire to 'transform all that is alive into dead matter'; a necrophile, as Brian Masters puts it, is 'a man for whom death is the ultimate beauty'.

Thus when Nilsen considered and dismissed necrophilia in attempting to understand his motives for the murders he was using too narrow an understanding of the term. A 'necrophiliac?' he said, 'the thought of sex with the sacredness of a dead body turns me right off'. He later wrote, 'I made another world and real men would enter it and they would never really get hurt at all in the vivid unreal laws of the dreams. I caused dreams which caused death. This is my crime.'

In the months that followed his first murder Nilsen was astounded that there were no repercussions. Not only had the police not come knocking at his door, but his victim's disappearance had gone entirely unnoted. Not that this encouraged Nilsen to repeat the act, as far as he was concerned the event was strictly a one-off. He stopped drinking for a while and threw himself into his work, managing to forget that there was a rotting corpse under his floorboards. He continued to go to pubs and sometimes picked up men whom he brought home for the night, but there were no violent impulses or incidents. It was almost as if the murder had never happened. But the urges, temporarily satisfied, crept back up on him. The cycle had begun, and would not stop until he was captured. Soon Nilsen would stop thinking that the events were unique and resign himself to his incapacity to stop the killings.

Kenneth Ockenden had recently graduated from university in Canada and was in England for a three-month holiday in the winter of 1979. On 3 December Nilsen met the twenty-three-year-old in a pub – the Princess Louise – and after some chat offered to take him to see some of the tourist sights in London. After sight-seeing together that afternoon, Nilsen invited Kenneth to Melrose Avenue for dinner. Back at his flat Nilsen cooked for the two of them, and they settled down to watch television and listen to music through Nilsen's headphones, enjoying each other's company. Both were lonely: Nilsen perpetually so, and Kenneth in a place far from home.

Nilsen later told both the police and Brian Masters that he could not remember killing Kenneth Ockenden. 'It was well after midnight – maybe one or two in the morning. I was dragging him across the floor with a flex around his throat. I was saying, "Let me listen to the music as well." He didn't struggle.' He does remember, however, that 'I was amazingly strong'. As Dr Brittain says, during his murders the serial killer is 'transformed into a very different person from the shy, timid, withdrawn individual he so often appears' as his 'sexual drive and his desire for power take control over his actions'.

After having killed Kenneth, Nilsen sat down and listened to music and continued drinking Bacardi: 'With the music and the drinking I could get away from what was around me.' After calming down, Nilsen began his ritual. He stripped and bathed his victim's body and then lay down with it on the bed: 'No sex, only caressing etc.' In the morning, finding Kenneth's body stiff and cold, Nilsen put it in the cupboard before going to work as usual. When he returned that evening, having bought a Polaroid camera, Nilsen removed the body from the cupboard, dressed it, put make-up on the face, and took some photographs. After this he told Brian Masters how the post-mortem ritual developed:

> I lay in bed fully clothed with him lying spreadeagled on top of me as I watched television. I would sometimes speak to him as though he were still listening. I would compliment him on his looks and anatomy. By crossing his legs I had sex between his bare thighs (although no penetration of the body occurred). I wrapped him well before putting him under the floorboards. I took him up on about four occasions in the next two weeks ... I would sit him in the other armchair next to me as I watched an evening's TV.

This was the purpose of the murder. Nilsen bore no animosity to Kenneth himself or to any group that he represented – quite the opposite; on one occasion, hearing the music he had been listening to with Kenneth before he murdered him, Nilsen became overcome with emotion and 'raised the floorboards and begged his forgiveness'. But he desperately wanted a body.

Unlike Nilsen's first victim, Kenneth Ockenden was not a homeless drifter who had nobody to notice his absence. He had a loving family who knew that something was wrong almost immediately. As Christmas approached with no word from Kenneth, who was meant to be returning home, his family became increasingly anxious and informed the police, who began to investigate his disappearance. In February his parents flew out to join the search. The police had mounted a full inquiry: prisons, hospitals, squats and pubs were canvassed, a reward was offered, there were public appeals for information, and the Ockendens' Canadian Member of Parliament became involved. But Detective Inspector Roy Davis finally had to admit that, 'Circumstantially, all evidence points to Ken Ockenden being dead ... There is a very strong possibility that this young man was murdered and his body, so far, successfully concealed.'

Dennis Nilsen leaves Highbury Magistrates' Court, London, escorted by police, as the search continued for the remains of his victims. (POPPERFOTO)

95 Melrose Avenue, where Dennis Nilsen killed thirteen young men. (ANNA GEKOSKI)

23 Cranley Gardens, where Nilsen killed his last three victims. (ANNA GEKOSKI)

Robert Black at a Christmas party. (REX FEATURES)

Robert Black being led away from court, having been found guilty of the murders of three young girls. (REX FEATURES)

31 West Bank, where Robert Black rented the attic room from 1972-1990. (ANNA GEKOSKI)

Robert Black at the time of his arrest in 1990. (REX FEATURES)

Colin Ireland as a boy.
(REX FEATURES)

Colin Ireland in his
survivalist's gear.
(REX FEATURES)

Colin Ireland at the time of his arrest. (REX FEATURES)

The front page of the *Sun*, the paper that Ireland contacted to confess to his crimes.
(REX FEATURES)

Above left, Frederick and
Rosemary West.
(REX FEATURES)

Above, Cromwell Street,
where the Wests lived for
over twenty years.
(ANNA GEKOSKI)

The walkway that was
built after 25 Cromwell
Street was demolished.
(ANNA GEKOSKI)

The West family in
the cellar of 25
Cromwell Street,
celebrating Anne
Marie's wedding
in 1984.
(REX FEATURES)

25 Cromwell Street
after the search for
bodies had begun.
(REX FEATURES)

Fred West (left) at the time of his arrest. (PA NEWS)

Rose West (below left) leaving Gloucester Magistrates' Court in December 1994, after being charged with nine murders. (PA NEWS)

Fred West (below) leaves Gloucester Magistrates' Court with prison officers. (PA NEWS)

His disappearance was to remain an enigma for three years.

The gaps between the murders began to narrow: it was just five months after the murder of Kenneth Ockenden that Nilsen claimed his third victim on 17 May 1980. Sixteen-year-old Martyn Duffey had run away from his home town of Birkenhead on 13 May and had been sleeping rough in railway stations in London when he met Nilsen, who was on his way home after attending a conference in Southport. Glad of the company in this big, strange city, Martyn was happy to accept an invitation to a warm flat for some food and drink.

Back at Melrose Avenue Martyn soon became tired and after just a couple of drinks he was eager to go to bed to get some sleep. Again Nilsen claimed to the police to have no memory of the murder: 'I don't remember any violence at all. I woke up the next morning and there was Duffey dead on the floor. He had my tie around his neck.' Once again Nilsen was more frank with Brian Masters: 'I remember sitting astride him (his arms must have been trapped by the quilt). I strangled him with great force in the almost pitch blackness.'

When Martyn was unconscious Nilsen lifted him off the bed, filled the sink and held his head under the water until he drowned. He then began his ritualistic cleaning of the body, this time getting into the bath with his victim and laying Martyn's body on top of his. After the cleansing was over, Nilsen dried them both and put the body on top of the bed. 'I talked to him and mentioned that his body was the youngest looking I had ever seen. I kissed him all over and held him close to me. I sat on his stomach and masturbated.'

Nilsen later wrote that 'sex was not a factor of continuity with the victims ... the only similarity was a need not to be alone'. But what counts, exactly, as sex? For that matter what counts as being alone? Sexual activity and companionship, and the emotions associated with them, had become so confused and distorted in Nilsen's mind, that he was no longer able to discern exactly what sex entailed, or what counted as being in company. He seemed to have lost grasp of the inescapable fact that a dead body is not a person. To deny that masturbating with a corpse is a form of sex, or to think that one can only overcome loneliness in the presence of the dead, suggests category mistakes of the broadest and most mentally dislocated sort. Thus Nilsen began to settle into his new life, his flatmates and sexual partners conveniently tucked away under the floorboards, until the process of decomposition rendered them inaccessible to the dictates of love.

By that summer the bodies of Kenneth Ockenden and Martyn Duffey were beginning to cause a problem. As they decomposed they began to smell so badly that the other tenants in the house started to comment upon it. Nilsen knew the bodies had to be disposed of, and decided that the best way to do this was to dismember them, put the parts into carrier bags, and put the bags into suitcases, and store them in the garden shed (where they remained until he made a bonfire some months later). Nilsen later admitted that the dissection of the bodies caused him no real problems: 'The flesh looked like just any meat one would see in a butcher's shop and having been trained in butchery I was not subject to any traumatic shocks'. When Brian Masters later voiced his incredulity that a man could dissect a human body, Nilsen told his biographer that his morality must be askew if he was more horrified at the dismemberment of a corpse – which, after all, had no feelings any more – than he was at the act of murder itself. In a much-quoted phrase Nilsen proclaimed that, 'The victim is the dirty platter after the feast and the washing-up is a clinically ordinary task.'

In 1980 Billy Sutherland, who had just moved down from his home in Edinburgh, was living rough on the streets of London, resorting sometimes to theft and more often to prostitution to earn money. Nilsen could not remember precisely when he had met Billy in a West End pub and embarked upon a pub crawl with him, but he thought that it was some time between July and September. After a night's drinking Nilsen decided that it was time to go home, alone, but as he bought his ticket at Leicester Square tube station he found his new friend standing next to him, informing him that he had nowhere to stay for the night. Telling Billy that he could sleep at his flat, Nilsen bought him a ticket. Nilsen's account of the murder is matter of fact: 'We had a great [alcoholic] binge and I killed Billy Sutherland. I remember having a tie round his neck and pulling the tie. I don't recall him struggling but I think he must have.' Like the others before him, Billy went under the floorboards.

To this day the identities of Nilsen's next six victims have never been established, as there was simply nothing – or not enough – left with which to identify them. The police were only able to establish through Nilsen that he had murdered six men between September 1980 and September 1981, a rate of roughly one every two months. He remembered fragments of the murders but could not supply the police with his victims' names. After all, 'when you go on the piss you can't remember', Nilsen told police. It was evident, however, that the same basic ritual had recurred with each victim. His MO was unwavering: he approached his victims in pubs, started a conversation with them, bought them drinks, took them home with him, then – after more drinking and listening to music – when they fell asleep he would strangle them (usually with a tie), and sometimes he would drown them to ensure they were dead. He would not gain any satisfaction from the act of killing itself, 'I get nothing from inflicting pain ... It [the killing] was quick.' It was afterwards that the real pleasure began when he would wash and dry his victim's body, take it to bed with him and touch it, sometimes masturbate over it, often talk to it, perhaps watch some television, take some photographs. This was his signature.

Nilsen does remember his eleventh victim in some detail, probably because the circumstances of the initial meeting were atypical. As Nilsen left for work on the morning of 17 September 1981 he came across a distressed-looking Malcolm Barlow. When Nilsen approached him and asked whether he was OK, Malcolm replied that he was an epileptic and that the medication which he took to control the condition had resulted in a loss of feeling in his legs. In an act of pure altruism, Nilsen helped Malcolm inside his own flat and called an ambulance to take him to hospital, making him a cup of coffee while they waited. The next day Nilsen was surprised to find Malcolm outside his house when he returned from work, waiting to thank him for his help the day before. Nilsen asked him in, cooked Malcolm some dinner, and they had a couple of drinks. Perhaps due to the effect of mixing alcohol with his medication, Malcolm fell into a deep sleep from which Nilsen could not rouse him.

Nilsen later told the police, 'At that moment I had a problem and I dealt with it. I didn't want to deal with the ambulance-men asking silly questions like "Why did you let him have a drink?"' He decided that the best thing to do was simply to get rid of Barlow. Nilsen told Brian Masters that:

> Putting my hands around his throat I squeezed tightly. I held that position for about two or three minutes and released my hold. I didn't check but I believed him to be now dead ... I finished my drinks, switched the TV off and climbed back into bed. The next morning, not feeling much like prising up floorboards, I dragged him through the kitchen and put him under the sink and closed the door. I went to work.

The Malcolm Barlow murder was the most cold-blooded and calculated of them all: Nilsen was not overcome by lust, he was simply annoyed and inconvenienced by Malcolm's presence. He had now killed ten men, what did another matter? And who would miss an orphan who had spent his life in a series of institutions and on the streets? Nilsen reasoned in self-justification that 'I felt I was doing him a favour. I felt his life was one long struggle.' Due to the circumstances of the killing, it is unlikely that any sexual activity took place.

This was to be Nilsen's last murder at Melrose Avenue. He had been having trouble with the landlords, who wanted to evict the tenants in order to refurbish the house, and his flat was broken into and ransacked on one occasion. But they hadn't counted on Nilsen's inherent stubbornness; he refused to let these bullying tactics work. Finally an amicable arrangement was made; Nilsen was offered a flat at 23 Cranley Gardens and £1,000 for his trouble. He moved out at the beginning of October, after he had dismembered the victims under his floorboards and disposed of the parts. Some were put in plastic bags and placed in bins near to his house and the rest were burnt in a bonfire.

At first Nilsen was determined to make a new start. He was

in a new place where there were no material reminders of his old activities. Of course the most important reminders were internal, and the urge to kill in order to have a body to commune with was not contained for long. In March 1982 the inevitable happened. Nilsen later wrote from prison that 'The need to return to my beautifully warm unreal world was such that I was addicted to it even to the extent of knowing of the risks to human life ... The pure primitive man of the dream world killed these men ... These people strayed into my innermost secret world and they died there.' This is a wonderfully accurate description, with a surreal pastoral edge; while it seems to deny responsibility for the killings, in fact it more accurately assigns responsibility to the world of the unconscious. And Nilsen experienced this world, which we might be tempted to think of as harbouring the murderous shadow side of the self, as an Edenic refuge of peace and harmony; his victims, far from being annihilated, were issued special invitations to come within the magic circle and find love.

Nilsen's first murder at Cranley Gardens, and his thirteenth in all, was of a man whom he described only as 'John the Guardsman from High Wycombe'. Police later identified him as John Howlett, a former convict and itinerant, not as he told people, an ex-guardsman. Like the men before him, John was invited back to Nilsen's flat for drinks. After a time John became tired and went to the bedroom. When Nilsen went to wake him later to tell him that it was time to leave, John protested that it was late and he wanted to stay. Nilsen became annoyed: 'I didn't feel like getting into the bed with him in it', he told the police. So he fetched an upholstery strap from one of his chairs and began to strangle John with it. Although his guest was strong and fought hard for his life, Nilsen finally rendered him unconscious by hitting his head against the head-rest of the bed. He then drowned him in the bath.

John's corpse was put in the wardrobe, but only as a temporary measure, because Nilsen had a friend coming to stay. He decided to dismember the body. The larger pieces, such as the head, were boiled in a pot on the cooker to separate the bones from the flesh; others were put 'out with the rubbish' in bin-liners or put in bags and stored in his tea-chest. The smaller 'pieces of flesh and organs' were flushed down the toilet.

Of his final two victims Nilsen's memory is scant. Graham Allen, a twenty-eight-year-old Scot, met Nilsen on Shaftesbury Avenue in late 1982, and later apparently fell into a drunken sleep at Cranley Gardens in the middle of eating the omelette that Nilsen had prepared him. 'I remember going forward and he was dead. I don't know whether the omelette killed him, but in going forward I intended to kill him and an omelette doesn't leave red marks on a neck.' Like John Howlett, Graham Allen was dismembered, and the parts put in the tea-chest and flushed down the toilet.

Nilsen's last victim was twenty-year-old Stephen Sinclair, a homeless drug addict and ex-convict whom he met in Leicester Square. Similarly to the fourteen victims before him, Stephen went to sleep at Nilsen's flat after a few drinks while listening to music. Nilsen told police: 'I can't remember anything else until I woke up the next day. He was still in the armchair and dead. On the floor was a piece of string with a tie attached to it.' He then began the ritual which gave the killings their meaning: he washed the body, dried it, and laid it on his bed. 'I had an erection,' Nilsen told Brian Masters, 'but felt he was far too perfect and beautiful for the pathetic ritual of commonplace sex.'

After he had finished with Stephen's body, 'I put the head into a pot, put the lid on and lit the stove. When the head was coming to the boil I turned the pot down to simmer. Then I took the dog for a walk.' By this time the toilets had started playing up, the drainage system unable to cope with the amounts of flesh that had been flushed down it. Nilsen knew he would soon be captured. He could have tried to dispose of the evidence but chose not to. After dissecting Stephen's body, he put it in bags in the wardrobe and waited for the inevitable.

Although Nilsen had admitted his crimes and given the police a detailed confession, like Peter Sutcliffe he entered a plea of not guilty to murder, but guilty to manslaughter on the grounds of diminished responsibility. The difference between the crime of murder and that of manslaughter is the defendant's state of mind – the *mens rea* – at the time of committing the acts. The defence's case was that Nilsen was suffering from such abnormality of mind as to substantially impair his responsibility for his actions, in accordance with Section 2 of the 1957 Homicide Act, making him guilty of the lesser crime of manslaughter. The prosecution were to uphold the charge of murder, contending that Nilsen's crimes were the work of a cold killer. Nilsen was 'not a man with moral blindness. The man enjoyed killing people', alleged the Crown. And 'even if there was mental abnormality, that was not sufficient to diminish substantially his mental responsibility for these killings'. The reading of the term 'substantially' was to become the crux of the case.

Mr Allan Green, leading for the prosecution, began his case by telling the court the details of Nilsen's arrest. Using extracts from Nilsen's statements to police he then took the court through each of the fifteen killings, laying particular emphasis upon the casual and cold-hearted way in which the defendant had described the murders. When asked how he had killed his victims Nilsen mordantly replied, 'I think I started off with about fifteen ties. Now I've only got one left and that's a clip-on.' (He had been forced to borrow a tie from Brian Masters for the trial.) In a similar tone, when asked how many bodies were under the floorboards at one time, Nilsen had told the police, 'I don't know. I didn't do a stock-take or anything. It was a bit of a jumble.' After the murder of his tenth victim, he told police, 'That was that: floorboards back, carpet replaced, and off to work'; after killing his eleventh victim he said 'I went off to bed: the end of the day, the end of the drinking, the end of a person'. Green told the court how Nilsen had killed Malcolm Barlow because he was an inconvenience; John Howlett because he 'didn't feel like getting into the bed with him in it'.

Green then moved on to the testimony from the survivors: Douglas Stewart, Paul Nobbs and Carl Stotter had all been identified as men whom Nilsen had attempted to murder during the past four years. These witnesses were of fundamental importance to the court as they were the only people, except for Nilsen himself, who could give evidence as to his state of mind at the time of the (attempted) killings. All three men had met the defendant in a pub, gone home with him, had some drinks, and fallen asleep. At some point during the night Nilsen had attempted to kill them. Douglas Stewart awoke with a tie around his neck, with a calm and expressionless Nilsen attempting to strangle him. Luckily he was able to fight him off. Paul Nobbs slept through the attack upon him and awoke the next morning feeling terrible. On Nilsen's advice he went to see a doctor only to be told that somebody had attempted to strangle him. Nobbs was puzzled: it could only have been Nilsen, but he had seemed so normal and unaggressive. Carl Stotter awoke in the night with something caught around his neck, and was then submerged in water. As he lost consciousness he was sure he was dying. He was surprised to awake hours later with Nilsen concerned and fussing over him: uniquely and inexplicably, his executioner had become his saviour.

The prosecution presented the calmness which accompanied the brutal attacks as indicative of a killer who felt no emotion. The defence responded that the radical change in Nilsen's behaviour, from pleasant and intelligent to murderous, signified a dangerous mental instability, which they were later to term a 'severe personality disorder'.

Nilsen had indeed killed, but he had not murdered, contended Ivan Laurence for Nilsen's defence. To be convicted of murder, one of the criteria in addition to malice aforethought and intent, is that a person must be of 'sound mind and discretion' at the time of the acts. If the accused is not of sound mind, if he or she is found to have a mental abnormality of such gravity as to substantially diminish his or her responsibility for the acts, then he or she is to be found guilty of the lesser crime of manslaughter.

Such mental abnormality can comprise of a multitude of disorders that stop short of actual insanity. Sutcliffe allegedly suffered from paranoid schizophrenia; in Nilsen's case, the psychiatrists for the defence called his condition a 'severe personality disorder'. Dr MacKeith's diagnosis was that Nilsen was suffering from a personality disorder of a type which wasn't described in any of the already recognized categories. The defendant clearly, however, showed 'maladaptive patterns of behaviour' and 'retarded or arrested development of mind'. Several elements of his personality and actions indicated this. Firstly, Nilsen could separate his mental life from his material behaviour, a phenomenon known as 'dissociation', which he displayed when he killed and dismembered his victims. His dissociation was also evident in his ability to lead an ostensibly normal life with corpses around him, and in his calm demeanour at the time of his crimes (to which the surviving victims testified). A second indicator of Nilsen's personality disorder was his feeling of grandiosity: he saw himself as the most important person in a world where other people were merely objects to be treated as he saw fit. Thirdly, he had a long-standing obsession with death and sexuality which manifested itself, for example, in 'bizarre' fantasies which he presented as if they were real events. Finally Dr MacKeith said that although Nilsen craved close personal relationships, he had great problems forming them, as he could never adequately express how he felt and was unduly paranoid about others. These particular features of Nilsen's behaviour were suggestive of a person with a severe personality disorder. He was not insane, but he was 'very close' to being so.

Dr Gallwey, the second psychiatrist called for the defence, gave the disorder a name: 'Borderline False Self As If Pseudo-Normal Narcissistic Personality Disorder' (the 'False Self' syndrome for short), and he told the court that he had made a special study of it. Those afflicted with the False Self syndrome, testified Gallwey, have strong paranoid and schizoid tendencies which can usually be kept under control so that the person can operate in society in a normal way. On occasion, however, the repression of these tendencies becomes too burdensome and the result of this emotional overload is seen in 'outbursts of irrational violence, often with bizarre or quasi-sexual features, always apparently motiveless'.

According to Gallwey, Nilsen's murders and attempted murders were instances of his periodic breakdown of control. He was 'clinging on [to reality and normality] like a man drowning in nightmares' until he had to give in to his fantasies and thus to his crimes. 'The world of his imagination, which turns out to be horrific, captured him more and more.' He was thus 'a cold-blooded killer' but one 'who is not responsible for his acts'. (Disagreeing with his defence, Nilsen himself was quoted as saying that 'I cannot allow the buck to travel outside my responsibility ... I deserve punishment for their deaths.')

In rebuttal, the Crown called their own psychiatric expert, Dr Bowden, who testified that he could find no evidence of the dissociation, paranoia, identity problems, abnormal sexual behaviour, alcohol abuse, grandiosity and relationship difficulties which the defence had listed as the basis of Nilsen's alleged disorder. Rather, he contended, Nilsen was a cool, scheming and remorseless murderer who simply enjoyed killing people. He was not 'overcome by outbursts of irrational violence', but was in complete control of when he killed and when he didn't. Some men left his flat unharmed, after Nilsen had assessed the consequences of killing them. Dr Bowden agreed with Nilsen's own version of his motives: the 'overwhelming desire to kill', the enormous sense of power it gave him, and the transference of his guilty feelings about homosexuality: 'By killing, he was able to transfer his feeling of criminality so that it was no longer because of his homosexuality but because of the fact that he was a murderer.'

Bowden testified that obviously a man who kills fifteen people is 'a very rare animal' and 'there is an abnormality of mind reflected in his behaviour'. Although this latter statement might sound like a concession to the defence's argument, it is not. Nilsen's abnormality, said Bowden, was not so severe as to *substantially* diminish his responsibility. In any case, Bowden continued, the argument of the defence was a circular one: to say that Nilsen had a mental abnormality because he killed and that he killed because he had a mental abnormality is tautological. It restates rather than explains.

Putting psychiatric jargon aside, as Ivan Laurence for the defence said, 'If that kind of behaviour does not indicate that the defendant is not all there, it is very difficult to conceive of any behaviour short of insanity that could.' Nilsen killed fifteen men, he dismembered them, he watched television with and talked to them, surely 'the thing speaks for itself'? But the *res ipsa loquitar* argument is not good enough: to show a person's monstrous behaviour is not, in itself, evidence of mental abnormality. So which of the experts' testimony was to be believed?

The jury were sent away to decide, only to return the next day (having spent the night in a hotel) to announce that they were having some difficulty in reaching a unanimous verdict. They simply couldn't agree on Nilsen's state of mind. Before telling them that a majority decision would be acceptable, Justice Croom-Johnson brought the lofty matters down to layman's terms, telling the jury that 'You will almost certainly say his mind was evil. A mind can be evil *without being abnormal*. Bear that in mind.' As he had said in his summing up, 'A nasty nature is not arrested or retarded development of the mind.' It did not take a legal mastermind to see where Justice Croom-Johnson stood.

Later that day the jury returned their verdict. They found Dennis Nilsen guilty on all six counts of murder by a majority of ten to two, for the attempted murders of Douglas Stewart and Carl Stotter they found Nilsen guilty by a majority of ten to two, and they were unanimous in their verdict of guilt for the attempted murder of Paul Nobbs. After sentencing Nilsen to life imprisonment, the mandatory term for murder, Justice Croom-Johnson recommended that he serve a minimum of twenty-five years.

The fact that a hardworking civil servant had been picking up, strangling, and dismembering young men for the past four years was almost beyond comprehension. It was inevitable that the question would be asked: why had the police not even been aware that a serial killer was at large? Surely there must have been some sign of what was going on? A headline in the *Daily Mirror* was typical: 'GUILTY OF MASS MURDER: THE MISSED CLUES THAT LEFT A KILLER AT LARGE'. The police were quick to defend themselves: the vast majority of the victims were never reported missing nor were any bodies found, so how could they have known that there was a serial killer operating? As the *Guardian* put it:

The reason why nobody knew that Nilsen was killing was that nobody, except Nilsen, knew that any killings were going on. Thirteen of the fifteen he killed were never even reported missing ... The crucial step that Nilsen took with each victim was to dispose of the body. A basic ground rule for an overworked police force is that if there is no body there is no murder inquiry.

But Nilsen hadn't always been careful in his disposal – the remains of some of his victims had been found in August 1981, not far from his home. On the night of 23 August Robert Wilson had been walking his dog through Gladstone Park, less than half a mile from where Nilsen lived at 195 Melrose Avenue. As he came out of the park something on the pavement caught his attention: spilling from a plastic bag which had fallen from a bin were what looked distinctly like human remains. Robert later told the press that 'I saw a load of meat-type stuff, flesh glistening in the light, so I prodded at it with a stick. I couldn't see exactly what it was so I went home to get a torch so I could check properly. There was no mistaking what I saw: a heart, lungs, windpipe and larynx, all attached together. It was all wet and covered in blood.' Wilson was sure of his identification as he was a microbiology graduate and had seen human organs before. He immediately called the police, who sent two cars out. After inspecting the grisly package, the officers told Robert that they would take care of the matter and told him that he could go home, after taking his name and address. When Robert went to check the next morning the bag was gone.

Nilsen later told officers that because he had had an excess of his victims' remains to get rid of in August 1981 – as he was moving flat – he had disposed of some of the body parts in plastic bags which he put in bins near his home. In the as yet unpublished autobiography – *History of a Drowning Boy* – that Nilsen has written in prison (excerpts of which have been printed in the *Daily Mirror*) he says:

The bag was taken to Willesden Police Station where the duty Old Bill thought it might be butchered animal entrails and it was subsequently destroyed. Had it been subjected to a closer examination by a qualified pathologist the alarm bells would have rung loud and clear. My bloody finger-prints were all over the bag and could soon have been matched with mine on file. This prolonged my arrest by eighteen months and four deaths.

There was also the matter of the five men whom Nilsen had unsuccessfully attempted to murder and whose complaints should have alerted the police to Nilsen's sinister behaviour. As they had no real memory of the incidents, neither Paul Nobbs nor Carl Stotter initially went to the police, although they testi-fied at Nilsen's trial. But Andrew Ho, Douglas Stewart and Toshimitsu Ozawa, who were all attacked by Nilsen in almost identical circumstances to his other victims, did report their ordeals to the police.

When Andrew Ho reported the incident, the police visited Nilsen but as his story was in direct contradiction to Andrew's it was decided that the matter would be dropped. Douglas Stewart also complained to the police, but again Nilsen denied every-thing and painted the picture of a homosexual quarrel that had got out of hand. The police assured Douglas that they would be in touch, but according to him they never were. He later told the *Daily Mirror*, 'I never heard from the police again ... I wanted them to charge Nilsen with attempted murder there and then, but they did not. If they had done so, then possibly several people who are now dead would be alive. The police made a bad mistake.' The police insisted that they left him messages, but when he didn't return their calls they assumed that he was content to let matters lie. Toshimitsu Ozawa similarly complained to the police about Nilsen, showing them the red marks around his neck. However, when the procedures for pressing charges were explained to him, Toshimitsu – whose English was not very good – decided that pursuing the incident was more trouble than it was worth. The police didn't attempt to change his mind.

Around the same time there was another attack which, although not an attempted murder, was certainly serious enough to result in a complaint being made to the police about Nilsen's conduct. A ten-year-old boy who lived near Nilsen in

Cricklewood told his parents that Nilsen had indecently assaulted him. The parents went to the police to make a complaint, but eventually decided not to proceed with it. As so often happens in cases involving children, the parents decided that their son had been through enough, and didn't want to subject him to the ordeal of testifying in court.

Three men, on three separate occasions, had complained to police that Dennis Nilsen had attempted to strangle them; in addition a boy's parents had complained that he had molested their son. Yet the cases were never linked, and the chain of murder went on, unbroken.

7

ROBERT BLACK

Robert Black never knew his parents. When Jessie Hunter Black gave birth to her son on 21 April 1947, she refused to put his father's name on the birth certificate. And Jessie herself, twenty-four and unmarried, earning a meagre amount as a factory-worker, was really in no position to care for an illegitimate baby, still a stigma in 1947. Within days of Robert's birth, Jessie decided to have him fostered. Years later Robert Black, by this time a man in his forties, told psychologist Ray Wyre, 'I don't know whether it was pressure from her parents or whether she just didn't want me. I don't know. I was fostered at six months.'

Within the year, Jessie had married. She and her husband, Francis Hall, were to have four children together – none of whom were told they had a half-brother – and to emigrate to Australia, where Jessie died in 1982. Francis Hall's niece, Joyce Bonella, recalls that Jessie 'didn't like it to be generally known that she had had a child out of wedlock. I don't think she ever told anyone who the father was'. From the time that she gave Robert up, Jessie never had any contact with her son again.

While Jessie was settling into married life, Robert was being cared for by his new family. Jack and Margaret Tulip were both in their fifties, and had fostered children on several occasions previously. Robert had been born in Grangemouth, about twenty miles from Edinburgh, on the Firth of Forth; the Tulips lived in Kinlochleven, near Glencoe in the West Highlands. Robert lived here for the next eleven years, the majority of which were spent in the care of Margaret Tulip, as Jack died when Robert was just five. Black claims to have no memory of him, indeed, no memories at all before the age of five. To Ray Wyre, this unusual memory block suggests the presence and repression of some sort of emotional or physical trauma to which Black had been subjected as an infant, probably at the hands of his foster-father. After all, Wyre says, 'most of us can recall something, some vague, impressionistic sense of who we were' before we were five.

Although locals remember how Robert Black was frequently heavily bruised as a boy, Black himself cannot recall how he got these injuries. He recalls no abusive behaviour from Jack, though he does remember how Margaret used to lock him in the house as a punishment for bad behaviour, or alternatively, pull down his trousers and underwear and spank him with a belt. At nights Robbie was frightened that there was a monster under his bed waiting to get him, and used to suffer from a recurring night-mare featuring a 'big hairy monster' in a cellar full of water. When he awoke he frequently found that he had wet the bed, which invariably provoked a beating.

To his classmates at primary school Robert – or 'Smelly Robbie Tulip' as he was known – is remembered as having been an aggressive and slightly wayward boy. 'A bit of a loner but with a tendency to bully', was how one old primary school mate, Colin McDougall, put it. It seems that Black didn't 'mix in with the normal playground games', preferring to spend time with children younger than himself whom he could easily dominate. As Colin McDougall also remembers, 'We had a gang but he insisted on being leader of his own gang. The members were always a couple of years younger than him.' Another classmate, Jimmy Minnes, remembers an incident where Black gave a boy with an artificial leg a beating: 'He gave the poor lad a terrible hammering. He just jumped on top of him as he was walking over the bridge to school one day. Black just punched and kicked him for no reason.' Sudden, mindless violence perpetrated against those physically less able than himself was typical of Black as a boy.

As he grew older his reputation as a bit of a ruffian grew. The local bobbie, Sandy Williams, later said that Black was a 'wild wee laddie' who 'didn't give a damn – no respect for authority. He had a dangerous spirit' and 'needed a smack round the ear to keep him in line'. Having said this, in the period that he was living with the Tulips, Robert never really got himself into any serious trouble: he had childish fights, played up at school, and bullied the younger children, yet he seemed to avoid anything more serious than a rebuke from Williams for swearing in front of ladies.

In addition to this propensity towards petty violence, Black was also developing a precocious sexual self-awareness. Years later Black remembers the emergence of a practice which began while he was living with the Tulips and would continue, and intensify, as he matured: 'I used to push things up my anus,' Black told Wyre, 'I was eight years old.' When asked what objects he would use, Black replied – holding his fingers about eight inches apart – that it was usually 'a little piece of metal'. After his arrest in 1990 police found photographs that Black had taken of himself: one showed him with a wine-bottle up his anus, another with a telephone-handset, yet another with a table leg. Black explained to the incredulous officers that he wanted to see just how much he could fit up there. At around the same age Black also remembers fantasizing about excreting on his hands and then rubbing the faeces into them. He also always had an uneasy feeling that he would have preferred to have been a girl – although there was certainly nothing feminine about his behaviour – he simply hated his penis and would have preferred to have had a vagina. We have here a nice inversion of the usual Freudian model, wherein women envy men the presence of the penis, whereas the lack, or absence, that Black experienced all of his life was that of the vagina. His life-long practice of self-penetration seems to have been an enactment of this vagina-envy.

However he was by no means homosexual in his desires. Not only did his auto-erotic sex life begin early, so did his experimentation with the opposite sex. His first sexual experience, which is one of his first memories, dated from when he was only five. Black vividly recalls himself and a little girl undressing and looking at each other's sexual parts. Then at the age of seven, at his Highland Dance classes, he remembers being far more interested in lying on the floor and looking up the girls' skirts than dancing. At the age of eight while looking after a neighbour's baby, he took off her nappy to look at her vagina. Both vaginas and anuses fascinated him, and he was obsessed with discovering how big they were, how much they could hold.

It is interesting to speculate what he was looking for – what could the orifices hold that he might discover? To search the vagina for some large hidden content is like a regressive version of the fantasy of searching for the origins of the self. If one looks up there, knowing how much it will hold, might one not encounter the ultimate secret: the baby, oneself? For one who had never known his parents, never had access to his birth-mother, and may subsequently have been abused, what a compelling obsession, to look into that darkness to see what it might have contained.

There is the further fascination, of course, with the anus, which may be thought of as the Thanatos to the Eros of the vagina. But a child's first fantasies are cloacal, it is the hole that fascinates, and the functions are not so closely differentiated in infantile fantasy. As the child grows more self-aware, the anus, of course, is differentiated as the remover of waste, though it may continue to exercise its old childish fascinations – so much so that Freud calls an entire personality type, formed round a matrix of characteristics such as tightness and the tendency to withhold emotion, the anal personality type. That Black was universally characterized as messy and smelly his entire adult life, also suggests some further manifestation of his compulsion to play about with the 'dirty' part of himself.

Margaret Tulip died in 1958. It was the worst possible thing that could have happened. Black was only eleven, and was once again deprived of a mother. Although a local couple offered to take him in, it was decided that Black would go to the Redding Children's Home near Falkirk, close to the place of his birth. It was during Black's time there that his fascination with sex, and particularly with the vagina, finally drove him across the line from childish experimentation to criminal behaviour. The fasci-nation with the secret of birth, the hidden contents of the womb, was clearly exacerbated by the loss of the second mother. At the age of twelve, Black made his first inept attempt at rape. He told Ray Wyre: 'Me and two other boys went into a field with a girl the same age. We took her knickers off, lifted her skirt and all tried to put our penises in.' Finding that they couldn't complete the act of penetration, the boys contented themselves instead with touching the girl's vagina. When asked if she was consenting to this, Black told Wyre: 'I was forcing her, like, you know?' The incident was exposed and the authorities decided that Black would be better suited to a home with stricter discipline, not to mention an all-male environment.

On the move again, Black was sent to the Red House in Musselburgh. Here, having entered as an abusive bully and potential rapist, Black swiftly found that he had changed roles. For at least a year, possibly two, out of the three that Black was at the Red House, a male member of staff – now dead – regularly sexually abused him. The man's custom, apparently, when the time approached for his current victim to leave, was to force him to recommend another boy to take his place. Robert Black was recommended. Black later described the form that the abuse took: the man, he said, 'Made me put his penis in my mouth, touch him, you know ... He did try to bugger me once, but he couldn't get an erection.' Even before his time at the Red House, Black had associated sex with dominance and submission. This association was now cemented in his mind. Now in the position of victim himself, he empathized and identified with his abuser: from the abuse perpetrated upon him, Black concluded that it was acceptable to take what you wanted without regard to other people's feelings.

During this time Robert had obtained a place at Musselburgh Grammar School. He was slightly above average academically, but it was sport that he was really interested in, especially football, swimming and athletics. When he later moved to London, in his early twenties he was given a trial for Enfield Town. Unfortunately his poor eyesight put a career in professional football beyond his reach. His love of swimming continued throughout his adult life, and he even worked as a life-guard for a time which was ideal fuel for his paedophilic fantasies. As a boy at the Red House Robert often walked from Musselburgh to nearby Portobello where there were two swimming-pools in which he would practise. Over twenty years later a little girl called Caroline Hogg was to be abducted from Portobello, and later murdered. Caroline's house was on the route between the two swimming-pools.

In the summer of 1962 when Black was fifteen, his time at the Red House finished. With some help from the authorities, Black got a job as a delivery boy and found a room to rent in a boys' home in Greenock, outside Glasgow. He later admitted that while he was doing his delivery rounds he molested thirty or forty girls. He told Ray Wyre that if 'there was a girl on her own in the flats where I was delivering, I'd like sit down and talk to her for a few minutes, like, you know, and try and touch her: sometimes succeeded, sometimes not.' Amazingly none of this behaviour seems to have been officially reported, and it was not until a year later that Black's first conviction came about. The charge was for 'lewd and libidinous' behaviour with a young girl; it should have been for attempted murder. Black, who was now seventeen, had approached a seven-year-old girl in the park, asking her if she would like to go with him to see some kittens. The girl trustingly followed him as he led her to a deserted building. Black told Ray Wyre that:

> I took her inside and I held her down on the ground with my hand round her throat ... I must have half-strangled her or something because she was unconscious ... When she was quiet I took her knickers off and I lifted her up so as I was holding her behind her knees and her vagina was wide open and I poked my finger in there once.

He then 'laid her down on the floor and masturbated' over her inert body. Her lack of consciousness, far from detracting from his pleasure, seems to have enhanced it. When he left the girl in that derelict building he didn't know – nor, it seems, care – whether she was unconscious or dead. She was later found wandering the streets: bleeding, crying and confused.

The case was brought to court and astoundingly Black was given an admonishment, a verdict particular to Scottish law which is effectively no more than a warning to be on good behaviour in the future. A naive psychiatric report had been prepared for the court which said that the event was an 'isolated' one, highly unlikely to recur or to mar Black's normal development. Thus by the time he was seventeen, Black had attempted to rape one girl, left another for dead, molested many others, and got away with it.

Unlike the psychiatric report, however, the Social Services probation report viewed the incident as more serious and it was decided that Black should leave Greenock and return to Grangemouth to make a new start. Here he got a job with a builders' supply company and rented a room with an older couple. He also met his first (and last) real girlfriend. According to Black, Pamela Hodgson and he fell in love, developed a sexual relationship and decided to get engaged. Years later he still remembers the 'devastation' he felt when a letter arrived from Pamela after some months telling him that it was over. Perhaps she had heard some of the gossip that was circulating about her boyfriend and his sexual preferences. Or, indeed, she may have been beginning to experience them at first hand.

In 1992 after Black had been served with ten summonses – including three for the murder of three little girls – in an attempt to shift the moral liability he told officers: 'Tell Pamela she's not responsible for all this.' This, of course, implied the opposite: that the break-up of their relationship had left him so devastated that she had driven him to murder.

Although Black claims that while he was seeing Pamela he did not molest any girls, he was forced to leave Grangemouth for just that. Black's mounting obsession with little girls, and his fascination with their vaginas, would not have disappeared during his relationship with Pamela – although he may have had less opportunity to act out his desires – and the cravings resurfaced in 1966. This time the victim was the nine-year-old granddaughter of his landlord and landlady. The abuse took the same form as it had previously, with Black looking at, touching, and putting his fingers inside the girl's vagina. She eventually told her parents, yet it was decided that the police would not be called. It was felt that the girl had been through enough and Black was ordered to leave the house.

Gossip spreads quickly in small towns. Sacked from his job without reason, and his place in the community undermined, Black headed back to Kinlochleven where he had been brought up. Again he took a room with a couple who had a young daughter, and again the inevitable happened. The seven-year-old girl was subjected to the same type of digital intrusion that was typical of Black's behaviour. When the abuse came to light Black was not so fortunate as he had been in Grangemouth, and the police were called to deal with the situation. In March 1967 Black was found guilty of three counts of indecent assault and sentenced to a year of borstal training to be served at Polmont, near Grangemouth.

On his release, Black decided to leave Scotland, where he was getting too well-known, and where his police record was expanding. It was time to go south, to the anonymity of London. Although he avoided any criminal convictions in the 1970s his obsession with young girls was growing, fuelled by his discovery of child pornography. During this time Black discovered that magazines such as *Teenage Sex* and *Lollitots* were clandestinely available, particularly in places like Amsterdam where the pornography laws were less stringent. When Black's room was eventually searched by police in the 1990s they found more than a hundred child pornography magazines and over fifty video tapes, with titles such as *Lesbian Lolita*. When Ray Wyre asked Black what he thought the age of consent should be, Black replied approvingly that someone had once told him that his motto was, 'When they're big enough, they're old enough.'

When he first arrived in London, Black lived in cheap bedsits and took casual work where he could find it. His favourite job was that of swimming-pool attendant, where he was sometimes able to go underneath the pool and remove the lights to look at little girls as they swam. At night he used to break into the baths and swim lengths – with a broom-handle lodged up his anus. It wasn't long before Black became the subject of a complaint from a girl who claimed that he had fondled her. The police were called but luck was on Black's side and despite his record he was not charged with any criminal offence, although he lost his job.

When he was not working, Black had developed a liking for darts and was a distinctly useful player. Most of his spare time was spent in pubs: drinking (although never heavily), playing in various darts teams, or doing part-time bar work. Although he enjoyed going to pubs, Black never made any good friends as he was a solitary man. Michael Collier, the former landlord of the Baring Arms in Islington where Black played for the pub team, recalls that:

> for all the years he drank in my pub you would never have called him a mate. He always drank pints of lager shandy but he never got involved in rounds. When he wasn't playing darts he just stood by the fruit machine. He was a bit of a wind-up merchant and enjoyed irritating people, particularly women ... He never talked about himself and he never spoke about his interests or joined in conversations.

The former world darts champion, Eric Bristow, who knew Black from the amateur darts circuit in north London, similarly remembers him as 'a loner' who 'never turned up with a girl-friend or anything. He just wasn't the type. He was a regular guy who would come into the pub and play darts.'

Black met Eddie and Kathy Rayson in a pub in Stamford Hill in 1972. They got chatting and Black told them how he needed a place to live. The Raysons' attic room was free, and although Eddie wasn't too keen initially, Kathy said that Black seemed like a 'big softie' so they decided to take him in. After Black's conviction in 1994, Eddie Rayson remembered Black as 'a perfect tenant. He always paid the rent on time and never caused us any problems'. He used to eat meals with the couple and their children (who had nicknamed him 'Smelly Bob'), and they occasionally went up to his room to listen to music or play cards, but other than that they rarely saw him. Although Eddie Rayson says that he 'was a bit like a father to him', Black never talked to him about personal matters or his past. Eddie and Kathy's son, Paul, says of Black, 'He was a bit odd and as kids growing up we called him names mainly because he smelled. But he was an ideal tenant.' In fact, he was 'more than just a tenant but not what you would call a friend ... not the sort of person you would ever be able to get close to, or would want to'.

The Raysons say that Black was a keen photographer and they sometimes jokingly called him David Bailey. It later transpired that one of his favourite pastimes was to go to the seaside or to a playground which was frequented by young children and video them playing or take snap-shots of them. Photography not only serves as a source of images that can be chosen to excite but it is also frequently used in a documentary sense: to provide the killer with a chronicle of his own history. As such, of course, the killer becomes the hero of his own world: the maker of it, the director, the protagonist.

In 1976 Black began to work for a firm called Poster Dispatch and Storage (PDS) as a driver. His job was to deliver posters to various depots around England and Scotland. It was ideal work for him: he was a bad time-keeper so it suited him to keep more or less to his own schedule, and as a loner he found driving for hours by himself an agreeable way to earn a living. He worked for PDS for the next ten years until his employers were forced to dismiss him because he was constantly getting involved in minor accidents and costing the company a fortune in insurance payments. Luckily for Black, shortly after his dismissal PDS was bought out by two employees who gave him his job back. He continued to get into scrapes, but he was a hard worker and was always glad to cover for his work-mates, doing the longer runs which the other drivers disliked because they interfered with their family commitments. Black frequently did the London to Scotland run, often stopping in the Midlands on his way back to see the Raysons' son John and his new family.

In the back of his van he would keep various objects as masturbatory tools, to be inserted up his anus while he fantasized about touching young girls. He later told police that he would get into the back of his van on night runs and dress himself in girls' clothing, particularly swimming costumes, while he was masturbating. He told Ray Wyre that over the years the recollection and image of the assault in which he had left the seven-year-old girl for dead kept returning. The assault would have been replayed and extended in Black's mind so often that when it finally drove him to his first murder it seemed a perfectly natural progression to him. But the fantasy is never totally fulfilled, the deep anger and frustration never finally resolved and tragically the cycle of fantasy and murder repeats itself. There is always the desire to re-enact the sequence in the quest for ultimate fulfilment.

The FBI maintain that serial killers actually murder because of their thought processes, which constitute their motivation: 'fantasy assumes a crucial role in sexual murders ... these men murder because of the way they think ... these cognitive acts gradually lead to the conscious planning and justification for murderous acts'. But surely citation of the primacy of fantasy and its enactment cannot answer a causal question, so the further question of what triggers the fantasy remains. Fantasies and thought processes must originate somewhere, and we must assume that these origins are to be found in the killers' personal histories. The history of Robert Black as a child – his double loss of the mother, lack of a father, his feelings of rejection, and of being unloved, the constant moving from place to place, and his sexual abuse from an older adult meant to be in the role of carer and protector – was a reality so devoid of either love or hope that fantasies involving domination and the perverse search for the lost mother/child are, if not inevitable, at least understandable.

It was a hot afternoon on the penultimate day of July in 1982, and eleven-year-old Susan Maxwell had asked her mother, Liz, if she could cycle to the tennis game which she was going to play with her friend Alison Raeburn. Liz was reluctant to let Susan cycle on her own as she was worried about the traffic, but after some consideration she told her daughter that she could walk if she liked. Susan had never yet walked anywhere alone, but at some point a child has to be allowed to start the process of independence. The Maxwells lived in a farmhouse outside Cornhill on Tweed, a small village on the English side of the English-Scottish border. Susan's tennis game was across the border in Coldstream, about two miles from her home, and on a route where Susan would know almost everybody she passed on the way. It was an area where people looked out for one another – particularly for the children.

In the end Susan didn't walk to her game because one of the farm-workers going into Coldstream offered her a lift, but she planned to walk back. When four o'clock came and it was time for Susan to be walking home, Liz decided to go and pick her up. Liz remembers, 'She wasn't expecting me. But I thought, "It's a very hot afternoon; after she's been playing tennis for an hour, she'll be hot and sticky and too tired to walk back." So I put the wee ones in the back and we went over.' As they drove down the road, where Liz was expecting to encounter Susan walking home, there was no sign of her. At the Lennel Tennis Club, and on the return journey to the farm, Susan was still nowhere to be found. A phone call to Susan's friend Alison quickly established that she had left Susan making her way home. 'I started to panic then,' said Liz, 'and Fordyce [her husband] said to just phone the police straight away.'

The police were called and inquiries swiftly began. Many people had seen Susan that afternoon, both people who knew her, and people who simply remembered a little girl, dressed in yellow, swinging a tennis racket. These sightings of Susan were numerous until a certain point just over the Tweed bridge, yards across the border into England. She was seen as she crossed the bridge by several people at about half past four and then she was gone. Nobody had witnessed her abduction, but in the space of a moment she had vanished.

The days after Susan's presumed abduction were spent meticulously combing the countryside and looking for clues to her disappearance. After the Northumbria police appealed for volunteers nearly two thirds of the population of Cornhill joined in the search. Fordyce himself went out every day with the search parties. As the Maxwells were journalists themselves, they spoke to the press constantly in the belief that it could only be beneficial to keep the case in the public eye. It was after one such media event that the news which they had been dreading finally arrived, two weeks after Susan's disappearance. On Friday 13 August Liz and Fordyce had been on Radio 2 talking of Susan's abduction and appealing to the public for information. When they returned, the police were waiting for them. Liz recalls: 'He [the officer] said they'd found a little girl. And I remember he wouldn't say the word "dead". He just said: "This little girl is not alive". And that was when the sort of coldness spread right through me.'

A man named Arthur Meadows had found Susan's body in a ditch next to a lay-by on the A518 at Loxley, just outside Uttoxeter in the Midlands, 250 miles from where Susan had been abducted. When Liz and Fordyce asked if they could see their daughter's body, the officer – as tactfully as he could – replied that the weather had been very warm. The body had decomposed beyond recognition after two weeks in the hot summer sun, meaning that Susan could only be identified by her dental records. The pathologist was not even able to determine how she had died. The only clue was that Susan's pants had been removed. Her shorts were then replaced, her pants folded beneath her head. This confirmed suspicions that the motive for the attack was sexual, though what form this took has never been established.

As Susan's body was found in Staffordshire it was the job of the Staffordshire police to lead the murder hunt, although they worked closely with the Northumbria force. Witnesses to Susan's 'final walk' were re-questioned, and people who had been in the area where Susan's body had been found were located and interviewed. Photographs of the girl were widely distributed and a reconstruction staged to prompt flagging memories; hotels and caravan sites were visited to elicit information on visitors to the area at the time of the murder, and these were subsequently questioned. Drivers from transport firms between Scotland and Staffordshire were interviewed. One of the most promising leads came from Mark Ball, a psychiatric nurse, who claimed to have seen a little girl matching Susan's description hitting out at a maroon Triumph 2000 with a tennis racket on the day Susan was abducted. His evidence was finally dismissed by the police, although not until some 19,000 drivers of maroon Triumphs had been questioned.

After almost a year the inquiry began to draw to a close. The manual database now comprised 500,000 hand-written index cards. Yet despite all the data, the investigation had reached a dead end; like the Yorkshire Ripper inquiry, the investigation was also in imminent danger of swamping the police by generating an immense amount of un-computerized information. Tragically, as is so often the case, it took another murder to provide the police with new information to get the investigation under way once more.

A year later, on 8 July 1983, in the seaside resort of Portobello on the outskirts of Edinburgh, five-year-old Caroline Hogg had been having a nice day. That afternoon she had been to a friend's party and after returning home for dinner she took her grandmother to the bus-stop with her mother, Annette. They returned just before seven o'clock that evening and Caroline, who was still full of energy, begged her mother to let her go down the road for a few minutes before bed-time. It was not unusual for Caroline to go to the playground, which was just a short walk from their house, and Annette said she could have a five minute play. Like Coldstream, Portobello is a small community where the residents all know each other. Besides, Caroline had always been told never to talk to strangers and was forbidden to go past the park to the promenade or to the permanent fairground, Fun City.

At 7.15 Annette, who had told Caroline to be just five minutes, sent her son Stuart to look for his sister. When he came back, unable to find her, Annette herself went out and soon the whole family were looking for Caroline. The police were called at just before eight o'clock. Many people had seen the little girl that night, and some of the sightings were of Caroline with her abductor. There were reports of Caroline holding hands with a 'scruffy man'. This man was seen looking at the girl in the playground, and then at Fun City, the place forbidden to her, where he paid for her to go on the children's roundabout. They were last seen walking out of the back entrance of Fun City, still holding hands.

As they had done the previous summer, the police quickly set up search parties. Caroline was abducted on Friday, and by Sunday the police had recruited more than 600 volunteers, who went over every inch of the local area for any sign of her. A week later this number had risen to some 2,000 people. It was the largest search ever carried out in Scotland but they would find nothing, as Caroline, like Susan, had quickly been transported many miles south. Unlike the Maxwells, Annette and John Hogg spoke only once to the media, in a press-conference at which

John begged her abductor, 'just bring her back ... Please, let her come home'; Annette, crying, told the public, 'We really miss her. I really miss her.' There seemed to be no leads, as Superintendent Ronald Stalker candidly told the press, 'I am afraid that all we have to say at this stage is that we have turned up nothing at all.'

Caroline's body was found on 18 July in a lay-by at Twycross in Leicestershire near the A444, the road that runs from Northampton to Coventry. Her body had been left some 300 miles from where she had been abducted, just as Susan's had been, yet they were found within just twenty-four miles of each other. It had been ten days since Caroline had disappeared and again the body was so decomposed from the hot weather that the cause of death was a mystery. She was identified by her hair-band and locket. This time the motive was clearly sexual: Caroline's body was completely naked.

Because of the obvious similarities between the murders of Susan and Caroline it was decided by the chief constables of the four forces now involved – Northumbria (where Susan was abducted), Staffordshire (where Susan was found), Edinburgh (where Caroline was abducted), and Leicestershire (where Caroline was found) – that the investigations into the murders should become a joint inquiry. In July 1983 the Deputy Chief Constable of the Northumbria police, Hector Clark, was put in charge. From the outset Clark had been told that part of his objective in this inquiry was to see how computers could be used to aid such an investigation. It was the first opportunity since the Yorkshire Ripper inquiry for the police to determine whether the early use of computers in a serial murder investigation could be helpful.

As the amount of data from the Susan Maxwell investigation alone was immense, Clark thought that the joint inquiry would be most efficient if it was computerized, which would involve transcribing all the manual files onto a computer database. The information relating to the Caroline Hogg inquiry would be fed into the same database as it progressed. The approach was sound, yet it was not given the go-ahead, as it was felt that too much time would be spent in back-converting the files. Instead a computer programme was written for the Caroline Hogg inquiry alone, and it was decided the Susan Maxwell investigation should remain manual.

In Portobello, witnesses on the promenade and at Fun City were interviewed, and house-to-house inquiries were made; in Leicestershire, officers sat for weeks by the A444 taking down the registration numbers of passing cars. LIOs (local intelligence officers) from every force in the country were asked to draw up lists of possible suspects. The houses of men who were believed to have been on the promenade that night for 'immoral purposes' were searched; holiday-makers from as far as Australia were asked to send in rolls of camera- or cine-film they had taken in Portobello. A reconstruction of Caroline's last journey was staged; parking tickets issued in Edinburgh were examined; and an artist's impression was drawn up of the 'scruffy man' – which prompted more than 600 names to be put forward by the public. Perhaps the most hopeful lead was from a Mr and Mrs Flynn who saw a blue Ford Cortina with a man and a 'scared-looking' young girl in it. 20,000 drivers of blue Cortinas were interviewed. Unfortunately, as had happened with the maroon Triumph, the lead turned out to be a red herring.

At the beginning of the summer of 1984 the police found themselves in a similar situation to that of the previous summer. They had been diligent, they had collated a huge amount of information, yet they had no real leads, and no likely suspects.

There was now a three-year gap until the next murder in the series of child killings that was already being dubbed by the press as the most horrific since the Moors Murders. On 26 March 1986, ten-year-old Sarah Harper was the third little girl to be abducted. Sarah lived in Morley, Leeds, which was further south than the residences of the two other girls, but still in the north of England. At eight o'clock that evening just as *Coronation Street* was ending, Sarah's mother, Jacki, asked if one of her children would go to the corner shop and buy a loaf of bread. Sarah volunteered to go. Taking £1 from her mother and picking up two empty lemonade bottles to get the deposit on them, Sarah left her home in Brunswick Place to walk to K&M Stores on Peel Street, just over a hundred yards from her house.

At K&M the proprietor, Mrs Champaneri, clearly remembers

Sarah coming in. The girl returned the lemonade bottles, and bought a loaf of white bread and two packets of crisps. She left the shop at 8.05 and, shortly afterwards, two girls who knew her saw Sarah walking home towards the 'snicket', an alley used by locals as a short cut. Then, like Susan and Caroline, she disappeared.

At about 8.15 Jacki started to worry, as the journey should have only taken Sarah five minutes. Although Jacki thought that Sarah was probably just 'dawdling' or eating crisps in the alley, she sent Sarah's sister, Claire, out to look for her. When Claire came back with no news of her sister, the family went out in the car to search for her. At nine o'clock the police were called and once again searches and inquiries were swiftly set into motion. Once again they proved fruitless.

On 19 April David Moult remembers how he was walking his dog by the River Trent in Nottingham when he spotted 'something floating in the river. I thought it was a piece of sacking then the current turned it round and I realized it was a body.' Using a stick, Moult managed to drag the body over to the side of the river bank. He then called the police. It was later determined that Sarah Harper had been put in the river at around junction twenty-four of the M1 when she was still alive. The pathologist who examined her body described the injuries, which had been inflicted pre-mortem, as 'terrible'. As Ray Wyre later described it, 'Sarah's assailant had violently explored both her vagina and her anus.'

Jacki Harper, like Liz Maxwell, vividly remembers being told of the discovery of her daughter's body:

> All he [the officer] could say was 'Would you like to make a cup of tea?' And all I kept saying was 'Will you tell me what you have to tell me?' I knew why they were there – it was obvious. But he wouldn't tell me: he just kept going on about this bloody tea. All I wanted him to say was 'Yes, we've found her.'

It fell to Terry Harper – Sarah's father, Jacki's ex-husband – to identify his daughter's body: 'It was worse than I ever dreamed of', he said.

Although Hector Clark was careful to keep an open mind, he believed at the time that Sarah's abduction and murder was not connected to those of Susan and Caroline. The differences, he said, outweighed the similarities. Susan and Caroline were both abducted on hot July days, in colourful summer clothes; Sarah was abducted on a cold, dark, rainy night in March, her small body covered with an anorak. Both Coldstream and Portobello are on, or near, heavily used main roads; Morley is not the sort of place you go to without a reason. This initially led Clark to believe that Sarah's abduction was committed by a local man who knew the area well.

In retrospect, however, the similarities, although perhaps fewer in number, were certainly more telling. All of the victims were young girls who had been skilfully abducted from public places for a sexual purpose. They were all driven south and murdered, their bodies dumped in the Midlands, within twenty-six miles of each other. Sarah may have been subjected to a more vicious attack than the other two girls (although the evidence is inconclusive), but if anything this pointed to, and not away from, the same offender being responsible. In serial murders the attacks frequently get more violent as they increase (this is true of Peter Sutcliffe, for instance) for the killer gains confidence and needs more and more elaborate acts of violation and mutilation to keep him aroused. Therefore it would not be surprising if the murder of Sarah Harper was more extreme in its sexual brutality than were the murders of Susan Maxwell and Caroline Hogg.

Initially the investigation into Sarah Harper's murder was conducted as a separate inquiry, led by Detective Superintendent John Stainthorpe of the West Yorkshire police. Yet close links were maintained to the joint Maxwell/Hogg inquiry in order to keep all avenues of approach open. The same painstaking inquiries were made in the case of Sarah Harper as had been with Susan and Caroline. House-to-house inquiries were conducted, people who had seen a white van parked near Sarah's house were interviewed, and an artist's impression of a strange man who was seen on the street and in K&M Stores was circulated. LIOs were again asked to draw up lists of men who had committed similar offences, all of whom were interviewed.

Yet this time the police had an advantage, as by now the Home Office Large Major Enquiry System had been established. HOLMES had been donated to the West Yorkshire police after the Yorkshire Ripper 'fiasco', and it was utilized from the first day of the Sarah Harper investigation. The system was designed efficiently to log, process, collate and compare information at the press of a switch. Once all the data from the investigation had been fed in to HOLMES, names of possible suspects or vehicle registration numbers, for instance, could be fed into the system, which would instantly tell the user whether the name or vehicle had come up previously in the investigation.

Despite this new technological efficiency, however, the police were getting no further in their investigation. Ultimately no matter how sophisticated HOLMES was, if the name of the offender was not stored anywhere in its memory it was useless. The police were relying on their killer's name being in the system; if it was, then the right questions to HOLMES would unearth him. Failing this, the computer was reduced to an efficient storage container. It would not identify a murderer.

After eight months of the Sarah Harper inquiry had lapsed, Her Majesty's Inspector of Constabulary decided that all three cases should be linked and that one database ought to be established. This was a gargantuan task. The Maxwell investigation had never been computerized at all; the Hogg investigation had been, as had the Harper, yet the programmes were incompatible. All three complete investigations had to be inputted, with the necessary conversions, into one database. The process took three years: in July of 1990 the job was finally complete.

It transpired, however, that there was no opportunity to test the effectiveness of a single database. Once again, as in many previous serial murder investigations, luck was to prove a key factor in the apprehension of the killer. As Clark said, 'Once we had exhausted all our lines of inquiry the best chance of catching the man responsible was if he struck again.' Clark added, 'My biggest hope, however, was that he would be caught before he went too far and killed a girl.' As with Peter Sutcliffe,

Black's apprehension came about during the course of an abduction which would certainly have turned into another murder.

It was 14 July 1990, a sunny day in the village of Stow in the Scottish Borders and six-year-old Mandy Wilson was walking to her friend's house to play. As she walked down the road one of her neighbours, David Herkes, watched her approach a van with its passenger door open. Herkes later told the police in his statement that as he bent down to look at his mower blades:

> All I could see were her little feet standing next to the man's. Suddenly they vanished and I saw him making movements as if he were trying to stuff something under the dashboard. He got into the van, reversed up the driveway the child had just come from and sped off towards Edinburgh.

David Herkes had the presence of mind to take the van's registration number, and then quickly rang the police. Police cars were promptly on the scene and the van's description was radioed to officers in the area. Herkes remembers what happened next:

> I was standing near the spot where the child had been abducted, briefing the police and the girl's distraught father about what had happened. Suddenly I saw the van again and shouted 'That's him'. The officer dashed into the road and the van swerved to avoid him before coming to a halt.

While officers handcuffed the man, who identified himself as Robert Black, Mandy's father, Mr Wilson, recalls:

> I shouted at Black 'That's my daughter – what have you done to her, you bastard?' But his reaction was nil, he had no expression. I could have got my hands round his throat there and then, but my concern was for my daughter, not him. Where was she? Was she alive or, God forbid, dead? I

went straight for a pile of rags just behind the seat and felt a little body inside the sleeping-bag ... I can't tell you how I felt as I unwrapped her from the bag and saw her little face bright red from the heat and lack of air. She was so terrified as I untied her and took the tape from her mouth that she didn't utter a word.

Before Black had tied Mandy's hands behind her back, covered her mouth with Elastoplast and shoved her into a sleeping-bag, he had sexually assaulted her. He later told Ray Wyre that, 'I pulled her pants to one side and I had a look. I thought I'd just sort of stroked [her vagina] ... but there was bruising on the inside – I don't know how.' He then told Wyre what he would have done if he had not been caught:

When I'd done the delivery in Galashiels down the road, I would have assaulted Mandy sexually. I would have probably stripped her from the waist down, but I would have untied her and probably took the plaster off her mouth. And if she called out when I was assaulting her, then I might have put the gag back on.

More specifically, Wyre quotes Dr Baird, psychologist for the Crown, whom Black told that:

he would have put things into her vagina 'to see how big she was'. He would have put his fingers in and also his penis. When asked about other objects, he agreed he might have put other objects into her vagina, and when asked for an example, he saw a pen with which I was writing ...

When Wyre asked Black how he could do such a devastating thing to a child while simultaneously claiming (as he had done previously) that he loved children, Black admitted that 'I wasn't thinking about her at all ... like, you know, what she must be feeling'. If she had died 'it would have been a pure accident'.

This extraordinary dissociation, which transforms the little girl into a mere object, is frequently to be found in the cases of other serial killers, but in Black's case it seemed to preclude the sadism that takes pleasure in the victim's sufferings. The child became a plaything, to be experimented with, poked, probed, and eventually disposed of. It seems to have been a matter of indifference to Black whether she objected to the process or not.

On the way to Selkirk police station Black told officers that the abduction was 'a rush of blood' and added, 'I have always liked little girls since I was a kid.' He said that he had just wanted to keep her until he had done his next delivery and then he would have 'spent some time with her', maybe in Blackpool. Then he would have let her go.

Robert Black's case came to trial the following month, on 10 August 1990. As the evidence in this particular case was over-whelming Black had little choice but to plead guilty. In light of the plea the job of the prosecution was simply to give the facts of the case, which the Lord Advocate, Lord Fraser, did, stressing that medical opinion said that Mandy would probably have been dead within the hour if she had been kept bound and gagged in the sleeping-bag. Dr Baird's report for the Crown said that Black was, and would remain, a danger to children. The task of the defence was to speak in mitigation. To this end, Herbert Kerrigan said that Black had admitted to liking little girls but had never before acted upon his desires. The abduction had been a one-off, and Black merely wanted to spend some time with Mandy. He did not intend to injure her, certainly not to kill her. Furthermore, Black had accepted that he was a threat to children and, said Kerrigan, 'wishes to engage in some sort of programme to get assistance'.

Dismissing the arguments of the defence, the Lord Justice Clerk, Lord Ross, described Mandy's abduction as being 'carried out with chilling, cold calculation'. 'This was', he said, 'no "rush of blood", as you have claimed. This is a very serious case, an horrific, appalling case.' Lord Ross sentenced Black to life imprisonment and told him that his release would not 'be considered until such time as it is safe to do so'.

Of course the abduction of Mandy Smith made Black a prime suspect for Hector Clark, as the MO was strikingly similar to that in the cases of Susan, Caroline and Sarah. When Clark first saw Black following his arrest in July 1990 he remembers,

> Slowly he looked up at me and my gut feeling was that this was my man. I had always thought that when I saw him I would know him and every instinct told me this was the guy. I knew by his body smell and his dishevelled appearance. Except that he was bald, he was just as I expected.

But 'gut feeling' and 'instinct' are not good enough. In spending so much time analysing such crimes, the police inevitably start to feel that they know the offenders in certain ways. They think they know what they will look like and how they will behave. George Oldfield, heading the Yorkshire Ripper inquiry, similarly said on several occasions that if he were in a room full of potential suspects he would instantly 'know' his man. As the Ripper investigation showed us, this is a dangerous assumption. Peter Sutcliffe was interviewed nine times during the course of the five-year investigation, but nobody 'recognized' him.

In the hope of eliciting some incriminating evidence, the police decided to interview Black. As he was already serving a life sentence they thought that he might be willing to talk about any other crimes he had committed. Interviewed in Scotland, Black talked candidly to officers about the offences for which he had previously been convicted, for the best part of six hours. He was frank about a variety of topics, including his one proper relationship with a woman, his attraction to little girls, the sexual abuse he had endured as a child, his fantasy life, and his masturbatory practices. Eventually however, when the officers asked Black about his work with Poster Dispatch and Storage and his whereabouts on the day of Caroline Hogg's abduction, he fell silent. When it came to the abductions and murders of the three little girls, Black would simply not talk to the police.

It was apparent that the police would have to find their evidence the hard way, through old-fashioned, painstaking detective work: they were going to have to look at Black's life over the past eight years. In most cases the tracing of a person's daily movements over almost a decade would prove an impossible task, but in this case the police were lucky due to the nature of Black's work. From a careful examination of work records, wage books, and receipts from fuel credit cards, the police were able to begin tracing Black's life.

Susan Maxwell's abduction had taken place in Coldstream on 30 July 1982. It was the task of the police to establish where Black was at every moment of that day. The first step in the process was to see whether PDS had records of journeys carried out by drivers dating that far back. The police were initially dismayed to find that potentially vital company records had been destroyed just months before, as was company policy after a certain length of time had elapsed. Yet new hope arose when it was established that the wage books from that time were still available. As different runs command different wages it was established – from the amount of money that Black received in his pay – that he must have done the London–Scotland run sometime between 29 July and 4 August.

The time still needed narrowing down, however. The police next looked at petrol receipts from the company's fuel credit cards that all drivers carried and it was established that Black had been in the Borders area on 30 July. He had filled up his white Fiat van just south of Coldstream before the time that Susan was snatched, and just north of Coldstream after the time of her abduction. The quickest route between the two garages was the A687, directly through Coldstream. Black had previously told his work-mates that when returning from a Scottish run he preferred not to take the most direct route (which was the M6 to the M1) but to get to the M1 via the A50 through the Midlands. Susan's body was found by the A518 in Staffordshire, not far from the junction with the A50.

The case against Black for the murder of Caroline Hogg was built in a similarly meticulous fashion. On 8 July 1982, the day of Caroline's abduction, it was established that Black had delivered posters to Mills and Allen in Piershill, just over a mile north of Portobello. Petrol receipts showed that he had filled up at a petrol station in Belford, Northumberland, and that the most obvious route from Belford to his delivery point in Piershill was through Portobello. The post-mortem had found that Caroline's body had been kept by her killer for four days after her abduction – dead or alive, they could not determine – making 12 July the first day on which her body could have been dumped. On this day Black had delivered posters to Bedworth, just over ten miles from where Caroline's body was found.

The circumstantial evidence for the case of Sarah Harper was equally strong. On 26 March, the day of her abduction, Black had delivered posters to a depot just 150 yards from the place where Sarah was last seen. Petrol receipts from the next day put Black driving directly past the spot on the A453 to Nottingham where Sarah's body had been deposited.

In addition to the growing mountain of circumstantial evidence another incident came to Clark's notice. On 28 April 1988, fifteen-year-old Teresa Thornhill had been to the park with some friends, and later walked part of the way home with one of them, Andrew Beeson. Just after she and Andrew had gone their separate ways, Teresa noticed that a blue van had stopped just ahead of her on the opposite side of the road; the driver had got out and was looking under the bonnet. As she approached, the man shouted to her: 'Can you mend engines?' Uneasily she replied that she could not and walked on. The next thing she knew, the man had grabbed her from behind, picked her up and was carrying her across to his van. She said later:

> I will never forget his hairy arms, sweaty hands and smelly T-shirt. He came over to me and got me in an all-encompassing bear hug which I could not get out of because he was very strong. I tried to struggle free and began shouting for my mum. I was looking around for something to hit him with, but there was nothing there. Then I grabbed him between the legs.

She also knocked his glasses to the ground, screaming all the while. Teresa's friend Andrew heard her screams and ran towards the van shouting, 'Get off her, you fat fucking bastard.' Teresa's struggle and Andrew's timely arrival meant that her attacker had little choice but to drop his victim and make his getaway.

Unfortunately, at the time there was nothing to obviously link Teresa's attack to the abductions and murders of Susan, Caroline and Sarah. Most importantly, these girls were aged between five and eleven, whereas Teresa was fifteen, nearly a woman. She looked far younger than her years, however: she was under five feet tall, with a girlish figure, and wore no make-up. She did not look like a teenager. If this had been taken into account at the time, the abductions would have seemed remarkably similar. If this case could be shown to be linked to the murders, then it was an important breakthrough, as Teresa's description of her attacker and his van matched Black exactly.

By the end of 1990 the police had gathered a mass of circumstantial evidence against Black, but unfortunately they had no forensic evidence and no confession. They decided to re-interview Black more rigorously, but for three days he refused to answer any of their questions, as was his right. The police had no real choice but to proceed with what they had. In May 1991 the police submitted their report to the Crown Prosecution Service who would decide whether to go ahead with a prosecution. In April 1992 Black was served with ten summonses.

Yet it would be another two years before the case was tried. Aside from the fact that there were twenty-two tons of evidence that had to be made available for the defence to examine, there were many difficult legal problems to sort out in the preliminary hearings. Firstly there were jurisdictional questions to clear up, given that the crimes had been committed across two countries with different legal procedures. Additionally, the prosecution's case relied upon being allowed to present the murders as a series, while the defence applied for severance of the charges. Finally, the abduction of Mandy Wilson was an issue under hot debate. The prosecution needed to present it as evidence of the defendant's unique MO, whereas the defence wanted it precluded from proceedings. The submission of a past offence as evidence of the commission of a present offence is called 'similar fact evidence' and is notoriously controversial. It is usually only permitted when the past offence is 'strikingly similar' to the present. In Black's case it was allowed. The pre-trial rulings were all made in the prosecution's favour and at last the case was ready to come to trial.

As most of his crimes had been carried out in England it was decided that this was where Black would be tried. Mr John Milford, leading for the Crown, began his opening speech at two o'clock on the afternoon of Wednesday 13 April 1994 in the Moot Hall in Newcastle. Ultimately he aimed to prove that the murders of Susan Maxwell, Caroline Hogg and Sarah Harper, and the abduction of Teresa Thornhill, were all part of a series committed by the same person; and that this person had to be Black. There was neither forensic evidence nor any admission of guilt from the defendant himself, so the case was to be based upon evidence which, while admittedly circumstantial, was still very strong. Black had been at all the abduction points, and in the places where the bodies had been disposed of at the pertinent times; descriptions given by witnesses matched Black's appearance at those times; on the days in question Black was driving the types of van spotted at the scenes; and he had already admitted to an abduction in 1990 which bore exactly the same unusual MO as the offences for which he was now being charged.

Milford highlighted to the jury the similarities between the murders in order to prove that they were all committed by the same man, which was his first essential point:

- All the victims were young girls.
- All were bare-legged, wearing white ankle socks.
- All were taken from a public place.
- Susan and Caroline were both abducted on hot July days.
- All the victims were abducted in a vehicle of some sort; Susan and Sarah were both abducted in Transit-type vans.
- After abduction, all the victims were taken some miles south.
- All the bodies showed signs of a sexual motive for the attack: 'Each victim was obviously taken for sexual gratification. Susan Maxwell's pants were removed, Caroline Hogg was naked and Sarah Harper was found to have suffered injury.'
- None of the victims suffered any 'gross bruising or broken bones'.
- Both Susan and Sarah had been unclothed and then reclothed; all three victims had their shoes removed.
- No real attempt was made to hide the bodies.

- All the bodies had been dumped in what became known to police as the 'Midlands Triangle', a twenty-six-mile area encompassing parts of Nottinghamshire, Staffordshire and Leicestershire.

These murders, said Milford, 'are so unusual, the points of similarity so numerous and peculiar that it is submitted to you that you can safely conclude that they were all the work of one man'. And this one man, as overwhelming evidence would prove, was Robert Black. 'The Crown alleges that Robert Black kidnapped each of his victims for sexual gratification, that he transported them far from the point of abduction and murdered them.'

Having outlined the similarities in the murders, Milford moved on to the charge of the abduction of Teresa Thornhill in Nottingham in 1988. This case clearly had the same features as the previous abductions: Teresa was a girl (who looked younger than her fifteen years) who was snatched off a busy street in the north of England by a scruffy-looking man driving a van. After detailing the similarities, Milford told the court that on that very day Black was delivering posters to a firm in Nottingham in his blue Transit van, and the description that Teresa gave to the police of her attacker matched photographs of Black at the time. When police searched Black's room after his arrest they found a paper from 1988 with a report in it about the attempted abduction. Teresa also told police that her attacker smelt strongly; the Rayson children had nicknamed their lodger 'Smelly Bob', and Eric Mould, Black's former boss at PDS, told the court that his workers used to complain that Black was unclean and had bad body odour.

Following Justice Macpherson's pre-trial ruling the court was next told of Black's arrest for the abduction and assault of Mandy Wilson in Stow in July 1990. Milford said that Black had admitted this abduction and assault and that it had all the hall-marks of the three murders and the abduction for which he now stood trial. In fact, the crimes were 'virtually carbon copies. At Stow he was repeating almost exactly what had happened at Coldstream.' Milford continued:

The little girl in Stow was wearing shorts when she was taken, was bare-legged and was wearing white socks. She was to be transported many miles south. Again it was the end of the week, it was July and it was hot. Stow and Coldstream are similar villages only twenty-five miles apart ... Even more remarkably, like Susan Maxwell, the little girl was wearing yellow shorts.

Black had admitted to the abduction of Mandy Wilson; this abduction was a 'carbon copy' of that of Susan Maxwell; the abduction of Teresa Thornhill and the abductions and murders of Caroline and Sarah were carbon copies of Susan's abduction and murder: ergo, Black committed the three murders.

The prosecution had made a good start. It had detailed striking comparisons which linked the murders of Susan, Caroline and Sarah, and the abduction of Teresa, as a series. It had also shown the similarities between these offences and the one to which Black had already admitted. It was an important beginning but by itself was not enough: they had established a series, but they now had to establish that Black was the perpetrator. The prosecution's next job was to go through the police inquiry for the court telling them exactly how the police had gathered the evidence which put Black at all the abduction and dumping areas at the salient times. At the end of this evidence, which lasted for some days, Milford sardonically concluded that either Black was the killer, or a similarly perverted 'shadow' of Black was following him around the country – a shadow who also had convictions for sexual assaults on children and a penchant for child pornography. The murders of Susan, Caroline and Sarah, and the abduction of Teresa, were all committed by one man and Robert Black had been present at all the pertinent sites at the critical times.

Deputy Chief Constable Hector Clark was saved for last. Clark described the mammoth investigation as 'the largest crime inquiry ever held in Britain'. The computer held details of 187,186 people (of whom 59,483 had been interviewed), and of 220,470 vehicles. When Milford asked Clark how unusual it was for three children to have been abducted, murdered and then had their bodies dumped a relatively long distance away, Clark replied that in his thirty-nine-year career as a policeman, 'I have no knowledge of any other cases with these features.' The case for the prosecution was closed.

There had been much speculation as to how Ronald Thwaites would conduct the case for the defence. Certainly the prosecution had no forensic evidence nor did it have any help from the defendant himself, but equally Black had not offered any alibis which the defence could use, nor did it have any other alternative suspects. Thwaites also had a self-admitted child abductor and molester to defend. The only realistic path to take was to acknowledge Black's previous known offences and admit to the court that yes, this was a 'wicked and foul pervert' but argue that this did not necessarily make him a murderer.

Thwaites said that Black had become 'a murderer for all seasons', a scapegoat for the desperate police who, after an eight-year investigation, had hardly got further than from where they had started. 'This series of cases,' said Thwaites, 'reeks of failure, disappointment and frustration.' When Black was arrested for the abduction in Stow, officers 'set to work to dissect the whole of his life', with total disregard for anything that didn't fit into their picture of events. Thwaites told the jury of Black's previous convictions in Scotland for 'lewd and libidinous' behaviour, and spoke of the paedophilic pornography found in Black's room. Of the abduction of Mandy Wilson he said that, 'The judge saw it fit to give him a life sentence. No one can be surprised by that and everyone must applaud it. Black's lifelong interest in children is further confirmed by the haul of pornography in his home. It is revolting and sickening to look at.' But, he said:

However wicked and foul Black is, and I am not here to persuade you to like him or find any merit in him at all, it is not unreasonable to suppose that there might be some evidence to adorn the prosecution's case other than theory. This case has been developed before you using one incident or abduction, which he admitted, as a substitute for evidence in all these other cases. There is no direct evidence against Black.

By evidence of course, he meant that of a forensic variety, as there was plenty of other evidence to link Black to the murders. Although it was the prosecution who had called James Fraser of the Lothian and Borders police forensics laboratory, in fact his testimony benefited the defence. Fraser testified that he and four to six other scientists had spent six months working solely on this case, examining over 300 items belonging to Black, 'almost all his worldly goods'. When Thwaites asked him, cross-examining, 'Have you been able to make a scientific link between this man, Black, and any of these murders?' Fraser replied, 'No.' (The prosecution did, however, regain some credibility by asking Fraser if he would *expect*, after a decade, to find any significant forensic evidence, to which Fraser replied that he would not.)

Thwaites alleged that as both the police and the prosecution were so certain that Black was their man they refused to look elsewhere. The Crown had 'tried to match together a new suit made from oddments, but it is full of holes whereas the original suit has been left – until discovered by my team.' Black himself, said his defence, would not be testifying on his own behalf as nobody could be expected to remember routine details of their lives going back over ten years. But the truth was that the girls' killer or killers were still out there.

In an attempt to convince the jury of this the defence called Thomas Ball as their star witness, who testified that on the day of Susan's abduction he had seen a young girl hitting a maroon Triumph with a tennis racket. 'She was making quite a lot of noise,' he recalled. 'It seemed to be a child throwing a fit of temper.' He said that there were two or three people inside the car; the driver was a teenager with a wispy beard. When later shown a photograph of Susan by police he said he was 'certain' it was the child he had seen.

Other defence witnesses included Sharon Binnie, who told the court how she and her husband had seen a dark red saloon car like a Triumph 2000 parked in the same place that Thomas Ball described; Joan Jones and her husband, who had also seen a dark coloured car in a lay-by; and Alan Day and Peter Armstrong who had similarly seen red saloon cars. Michelle Robertson, who was a young girl at the time of the murders, testified seeing a 'scruffy' man in a blue Ford Escort; Kevin Catherall and Ian Collins claimed to have seen red Fords. This evidence did not further the case of the defence, however, as none of the people associated with these cars were doing anything remotely suspicious, they were simply in the vicinity of the abductions when they occurred.

Ultimately the question for the jury to decide, said Thwaites, 'is whether it may be proved he graduated from molester to murderer. There is nothing automatic about that.' 'The prosecution,' he said dramatically, 'has conducted their case here from beginning to end without letting you into an important secret. The secret is that there is no evidence against Black.'

On Tuesday 17 May Mr Justice Macpherson sent the jury away to begin their deliberations. It was not, however, until the morning of the third day – the 19th – that the jury finally agreed upon a verdict. When they found Black guilty on all counts, a sigh of relief went around the courtroom. Mr Justice Macpherson sentenced him to life for each of the charges, adding that for the murders, 'I propose to make a public recommendation that the minimum term will be thirty-five years on each of these convictions.'

As Black was being taken down he turned to the twenty-three officers who were there to hear the verdict and said, 'Well done, boys.' At a cost of some £1m to the tax-payer the trial was over and Black would not be eligible for parole until he was eighty-two, in 2029. To this day Black has never admitted his guilt to the police. But in his last talk with Ray Wyre, when Wyre asked why Black had never denied the charges to him, Black replied that he hadn't done so because he couldn't.

Once Black had been convicted the recriminations began. Everybody wanted to know why it had taken eight years for Black to be apprehended, three years longer than it had taken to catch Peter Sutcliffe. An amazing time, one might think, considering Black's past. And unlike the Sutcliffe case, computers in general, and HOLMES in particular, were used to track Black. Partly, of course, the problem was that the murder investigations were not initially stored on one database, which meant that information between cases could not be adequately cross-refer-enced. When all three cases were eventually conjoined on one database, by this time Black had already emerged as a suspect. Thus the effectiveness of the new system had not been tested.

However although one database would have been invaluable in data storage and comparison between the investigations, it probably would not have caught Black. HOLMES might well have played a vital part in catching Sutcliffe, as one of the major downfalls of that investigation was that poor cross-referencing meant that when questioning Sutcliffe officers simply didn't realize that he had been interviewed many times before. If they had realized this there is little doubt that Sutcliffe would have emerged as a strong suspect. Yet since the police had never inter-viewed Black in connection with the murders, he was simply not *in* the system as Sutcliffe had been. Black was not in HOLMES for the Harper inquiry, nor had his named cropped up in the Maxwell or Hogg inquiries. The single database would not have changed this.

The question is really why Black was not identified as a suspect at any stage. After Black's trial, criticism was directed at Hector Clark from the media and, more distressingly, from other officers on the inquiry, particularly Detective Superintendent John Stainthorpe (who had headed the Sarah Harper investiga-tion). Stainthorpe's criticism was that Clark had defined his parameters too narrowly when looking at men with records for sexual offences as potential suspects. Clark had confined his search to men who had been convicted of serious sexual offences: the attempted or actual abduction, rape or murder of a child under sixteen. Black, however, had been convicted of 'lewd and libidinous' behaviour – a charge which did not match the sever-ity of the offence – with a seven-year-old girl in Scotland in 1967. Stainthorpe said that if Clark had included *all* sexual offences, Black would have been a first-class suspect straight away, or at the very least would have been in the system: 'Black should have been arrested years ago, with his history and convictions.'

Clark was quick to defend himself to the press and public: 'We just couldn't check on everybody,' he said. 'It would have overloaded the system to an unmanageable extent.' He argued that criteria based on the most likely suspects had to be utilized, and given that the charges being investigated were for murder, looking at those offenders with convictions for highly serious offences seemed the most sensible way to proceed.

However, when we look at research done into the backgrounds of serial killers we see that if they have any past convictions they are hardly ever serious and usually not sexual. John Christie, Ian Brady, Colin Ireland and Fred West had previous convictions for offences such as theft, fraud and breaking and entering. Peter Sutcliffe, Dennis Nilsen, Myra Hindley and Rose West had no criminal records at all before their convictions for murder. But Black was not just – or primarily – a serial killer, he was also a paedophile, and unlike serial killers paedophiles often do have past convictions for sexual offences. These offences, however, may often be relatively minor. Thus if the investigation was to be centred around the creation of suspects based on previous form, Stainthorpe was right to say that even minor sexual offences needed to be included. Of course, this was not a viable way to conduct the inquiry. In this sense, at least, Clark was right: the creation of a database with all sexual offences committed in the past twenty years on it, and the subsequent investigation of the offenders, was not a task the inquiry could manage.

Just as the case of Peter Sutcliffe highlighted the need for a computer system such as HOLMES to replace the old manual system of data collation, the Black inquiry made apparent the need for a constantly updated national database of all sex offenders and killers. The police needed a system such as the FBI's VICAP which can search its memory of sex offenders and their MOs to match the case under investigation. As John Stainthorpe said, 'had Black been on a computerized criminal intelligence system, his name would have popped up like a cork out of a bottle'. And it probably would have, provided that the types of offence initially fed into the computer were comprehensive and went far enough back in time.

In a case such as Sutcliffe's where the killer has committed no past sexual or violent offences, such a system would be of little use in the identification of possible suspects. In Black's case, however, the system would have had a two-fold usage. It would have identified Black as a man with convictions for sexual assaults on young girls, and also have unearthed offences which he may have perpetrated but had not yet been linked to.

As it was it emerged only after Black's trial that he was almost certainly responsible for more than the three murders for which he was convicted. A serial killer like Black having killed Susan in 1982 and Caroline in 1983, is highly unlikely to then leave a gap of three years before the next murder. And Susan was unlikely to have been his first victim. At the age of seventeen Black had assaulted and left a seven-year-old girl for dead; his first murder allegedly occurred when he was thirty-five. But the incident in 1967 hadn't left him full of remorse or regret: these were things he told Wyre that he knew he should, but could not, feel. When looking back on the event all he felt was lust. The image of that day re-formed again and again in Black's fantasies; he relived it and improved upon it until it was just right. The compulsion to re-enact and refine the experience in reality would have been too deep and over-powering to leave for fifteen years.

In July 1994 a meeting was held in Newcastle, attended by the officers who had led the Maxwell, Hogg and Harper inquiries, and other officers from across the country who had outstanding murders of a similar nature. There were up to ten unsolved abductions and murders which bore Black's MO: April Fabb who was abducted from her bicycle in Norfolk in 1969; nine-year-old Christine Markham who was snatched in Scunthorpe in 1973; thirteen-year-old Genette Tate who disappeared in Devon in 1978; fourteen-year-old Suzanne Lawrence who was found dead in Essex in 1979; sixteen-year-old Colette Aram who was found strangled and sexually assaulted in a field in Nottingham in 1983; fourteen-year-old Patsy Morris who was found dead near Heathrow in 1990; and Marion Crofts and Lisa Hession. There were also unsolved murders in Ireland, Amsterdam, Germany and France which Black could have committed.

One senior officer was quoted in the *Express* as saying, 'We know he killed Genette Tate and April Fabb, and we believe that their bodies are buried somewhere in the Midlands Triangle.' John Stainthorpe said that in his opinion there was an eighty per cent likelihood of Black being involved in the disappearance of Genette. Inquiries into these murders have been re-opened. Had these abductions and murders been linked at the time to the cases of Susan, Caroline and Sarah, the police might have unearthed useful new leads. Had they had a national database Black might have been identified as a suspect. An enormous amount of fruitless work could have been averted, a quicker conclusion reached, and lives saved.

8

COLIN IRELAND

The case of Colin Ireland was never reported in the press with the kind of near hysteria that greeted those of Peter Sutcliffe or Fred and Rose West. Partly, this is because Ireland pleaded guilty to the murders of five homosexual men in 1993, and thus there was no lengthy trial to report, and few details about him emerged; partly, too, one suspects that the murders of a handful of gay men were unlikely to cause the sort of public outrage and fascination as the murders of young women or children. Whatever the reasons, no book has been written about him, nor have any substantial articles. I have been fortunate, therefore, to have been able to contact Colin Ireland directly and to have received extensive replies to my questions from him.

The following account is based largely on my correspondence with Ireland. He assures me that in his answers to my questions he has been entirely truthful, as 'I see no point in being otherwise', and I will take his word for that. But, of course, in such circumstances, one cannot testify unreservedly to the accuracy of the information, which can sometimes be distorted due to memory failure, suppression of information, or special pleading. Yet, there have been few cases in which serial killers in England have revealed themselves so forthrightly, and the gains of hearing first-hand why and how the mind of a serial killer has been formed, and operated, more than compensate for any possible inaccuracy in the material. The following account, then, is unique: it is, largely, Colin Ireland's own story.

The conception of Colin Ireland was unplanned. When Colin's natural father discovered that his seventeen-year-old lover was pregnant, he disappeared. Colin's mother – who has expressed her wish to remain unnamed – was upset, but unsurprised, and her partner's absence did nothing to change her mind about having the baby. When she gave birth to her first son on 16 March 1954, in West Hill Hospital in Dartford, Kent, she decided

217

not to name her baby's father on the birth certificate, and to this day Colin Ireland has no knowledge of him. Earning a meagre wage as a newsagent's assistant, Colin's mother was too young to be able to cope with motherhood by herself, both financially and emotionally, but Colin's grandparents were supportive. They agreed that their daughter and new grandchild should live with them and Colin's uncle at Myrtle Road in Dartford.

And there they stayed until 1959, when the arrival of relations from abroad prompted their move. Colin's mother was now twenty-two, a little more mature, and she decided that she and her five-year-old son should be more independent of their relatives. It was not to be that simple, however, and their move to Birch Road in Gravesend that year marked the first in a long series of physical and emotional upheavals. During the next six years Colin and his mother were to move a total of nine times. Colin's mother desperately wanted to provide her son with a decent home, but every time they moved into a place of their own she soon found herself unable to cope, with a small child to support, and relying on part-time and unskilled work. Their stay at Birch Road was short-lived, and they returned to Myrtle Road to live with Colin's grandparents again within the year.

In 1960, when more money had been saved, Colin and his mother moved out of her parents' house for the second time, to Chester Road in Sidcup, Kent. Later that same year, however, having hit upon hard times once more, they had no choice but to move out. Unwilling to rely on the charity of her parents again, Colin and his mother were forced to live at Westmalling in Maidstone, which was, in Ireland's own words:

a camp for homeless women and children comprising of long wooden huts. In turn these contained small cell-like accommodation, one unit per family. Worse than any prison, Westmalling was degradation personified. I can still remember my mother's tears when we first arrived, a woman who does not cry easily.

They spent three months there until, unable to stand it any longer, Colin and his mother returned to her parents at Myrtle

Road. By the following year, they were again ready to move out. This time things were more hopeful, as Colin's mother had a new partner, and together the three of them moved to Farnol Road, in Dartford, where they would remain for the next three years. The couple were soon married, and Colin's surname was changed from his mother's maiden name of Ireland to his new step-father's name, Saker. Ireland remembers him with a mixture of fondness and exasperation: 'My first step-father was a harmless man ... He was humorous and unaggressive.' Unfortunately, however, 'He had little idea of responsibility and though he would treat me, he would also walk out leaving us penniless.' Although Colin's step-father was an electrician by trade, he only worked sporadically and was irresponsible with money, and the years with him were, Ireland says, 'financially, very unstable ... we were poor.'

Due to the family's constant changes of address, Colin never settled into school life. Between the ages of five and ten, he attended six primary schools, all in different parts of Kent.

> I would not say I enjoyed school. It was a chore. As to why not, I would say I was not given a chance. My primary education was a mess, unstructured is too nice a term. Disjointed an understatement. My secondary education was, I feel, hampered by my not going through primary education – with the boys. My start was also delayed, I walked into a class of boys who were half way through a class. They had been together for some time, several weeks at least. My 'new boy' status was duplicated. It went down hill from there.

Everywhere he went he was the 'new boy', the odd-one-out, who even looked different from the other boys. He told the police after his arrest, that he had always been a 'thin, lanky little runt – always getting the worst of it'. He remembers how, at school:

> I was subjected to verbal abuse. Serious physical abuse was very rare. The abuse would be due to my appearance,

both physical and my clothing, its general state equalled my school report: could do better! Physically I was very thin, though tall. My parents would supply me with school clothes, I just wore them out quicker than they could afford to buy them ... I can also remember being bow-legged and my mother telling me not to stand with my legs crossed.

To avoid bullying by the other children, Colin would frequently be absent from school. When he did go, he was nearly always late.

My absenteeism would take the shape of me asking not to go to school and it sometimes being allowed. I was never absent in a deceitful way. Not that I can remember anyway. The punishment for lateness, repeated lateness, was the cane and I'm surprised that I grew up to be a sadist and not a masochist.

Of course, it is often the case that those who have lacked power earlier in life seek the chance to grasp it later on. They identify with the aggressor, and abandon the role of victim.

Although the teasing abated when Colin's step-father went to the school to speak to his teacher about the problem, Colin was still constantly on the perimeter of the social world of the playground. He became a withdrawn and lonely boy who had few friends. 'I would not say I joined in with the others, I'm not a mixer. I would often be on my own, with one or two at most, no more than that.' He was 'very lonely at times. Often at the edge of things.' ('I still am,' he adds, without conscious irony.) When teams were chosen for football or cricket, he was one of those boys who would spend 'more time on the side line waiting to be picked' than playing, which was 'very humiliating'. His few friends were chosen because they were unthreatening: 'In many ways I was immature and tended to seek out immature associates.'

Although he was a member of the Sea Cadets for two years, which provided him with some social structure, he mostly played alone after school and at weekends. It was during one of these solitary games that Colin had an accident:

> My grandparents had a fireplace that had a raised surround. One day I must have been playing knights in armour or something as I was wearing a saucepan on my head ... I fell and hit my head on the fireplace surround. In the accident I lost or damaged teeth, the underneath of my eye was cut and scarred and in general I had a 'knock on the head'.

He believes that this knock rendered him unconscious for a time, but as his grandparents are now dead, his mother was at work when the incident occurred, and he himself has no clear memory of the event, he cannot say for sure. 'I do remember having my teeth corrected afterwards but do not remember the accident. Is this a pointer to being dazed or worse?' he asks.

In 1964, Colin's parents' financial situation eventually became so bad that they were evicted from Farnol Road due to non-payment of rent. Ten-year-old Colin and his mother were forced to go back to Westmalling for a time, and as men were not allowed, Colin's step-father went to live with his parents. When Colin's mother discovered that she was pregnant later that year, they knew they would be unable to cope with the increased emotional and financial strain. But she wanted the baby, and so it was decided that Colin would go into care until his parents' monetary situation improved. As Ireland puts it, more under-standing now than he was then, 'We lacked the structure that would allow us to be together'. Colin was sent to stay with a foster family in Wainscott, Kent. Of this period he simply remembers that, 'my foster parents were ordinary and during my stay with them I felt ordinary'. He was returned to his parents, who were now living in West Kingsdown, a few months later, once they were better able to cope with him and his new brother.

Throughout his childhood, despite – or perhaps because of – their relative poverty and constant upheavals, Colin was always very close to his mother, whom he remembers as an affectionate and benevolent force throughout his life. When the family were struggling for money he recalls how she would make sacrifices herself in order that her children could be fed and clothed. The children usually ate well, he says, but this 'involved my mother not eating so that we could on a number of occasions during the worst periods ... As a child I was shielded by parental sacrifices from the worst effects of our poverty'. He vividly remembers one Christmas:

> I can remember having extra presents. Through either the efforts of my mother and step-father, or a benevolent uncle, this would have been my uncle Alan, I had been provided with a train set! This Christmas I also received gifts donated to the NSPCC and I was told by my mother that I was not to mention the train set to their officer when he arrived. I can still remember that man's arrival in all of his uniformed splendour, knocking on the door ... He did leave me with a rather splendid tin plate toy American police car that did all sorts of things.

Their poverty, in retrospect, had one positive effect, as 'the shared adversity my mother and I faced helped to bond us further'.

Not long out of care, Colin's sense of security was again shattered when his step-father left. It was, he remembers, 'a time of great instability for me and I felt threatened by this'. Not yet an adolescent, he had already been abandoned by both his real father and step-father, moved home on nine occasions, been shipped from school to school, and been placed in care. It is hardly surprising that during this period: 'I felt a general distrust of the adults within my family. I was a child, I did not like the situation at the time and in a childlike simplistic manner put the blame on those who should have been solving the problem.'

Colin's mother had been unhappy in her marriage for some time, and before her husband left she had already met another man, whom she married when Colin was twelve. At the time, Colin was confused and angry, and refused to take his new step-father's name, reverting instead to his mother's maiden name. But although Colin was resentful of the constant changes in his life, his second step-father was clearly a good-hearted man who worked hard to provide for his family and, most importantly, loved his new wife and her children dearly.

> My mother's marriage to my second step-father has been a long and good one ... He has stood by my mother for many years and I have great respect for him. He does make an effort to get on with me and I now regard him as being my father. He has given my mother the life she deserved but had never had.

Colin's second step-father soon proved himself a source of stability in their lives, and in 1965 they all moved to Clyde Street in Sheerness, Kent, where they would stay for the next five years. At Sheerness Secondary School, at the age of twelve or thirteen, Colin began to be curious about sex, which he learned about from his peers, sex-education classes at school, and a book which he borrowed from the library and then discussed with his mother. He remembers that he started masturbating at around this age, but didn't utilize any pictorial images nor fantasize while doing so: 'I never knew enough about sex to fantasize, it was more along the lines of "I wonder what it would be like?" '

> The only pornography available to me at that time was a magazine called *Parade* which I remember seeing, and the ladies' underwear pages within my mother's catalogue. If I had never seen a woman but only seen a sixties *Parade* I would have thought they only had an upper torso. The ladies' underwear section was a source of erotica shared by most adolescent boys at that time. Neither forms played a role in my masturbation ... I did it because it felt nice and it was interesting.

These thoughts and practices sound normal enough, but Colin was also exposed to less healthy sexual experiences and situations as an adolescent in Sheerness. Four experiences clearly stand out in his mind. On each occasion he was approached by an older man who tried to entice him into sexual activity. Although Colin resisted their advances, the experiences left him with an anger that would not abate. The first occasion was during the family's first year in Sheerness when, despite Colin's new father being in regular employment, the family were still struggling financially. To help out, Colin began to work in the school holidays.

One of the methods by which I financed my family was to work in a fairground. I earned ten shillings a day. There was a man who during the summer season rented a lock-up that backed onto the fair. His trade consisted of cheap gifts which he sold to the visitors. A necklace and locket caught my eye as a possible present for my mother, but the price was beyond my reach. I spoke to the man about the item. He suggested that I visit him in his caravan. So I, a very lonely and vulnerable boy, went to the caravan as he had told me he may give me the necklace if I did. I half thought he may offer me a job, I also, to a point, knew his intention in that I knew it might be unpleasant. I wanted that gift. In the caravan the man pulled down my trousers, beneath them I was wearing shorts. I saw it at the time as 'bottling out' but did not allow him to remove the shorts and never received the gift.

The subsequent occasions were, Ireland says, 'of a lesser nature though I remember them as if it was yesterday'. The second event was when Ireland was twelve.

On my way home I stopped to use the toilet. I was sat in a cubicle when a man (late teens/early twenties) looked over the dividing wall and offered me seven shillings and six pence. He never specified what he wanted in return. I sat where I was for a while, he had withdrawn. It's difficult for me to come to terms with, but I may have considered his offer. I was very young and very poor and also inquisitive, but when I came out he had gone … That man was not gay, he was a paedophile. So was the first.

The third time that a man approached him in Sheerness was at the cinema:

> On another occasion while watching a film at the cinema, a man had been going from child to child offering them ice-creams and drinks. I reported this man to the only 'official figure' I knew, a probation officer named Mr Bridges. The man was a local optician and I am still uncomfortable in the company of male opticians. Mr Bridges was unable to do anything.

The situation, as remembered, has a curious dream-like quality, suggesting that – as is so often the case with formative childhood experience – it elicited sufficiently powerful feeling that something has been left out, repressed, or distorted in remembering it. Ireland's fourth example is more mundane. The last such event was:

> a man who worked for a second-hand shop, he would pull a barrow around the town. He befriended me and later made it known that for sexual services he would give me money, I declined. I was just a child, how many more did they approach? They saw my vulnerability and attempted to abuse that, though I was never abused.

Although there was never any direct sexual contact, Colin felt upset, violated, and angry. These experiences, it seems, undermined his already insubstantial confidence in the world in which he lived, and suggested to him that he was always likely to be a victim, prey to the impulses of older, strange and sometimes perverse people.

In 1970, at the age of sixteen, Colin committed his first crime. He had been unhappy at home and at school for some time now, and he stole £4, planning to run away to London with the money. He was caught, however, made the subject of a 'fit person order', and sent to Finchton Manor School, in Kent.

> Finchton Manor had two requirements: the boy had to be above average intelligence and have 'emotional' problems. It was a fee-paying 'free expression' school. I was one of the two boys paid for by the local County Council as part of a care order. The rest were paid for by their parents.

After some months, however, Colin was again subject to a form of bullying.

> I was sharing a room with two other boys. One of the boys would ridicule me because my parents could not afford to keep me there, he also poked fun at my accent. I decided on an extreme form of revenge and one day went into our room, placed crunched up newspaper around his belongings, then set fire to it. I then left the room and went down the stairs only to return to the door to listen to the crackle of the flames.

This interest in fire-setting was apparently a recurrent one during his childhood, and continued into his adult life. In his early teens he had began having:

> a series of fire based nightmares that have plagued me as an adult. As I have said this is a recurring dream and was preceded by a less than healthy interest in fire as a child. I can remember reading on a number of occasions a book on the fire brigade, as it was then. This was at school and I can remember, though quite young, what equipment did what.

Before the fire brigade arrived a member of staff managed to put out the fire before it did any substantial damage, but that evening a social worker arrived to take Colin Ireland away from Finchton Manor. No charges were brought against him.

Having left Finchton Manor Colin ran away to London, where he says,

I became involved in the 'Playland' scene. You may or may not have heard of Playland, it was an amusement (whose amusement?) arcade where paedophiles would pick up young runaways. Again, I was on the edge of things, I was never abused though many of my friends were, often exchanging their bodies not for money, but just for a bed for the night.

With neither money nor a place to live, he was in trouble again almost immediately. Although his offences were still relatively minor, they were steadily escalating, and at seventeen Colin was sentenced to his first stint of borstal training, having been found guilty of burglary. He was sent to Hollesly Bay, an open borstal, where the regime was sufficiently lax to enable him to escape. He remembers that 'I escaped in the early morning, it was the summer. I ended up in the corner of this field. It was a safe place to hide, my only companion a dead rabbit. I stayed there till the night. It was a long day, I had no food or water and could not move and the rabbit smelt.' He was not on the run for long, however, before being picked up by the police, and he served the rest of his sentence, from 1971 to 1972, under the stricter regimes of the Rochester and Grendon borstals.

After his release at the age of eighteen, Ireland was able to begin his first relationship with a woman, but it was not a happy period. He reports that he was in a confused and unstable mental state:

I was entering what I call the lost period. Common with those who suffer from psychopathy. Two examples – one fictional, one not – spring to mind. The fictional account is in the book *Catcher in the Rye*. The true account was the year Adolf Hitler disappeared when he was in Vienna. When he reappeared he had lost his coat; that is all that is known about that year. My own 'lost period' (my term) lasted a lot longer. In between custodial periods a lot of the seventies are a blur. I spent my time detached and wondering.

In December 1975, at the age of twenty-one, Ireland was again in trouble with the police. No longer a minor, when he was found guilty of two counts of burglary, stealing a car and damage to property, he was sentenced to eighteen months' imprisonment, of which he served twelve. The first part of his sentence was spent in 'crowded London prisons' where, he reports, he began to think that his name was 'oi you'. When, after a few months, he was moved to the more civilized Lewis, and greeted after his first night with the words 'good morning Colin' he could hardly believe it.

Shortly after he was released, Ireland met, and moved in with, a woman with whom he began his first real sexual relationship.

> The losing of my virginity was interesting. Again it was late, I was twenty-one–twenty-two, I think it was twenty-two, it was December 1976. I had got out of prison the November before and was living in Swindon. We met at our place of work. She was of a different race to me, she was a black West-Indian who had come to this country when she was sixteen. She was five years older than me and had four children. I stayed at her house for a while. During the second night I lost my virginity. She did not know I was a virgin, I never told her. As to if I enjoyed it I can only say I never had the chance to think about it as we made love for a second time shortly afterwards. I lived with her for two or three months and we planned to marry. We never did.

Seemingly unable to keep himself out of trouble, with neither skills nor direction, in 1977 Ireland was sentenced to a further eighteen months' imprisonment for 'demanding with menace'. Over the next few years he was constantly in and out of prison: in 1980 he was sentenced to two years inside for robbery; a year later he served two months for attempted deception; and in 1985 he was sentenced to six months for 'going equipped to cheat'. In between these periods of incarceration, Ireland worked sporadically in a variety of unskilled jobs, including work as a bouncer in various bars, including a gay club, as a volunteer fireman, a restaurant chef, and a volunteer in a shelter for the homeless.

In 1981, at the age of twenty-seven, while working as a chef in London, Ireland met his first wife, Virginia Zammit, at a lecture on survivalism, a topic in which he had been interested for some years. Its theme – how to survive in a hostile environment by using your strength and wits – obviously resonated with him: it was what he'd been trying to do all his life. He enjoyed going camping in marshes and woods, and eventually joined the Southern Rangers survival group, where he and the other members learnt how to live off the land by killing animals and eating berries.

At thirty-six, Virginia Zammit was nine years older than Ireland when they met, and she had a five-year-old daughter. They married in 1982 and initially were very happy together. Virginia had been paralysed at the age of twenty-four in a road accident, and remembers that Ireland 'saw me as the person I was – the person inside rather then somebody in a wheelchair'. She said that 'there were so many good things about him': he would spend hours playing with her young daughter, whom he adored, and helped the children at her school with their reading and art. On the Holloway estate on which they lived he was known as 'the Gentle Giant'. Nevertheless as Ireland was deeply unstable, the harmony was not destined to last, and Virginia soon tired of her husband's frequent prison sentences and increasing aggression. In 1987, after he had an affair with another woman, they were divorced.

Two years later, in 1989, Ireland met Janet Young at the Globe, a pub in Buckfast, Devon, where she was landlady. Within a week Ireland had moved into the pub with Jan and her eleven- and thirteen-year-old children, and three months later they were married at Newton Abbot Register Office. After just four months of marriage, Ireland drove his wife and her children to Jan's mother's house in Margate, and then disappeared, taking with him Jan's car, and some money from the pub and their joint bank-account.

After the collapse of his second marriage, in 1991 Ireland moved to Southend-on-Sea in Essex, where he began work in a shelter for homeless people, despite the fact that he was homeless himself for much of this period. The manager there, Richard Higgs, remembers that Ireland was well liked by the guests, as he could empathize with their predicaments. However in December 1992, Higgs said that a 'conspiracy' had developed amongst some of the staff who disliked Ireland. 'All sorts of unfounded allegations were made against him and eventually he resigned. Colin was absolutely devastated.' Unemployed again, Ireland went to an adult training centre where, according to Higgs, 'He found himself breaking up wooden pallets. It was very demeaning. He was troubled, frustrated, and didn't know what to do with his life.'

The Coleherne, a pub on the Brompton Road in West London, has a reputation amongst London's homosexual population as a likely place to find a partner for the night. The clientele wear colour-coded handkerchiefs depending upon their masochistic preference, submissive or dominant, to make cruising easy and to avoid misunderstanding. On 8 March 1993, Ireland was in the pub, playing the part of the 'top' or Master. He later told police, 'I went to the Coleherne that evening and I felt that if I was approached by one of the group that tended to trigger feelings in me – masochistic men – I felt there was a likelihood I would kill.' This surprising indicator of the violence of his fantasy life – up until now Ireland had only committed minor offences – can only be explained by the slow escalation of his inner rage to the point where it could no longer be contained.

Sadly, somebody did approach him, indirectly. Peter Walker, a forty-five-year-old choreographer who was working as an assistant director on the West End musical *City of Angels*, was a regular at the Coleherne. Walker made no secret of the fact that he was homosexual, nor that his sexual excitement was enhanced by being the submissive partner in an S&M relationship. Ireland and he met when Walker spilled his drink over Ireland by accident, and then begged to be chastised. Ireland needed no further invitation.

As the front of the Coleherne was covered by a security camera, Ireland led Walker out of the pub by the side door, and they made their way back to Walker's flat in Battersea. With little preamble, Walker undressed and allowed himself to be bound, handcuffed, and gagged (using knotted condoms). 'I tied him up', Ireland later told police: 'there was a four-poster bed ... four posts with knobs on the top and I tied him by his fists with cord. Specially-made cord.' Ireland had come equipped, prepared with a 'murder kit': a knife, some cord, a pair of gloves, and a change of clothes. Having rendered his victim helpless, Ireland proceeded to beat Walker with his fists, a dog lead, and a belt. The post-mortem later suggested that Walker may still have believed it was a game at this stage, within the boundaries defined by his fantasy life. It wasn't to Ireland. 'Once I had tied him up I knew my intentions were different to his. I'm not sure if I really set out to kill him ... but it went from there.'

After beating Walker, Ireland produced a plastic bag and placed it over his victim's head. He held it there for a time, taunting Walker, revelling in the God-like power he possessed: he could choose this man's destiny. 'I took the bag away and told him how easy it was to end it all.' Ireland told police:

> It was a fate thing and he said to me, 'I'm going to die' and I said 'yes, you are'. I think in a way he wanted to die. There was a lack of desire to carry on. I think he knew he was going to die ... he was quite controlled about it. In the end I killed him with a plastic bag. I put it over his head and killed him with that.

When Walker was dead Ireland burnt his pubic hair. He was curious, he explained to police, as to how it would smell. Meticulously, he then set about erasing all traces of himself from Walker's flat. An avid reader of true crime books and police – particularly FBI – manuals, Ireland knew that those criminals with some 'forensic awareness' would be more likely to escape detection. Ireland was a classic case of an organized killer: he wiped any surfaces he had touched with his bare hands, changed his clothes, and bagged the old ones, along with the cord he had used, to be disposed of later. Then, worried that he would attract too much attention by leaving at such a quiet hour, Ireland decided to stay until the morning, entertaining himself by watching television and rummaging through Walker's personal effects.

Amongst these he came across the information that his victim had been HIV-positive. This incensed Ireland, as Walker had obviously been planning sexual intimacy with him, and had not disclosed his condition. John Nutting, for the prosecution at Ireland's trial, later said that as an expression of his disgust Ireland 'got some condoms and put one in his [Walker's] mouth and another in his nostril. As a further humiliation he put two teddy bears on the bed in a "69" position.' Before he left the flat, Ireland remembers:

> I looked at myself in the mirror. Then I walked down the road and thought that anyone who looked at my face would be able to see I had just murdered somebody. I thought they must be able to tell by just looking at me. I remembered losing my virginity and I remembered the same feeling. You're always buzzing.

We recognize here that perverse association of sexuality and death that inevitably appears in the inner lives of serial killers, and eventually manifests itself in their behaviour.

Inconspicuously mingling with the crowds, Ireland left in the morning rush-hour to catch a train back home. He says his crimes were committed in London rather than in Southend in order to confuse the police. Recent research on serial killing, carried out at the Investigative Psychology Unit at Liverpool University, shows that serial killers have a 'home range' which, according to Samantha Hodges, 'allows us to say something about where the killer lives in relation to his crimes'. This home range – the optimum distance that a killer will live from the crimes that he commits – is seven miles in England. Some 90 per cent of killers live within this seven-mile area of operation. Knowing this, Ireland consciously decided to kill outside the defined range, in order that any offender profile drawn up of him would be inaccurate on this point, and thus mislead the police. 'I deliberately turned around aspects of profiling,' he told me, 'attempting to use a tool of law and order against itself. The watchdog biting the handler.' Another example of his attempt to baffle the police lay in his disposal of evidence: 'My method of disposing of incriminating matter was to throw it from the return train window and always within the boundaries of the London transport network, my one exception made necessary by the presence of another passenger.'

Walker's body was soon discovered, but the police had nothing to go on, as Ireland had cleverly covered his tracks. He had always dreamed of committing the 'perfect murder', and it seemed he had done just that. The most obvious interpretation of the death was that Walker, who was a self-confessed homosexual with S&M inclinations, had engaged in a sexual game which had escalated out of control. However, when the police started making inquiries about Walker's sexual partner on the evening of his death, they were met with resistance. The gay community is notoriously suspicious of the police, and unwilling to help an organization they feel is hostile towards them and reluctant to take allegations of assault against gays seriously, which was one of the problems encountered in the Nilsen case. In addition, just a day after Walker's body was found, the Law Lords ruled that S&M between consenting adults was illegal. Thus, numerous gay men were unwilling to come forward to offer information lest they become the subject of prosecution themselves.

Two days after Walker's murder, the Samaritans received a call from a man who told them that he was worried about Peter Walker's dogs. He had, he said, locked them in a room before he killed their owner. This eccentric behaviour ought not to be put down to a love of animals, however, and eager for publicity, Ireland didn't stop at one phone call. He then rang the *Sun*, telling them, 'It was my New Year's resolution to kill a homosexual. He [Walker] was a homosexual and into kinky sex. You like that stuff, don't you?'

Ireland intended to kill again, but he was careful, and waited for the police activity to die away, and potential victims' suspicions to calm. After just over two months, he returned to the Coleherne on 28 May. 'I had gone out quite prepared to kill the man ... and I was going to have him,' Ireland later told police of his second victim, thirty-seven-year-old librarian Christopher Dunn. Like Walker, Dunn told Ireland that he liked to be dominated, and they returned together to Dunn's flat in Wealdstone, where they settled down to watch an S&M video and have something to eat, before Ireland told Dunn to go and 'get ready'. When Ireland entered the bedroom he found Dunn naked except for a body harness and studded belt. Telling his victim to lie face down, Ireland handcuffed him and tied his feet together, asking him how he felt. 'Frightened but excited', Dunn answered. He was right to feel frightened. Ireland demanded the PIN number for his cash-card, telling him that he had better co-operate 'if he wanted to hear the birds singing the next morning'. After Dunn gave him the number, Ireland beat his victim with a belt, held a lighter-flame to his testicles, and then suffocated him by stuffing pieces of cloth into his mouth.

Nutting later told the court that Ireland stole from his victims 'to re-imburse himself for the costs of the last murder and re-equip himself for the next'. Ireland said, 'I made a point of disposing of any footwear I was wearing … I always disposed of the gloves I had worn. In the case of the shoes I would rip them apart and then buy another pair.' He was on the dole at the time, and thus unable to meet the expenses that the murders incurred. He stole £200 from Dunn's bank account although he was, he told police, 'tempted to steal more ... But I didn't in the end. I didn't want anything later on to be used as a pointer to me.' He tells me that 'One of my victims [Dunn] had a rare and valuable collection of Dinky toys. Let me say it took a great deal of will to leave them.'

After the murder, Ireland again went through the ritual of cleaning the crime scene and himself. He bagged the glass and plate he had used earlier, removed the cord from Dunn, and even threw away his torch batteries after wiping his prints off them. 'I had got that idea after watching *The Bill*,' Ireland told police; 'you know you ought to ban that programme ... it gave me lots of ideas.' He then stayed with the body until it was safe to leave. In his statement to the police he commented that sitting with the corpses:

affected me mentally to quite a degree. I think if I had just killed these people and gone I wouldn't have been affected so much. But sitting with these bodies like five or six hours on some occasions watching them gradually sort of blotch as they go cold. It wasn't something I think I could cope with quite honestly.

Dunn's body was discovered by a friend two days later, on 30 May. The connection to Peter Walker's murder was not immediately noted, however, as the officers who arrived at the scene were from a different station to those investigating the first murder. It was initially believed that Dunn had accidentally suffocated in a sex game, but when the police discovered that money had been taken from his bank account after his death, they thought that he might have been killed for financial gain. Again, they had neither forensic evidence nor witnesses.

The gaps between the murders began to close. On 4 June, just six days after he had killed Christopher Dunn, Ireland was again cruising for a victim at the Coleherne. This time it was to be thirty-five-year-old Perry Bradley III, son of a US congressman, himself a businessman from Texas and closet homosexual living in Kensington. Having met in the Coleherne, they returned together to Bradley's flat, where Ireland soon suggested that he tie his host up. Bradley didn't like the idea, however, as S&M didn't appeal to him. To gain his victim's compliance without suspicion, Ireland told him that without the S&M element he couldn't get aroused. Bradley was soon trussed up on the bed, face down, with a noose around his neck.

It was then that Ireland demanded his victim's money: 'I told him I was just a professional thief and I just wanted money from him.' He asked for Bradley's PIN number under threat of torture, telling him that he'd tortured another man with a cigarette lighter. Bradley, who was frightened and eager to co-operate, told him, 'I'm quite happy to give you anything you want to know' and even offered to accompany him to the cashpoint, which Ireland said 'wouldn't be allowed'. After Bradley gave Ireland his PIN number (which Ireland later used to steal £200, as well as taking £100 in cash from the flat), Ireland told him that he might as well go to sleep as he wouldn't be leaving for hours yet. Amazingly, Bradley did. 'I sat there,' Ireland told police, 'and at one point I was thinking of letting him go. Then I thought, "it's easier to kill him".' So, Ireland continued, 'I put a noose around his neck and tied it to something ... There was no way I could allow that man to wake up. That wasn't part of my plan anyway. My plan was to kill. While he was asleep I went round to his side of the bed.' When he pulled the noose, his victim 'hardly struggled'. Ireland placed a doll on top of Bradley's body.

Again, after the murder, Ireland carefully cleaned up. 'Anything I touched I put in a plastic carrier bag. In his flat there was a wine glass I had used and some food. I basically got rid of everything I had touched.' He spent the remainder of the night listening to the radio, and left in the morning. Once again, a different set of police investigated the murder, and the fact that it was part of a series went unnoted. No one remarked upon the similarities between the cases.

By this time Ireland was becoming frustrated: he had killed three times and the publicity he craved wasn't on the scale that he had anticipated. The police hadn't even realized a serial killer was operating. So it was just three days later, on 7 June, that Ireland struck again. His MO was firmly established by now. He met thirty-three-year-old Andrew Collier, a warden at a shel-tered housing complex, in the Coleherne, and they soon left together to go back to Collier's flat in Dalston. Like the others, Collier soon consented to being handcuffed and tied to his bed. Ireland later told police, 'By this time I was reaching the point where I was just accelerating. It was just speeding up, getting far worse, it wasn't making me angry, it was just like a roller coaster effect.' With Collier bound and helpless Ireland demanded his PIN number and cash-card. When he refused to surrender them Ireland strangled him with a noose.

After Collier's murder, Ireland began to look through his victim's effects, in an attempt to find his PIN number. Once again he was to discover that the man he had murdered was HIV-positive. Suddenly, Ireland felt as if the tables had been turned: 'That annoyed me. I was the killer and he had AIDS ... he didn't tell me about this, he didn't warn me – could have been me in five years ... I went fucking crazy.' Nutting told the court that to vent his fury, Ireland 'burnt various parts of the body and, as Mr Collier told him he was very fond of his cat, he decided to kill the cat as well.' He strangled the cat and then laid it across Collier's chest, placing the cat's mouth around Collier's penis – which he had encased in a condom – and the cat's tail – also in a condom – in Collier's mouth. He did it, he confessed, partly through anger, and partly to 'increase' the 'thrill of killing', and to leave Collier 'no dignity in death'. He told police:

> I wanted to know how you would react when you came across that scene. You're not thinking normally when you do something like this. But it was almost like a signature – to almost let you know I'd been there. I was reaching that point – you know where you feel you have to set up a stage each time.

The body of the dead cat reminds us of those other objects – the doll and the teddy bears – that were characteristic of Ireland's signature: deranged and defiled images of childhood loves, placed with unbearable poignancy on the death bed of the victim, symbolic suggestions of lost innocence. He left when the streets began to get busy, taking with him a mug he had used and £70 he had found in the flat.

At last two of the murders were linked: those of Andrew Collier and Peter Walker. The scenes were so similar, the strange signature with the condoms so distinctive, that detectives realized it had to be the work of the same man. Police from different areas of London immediately began to collate information on similar murders that had occurred in the area and to suspect that a serial killer was operating.

On 12 June Ireland called the Kensington police and told them that he had killed all four men, and that they had to stop him. He also called the Battersea police and asked them: 'Are you still interested in the death of Peter Walker? Why have you stopped the investigation? Doesn't the death of a homosexual

237

man mean anything? I will do another. I have always dreamed of doing the perfect murder.'

Ireland's fifth and final victim was forty-one-year-old Emanuel Spiteri (a 'leather type') who was a Maltese chef. Ireland remembers how he and Spiteri 'went from the Coleherne – via a couple of trains – to his flat' in Catford on 12 June. When they arrived at the flat, Ireland cuffed and bound Spiteri on his bed, putting a noose around his neck and demanding his PIN number. But by this time Ireland's desire to kill seemed to be wearing thin.

> Once at his flat I bound him, but he was becoming suspicious. The word had got around about the gay murders and he was getting a bit worried. By then it was too late. But he was a very brave man. He told me, 'Do whatever you are going to do.' I told him I wanted his PIN number. It wasn't my primary motivation to kill him. It was more finance, money really. But I couldn't allow him to stick around and recognize me so I killed him with a noose again. I put a noose around his neck and started to tighten it and I killed him.

Ireland had now killed four times in seventeen days. Again, he went through the ritual of eradicating forensic evidence, and once again waited until morning, watching television, until it was safe to leave. Before he left he added a final touch, attempting to set fire to the flat. Indeed, he thought of leaving the gas on, in the hope that the whole block might set alight, but decided against it. When asked later why he had set the fire, he told police, 'I once worked as a fireman – there is a bit of an arsonist in all firemen.' He added, 'I think there is something in me that's highly destructive, in some moods I would be quite happy to burn the world down.'

The next day, Ireland rang the police, telling them to look for a body at the scene of a fire in south London. He also told them: 'I have read a lot of books on serial killers. I think it is from four people that the FBI class as serial, so I may stop now I have done five. I just wanted to see if it could be done. I will probably never re-offend again.' This statement prompted numerous calls from the British press to (ex) FBI Agent Robert Ressler asking him whether his book *Whoever Fights Monsters* shouldn't be removed from the shops, as Ireland had obviously read it and it had caused him to murder. Ressler quite rightly answered that a person intent on committing a murder will seize upon any justification and encouragement for his actions.

While officers were searching for the body, on the early evening of 15 June a landlady in Catford rang the police to report that one of her lodgers was dead. It was Emanuel Spiteri, and there was evidence of a fire that had burned itself out in his room.

The publicity campaign now began in earnest. Late that same night a press conference was called, and Detective Superintendent Ken John reported that the murders of five homosexual men had now been linked as a series, both 'pathologically and forensically'. The murders of Walker and Collier had previously been identified as the work of the same man, but now Dunn, Bradley and Spiteri were being added to the series. Sitting next to a representative of the Gay London Policing Group, John appealed to the gay community to be wary, recommending that if they intended to go anywhere with a stranger they should tell a friend exactly where they were going. Detective Superintendent Albert Patrick added, 'I am extremely frightened that this man will strike again. There may well be other victims we don't yet know about, and heterosexuals may also be at risk.' He also surmised (wrongly) about the killer's motives that 'It is possible that the killer has AIDS and is taking revenge for his own HIV infection. I have a gut feeling that the men were lured for sex and then things went badly wrong.'

On 17 June, Ken John made an appeal directly to the killer, asking him to give himself up: 'Speak to me, I am willing to speak to you. I need to speak to you. This is something we can talk about. Enough is enough. Enough pain, enough anxiety, enough tragedy. Give yourself up – whatever terms, whatever you dictate, whatever the time, to me or my colleagues.' John told the press that a man had been in contact with the police, giving details of the killings, and they were very eager to talk to him. He said that the calls were factual; they were not, as many were speculating, 'baiting and mocking the police', but were more likely 'a cry for help'. John added that he wanted to protect the gay community in any way possible, and asked the media not to speculate about the killer's motives, as it might 'spark him off. The person may be disenchanted with the way he has been portrayed. That again can spark reaction.' Tread gently, he was pleading: 'We are dealing with a man who might need help. We are prepared to offer it to him. I need to talk to him.'

On 19 June, police were present at London's Gay Pride festival – which was attended by around 50,000 homosexuals – to distribute leaflets giving details of the murders of the five men, appealing for anyone with information to come forward, and warning gays to be careful in their casual encounters with strangers. The police said that the killer might well be present at the festival, in search of his next victim.

The police also sought the advice of psychologist Dr Mike Berry, whom they asked to draw up a psychological profile of the killer. Berry told police that the killer they were seeking was fuelled by violent fantasies. But with every murder there came only disappointment and frustration: it was not quite how he imagined it, he needed to keep refining his 'art'.

> The one thing about fantasy-driven offences is that the reality is never quite up to the fantasy. And therefore the serial killer has to do it again and again … This is a well organized serial killing and he takes great pleasure in it. I think that it is unlikely that this man is HIV positive and is taking revenge on homosexuals. This is not the underlying motive. This guy has been fantasizing about violence for a long time and has at last started.

Dr Jonas Rappeport agreed, suggesting that the killer might be pretending to be a homosexual in order to lull his victims into a false sense of security, but he was not a homosexual himself. The police, he said, should be 'looking for a large or physically very strong man. He is clearly confident in committing crimes, and I would suggest they should look for someone with other features of criminality in his personality.' Advice was also given by criminal psychologist Paul Britton, Michigan psychologist Dick Walter and Robert Ressler.

On 24 June, the police issued a description of a man seen with Emanuel Spiteri on the train from Charing Cross to Hither Green. The suspect was a white male aged thirty to forty, over six feet tall, clean shaven, with a full to fattish face, short dark brown hair, and dirty and discoloured teeth. An E-Fit (Electronic Facial Identification Technique), or Videofit, was subsequently issued. (E-Fits have replaced the old technique of photofits such as those used in the Yorkshire Ripper case. An E-Fit is a computer-generated likeness based on verbal descriptions, with many more features to choose from than the 800 possibilities available in the old photofits.)

Assuming that Spiteri and his killer had taken the train from Charing Cross, which is where they were sighted, the police were eager to view the film from the station security cameras for that night. On 2 July, the police released the picture they had found: it was of Spiteri and another man at Charing Cross Station, a man very similar to the one in the E-Fit. An appeal was made for the man to come forward to be eliminated from inquiries. John announced: 'Somebody in the community will know this man. My appeal to that person or these persons is: "Who is the man and where is the man?" I just need to identify him and talk to him.' To the killer he said, 'The lines of communication are not down, but very much open.' By the next day the police had received forty calls, some of them claiming that they had seen or talked to the man in the Coleherne.

On 19 July Colin Ireland walked into his solicitor's office in Southend-on-Sea, and told him that he had been with Spiteri that night. It was him in the picture, he said, but he was not the killer – he had left Spiteri in his flat with another man. As Robert Ressler says, 'That attestation might have worked, except that Ireland's fingerprints matched the one that had been left on the window ledge in the apartment of the fourth victim.' As careful as he had tried to be, Ireland had made this one mistake. Shortly after he and Andrew Collier had returned to Collier's flat, they had heard a noise outside and gone to look out of the window. When Ireland was clearing up after himself later he forgot that he had touched the window ledge. He was charged with Collier's murder on 21 July, and with Spiteri's two days later.

While on remand in prison, Ireland continued to maintain his innocence until 19 August, when he finally decided to confess to all five murders. He told prison officials, 'I am the gay serial killer. Tell the police I want to confess.' And so he did, and he was charged with the murders of Dunn, Bradley and Walker. A police officer later said, 'He wasn't off-hand but gave calculated descriptions in a very low-key manner. He showed no emotion.' Before he gave the details of the murders to the police he told them:

> I feel that there is a side to my personality that can only be controlled by my being restricted to a prison regime. I think long-term prison establishments are humane and they take good care of you. I feel I'm okay within this restricted environment. But I feel there are certain sides to my character – especially within the group that I was targeting – that means I may offend again. I want to remove that possibility. I feel there is a certain side of my character – not all of it by any means – but I'm probably sixty to seventy per cent quite a reasonable human being most of the time. However, there is a side of my character that is quite cold and calculating. I feel that because of the confession I am about to make that I face an extensive prison sentence and that will restrict me. That will stop me harming other people. When my case comes to trial any judge worth his salt is going to find me guilty and he will imprison me and by doing so allow me not to offend again for some time. That's all I really wanted to say.

He went on to emphasize four points in particular: (1) he had not been under the influence of drink or drugs when committing the murders; (2) although he had worked as a bouncer at a gay club in Soho, he was not gay or bisexual himself; (3) he had not undressed himself, engaged in any sexual activity with the men, nor got any sexual thrill out of the murders; (4) he had no grudge against gays particularly, they were picked because they were easy targets.

Ireland had both given a full confession and (unlike Christie, Sutcliffe and Nilsen who also did so) pleaded guilty to all charges. On 20 December, at the Old Bailey, the Number One Court was told by the prosecutor, John Nutting, of Ireland's 'exceedingly thorough', 'premeditated and meticulously planned' murders. 'Indeed,' said Nutting, 'it would seem this defendant set out to be a serial killer. He told others that in order to be classified, he knew he would have to commit at least four murders.' He targeted homosexuals because they were 'a vulnerable group' who would readily put themselves in compromising positions.

Ireland's barrister, Andrew Trollope QC, told the court that he could offer no mitigation for 'this series of truly dreadful crimes': two psychiatrists pronounced Ireland completely sane, and Ireland himself was under no delusion that he would ever be released from prison. Trollope emphasized to the court that Ireland had a good side – he worked with the homeless, and with children, and had looked after his disabled ex-wife – and offered as a reason for the crimes that: 'He was unable to stop himself killing – he was under a form of compulsion. He was not in control.'

Mr Justice Sachs told Ireland:

> By any standards you are an exceptionally frightening and dangerous man. In cold blood and with great deliberation you have killed five of your fellow human beings. You killed them in grotesque and cruel fashion. The fear, brutality and indignity to which you subjected your victims are almost unspeakable. To take one human life is an outrage, to take five is carnage. You expressed the desire to be regarded as a serial killer. That must be matched by your detention for life.

A friend of his later remarked that Ireland was approaching the age of forty and felt he had achieved nothing in his life. He wanted to be somebody, to be famous. In addition to these feelings of

243

inadequacy and the desire for recognition, he had also been harbouring a pool of deep hatred inside himself. What Ireland calls 'extreme male deviants', had disgusted him ever since his childhood brushes with paedophiles. After his experiences at 'Playland', his hatred had grown so intense that he resolved that at some point in his life he would kill such a man.

As an adult Ireland realized that paedophiles who target boys, are not necessarily homosexual. Therefore, gay men *per se* did not disgust him. He says that, 'My anger is not triggered by the behaviour of the conventional gay man, it's triggered by male deviancy. I do not regard the two as the same. The men I preyed on were deviants who happened to be gay.' The common 'deviant' factor that his victims shared was their interest in sado-masochism. Although Ireland is unable to articulate exactly why such behaviour is abhorrent to him, it is likely that he identified the sado-masochist's desire to give and to receive pain (within a relationship where one partner is dominant and the other submissive), with the pattern of behaviour with which he had come into contact as a child. In his mind the homosexual man who indulged in S&M became akin to the paedophile who has a similar 'relationship' with his victim: both are partnerships of power and acquiescence.

Another factor that added fuel to his hatred was his discovery that some of these men used 'rent boys, some of whom were very young. One way or another they would arrive on the "scene", some gay, some not, and within a short time be rendered a physical and mental mess. Two of my victims were known to have used rent boys.' Ireland was aware that the sexual activity between a 'rent boy' and his client is consensual – as it is in an S&M relationship – what he was responding to was the destruction of innocence, a theme which is evident in his crimes in the strategic placing of the teddy bears, the doll, and the cat.

If Colin Ireland is a lust-murderer, like the other murderers in this study, then we are talking about a different sort of lust. In all of our other cases, the men who have killed have done so for sexual pleasure. The victim, dead or alive, has been the killer's sexual partner, and the violence used was necessary to provoke sexual satisfaction. If Colin Ireland is to be believed – and there is no direct evidence to the contrary – the act of murder was not sexually motivated for him, and was unaccompanied by sexual excitement. Though it is clear that Ireland was targeting victims on the basis of sexual criteria – homosexuals with sado-masochistic tastes – this does not necessarily imply that the victims were also objects of desire. Indeed, according to Ireland, the reverse was true: they were objects of disgust. He regarded himself as ridding the world of vermin. He saw himself, in this perverse crusading sense, as cleansing society from sources of contagion. As his step-father said after his son's trial:

> Colin wanted to rid the world of those sick perverts. He was sickened by what they get up to behind closed doors and decided that it was his mission to wipe them out. He did what he did and makes no apologies for it. It is the sado-masochists, the really sick ones, he cannot stand.

There is a line of thought, beloved of Freudians and other students of the unconscious, that believes that a hatred as intense as Ireland's (given that he was never actually abused) is so irrational, that it is, in itself, a symptom in need of interpretation. The answer sometimes suggested is that the hatred is so intense because it involves a strategy of denial: I hate these people, therefore I am not like them. Might it not be that Ireland felt in himself impulses similar to theirs and that he was so deeply ashamed of them that he could not admit them even to himself? Thus they would lie in a state of profound repression, consciously denied, but posssessing a dark power that was always likely to be dangerous. Could it be that Ireland had to kill in order to confirm and to reconfirm to himself that he was not a homosexual? What he was killing, therefore, was symbolically a part and a version of himself, but so repressed as to be invisible to him. Thus the rage one feels against one's own dirtiness is turned against others rather than oneself.

It is a coherent line of thought, and one to which Robert Ressler subscribes: 'I thought it likely that, despite his denials, Ireland was a homosexual or bisexual ... and that he had committed his crimes after having fantasized about similar ones

245

for many years.' His sexual history shows the kind of anger and hostility towards his partners that suggests that he was, at the least, ambivalent about women as objects of desire. Furthermore, in his account of his first experience with a paedophile as a child, he talks of 'bottling out'; of the second such experience he says that, 'it's difficult for me to come to terms with, but I may have considered his offer'. It is possible, therefore, that Ireland never did 'come to terms with' the desire that such approaches had elicited. He denied it, and projected his anger at himself for feeling it onto the figures of those who had tried to abuse him, and later onto all types of male deviant.

Yet it is hard to know how to verify such a claim, as Ireland reports that he has neither homosexual experience nor fantasies. And a hatred of homosexuals is not uncommon in working class culture, and is easy enough to observe in pubs and factories, where gays are often subjects of discrimination and the objects of distaste. Just as feminism has produced a backlash of resistance to the gradual emancipation of women, so too the gay rights movement has concentrated the intensity of anti-homosexual feeling. And it is nonsense to suppose that every man who intensely dislikes gays is unconsciously homosexual, just as it would be irrational to suppose that those who hate Jews are latently Jewish.

As a young adult, Ireland was an avid reader of Nazi and fascist literature and propaganda which would have given him an exposure to this culture of hatred, and to the easy line of thought that distinguishes between a master race and an under-class of degenerates (homosexuals, Jews, blacks, gypsies and so on) who need to be cleansed in order to purify the master strain. To be a killer is thus to be an eradicator, a purifier, a preserver of what is good and worthwhile. For a poor, disenfranchised man, without self-esteem but full of fantasy, the conclusion is easy and inviting – one can find identity, and power, by identifying with this presumed master class.

It isn't a very big step from this kind of sad rationalization to produce the figure of the serial killer as hero. One of the features that distinguishes all serial killers is the aura of grandiosity that they generate and project: only they understand how important they are, while their detractors are fools or weaklings.

The lust-murderer needs to kill because it gives him sexual pleasure and power, so he becomes a killer until he is caught. He does not want to be caught, because he is, fundamentally, enjoying himself, pursuing satisfaction at the unacceptable boundaries of the pleasure principle. Colin Ireland, as we have seen, does not quite fit this picture. With him, the pattern is reversed: he kills because he wants to be identified as a serial killer: the murders are the product of desire, not for sexual satisfaction, but for recognition as a superior kind of person. He kills because it will make him noticed, and the murders are sources of regret to him in a way that they are not for, say, Robert Black.

So, after committing enough murders to 'qualify' as a serial killer, Colin Ireland really wished to be caught. He had done enough to acquire that perverse shadow celebrity for which he had yearned. In an era where the figure of the serial killer is so discussed, and such a source of fascination, we are left with a sense that Ireland is a product of that process: he is not so much a serial killer, as a lethal parody of one. As Dostoyevsky said a century ago, the typical crime of the future would not be the common criminal killing for gain of a material nature, but to *stake a claim to an identity*. Colin Ireland's name would finally be known, however darkly. He was somebody, after all.

9

FRED AND ROSE WEST

For generations the West family had laboured on the land of the Hereford countryside. Walter West had been raised in the village of Much Marcle, near Ross-on-Wye, a village so small and insular that, even today, a visit from 'outsiders' provokes curious, frequently hostile, stares. It was here that Walter started and raised his family with his second wife, Daisy. Daisy West, née Hill, was only seventeen and almost certainly pregnant when she married Walter in 1940, although they insisted that their first baby, Violet – who died the day after her birth – was simply born some weeks premature. Undeterred, Daisy fell pregnant again shortly after Violet's death, and on 29 September 1941, she gave birth to her first son, her golden boy, Frederick Walter Stephen West.

Shortly after the birth of Frederick – known as Fred or Freddie – Walter and Daisy rented Moorcourt Cottage which was to become their family home, where they would raise the six children who arrived in the next ten years. Life was hard. Moorcourt Cottage was attached to Moorcourt Farm where Walter, and indeed the whole family, worked. Everybody was expected to pitch in and help, whether it was with the dishes in the kitchen, the milking, lambing, or apple-picking. The cottage allowed little privacy, with three bedrooms for eight people: Walter and Daisy in one, the girls – little Daisy, Kathleen and Gwendoline – in the second, and the boys – Fred, Douglas and John – in the third. To say the facilities were basic is a kindly euphemism. A bucket, which was emptied at the bottom of the garden, served as a toilet; they were plagued by rats. Money was so tight that the children's packed-lunch (it was later said) consisted of a raw parsnip or turnip. Dinner was not infrequently an animal that had been running around just hours before. Like most children brought up on farms, the young Wests soon became accustomed to their food being killed in front of their eyes.

Daisy, who had been a carefree girl when she married, quickly lost her youth. She always seemed to be pregnant, had small children to look after, and a husband with a growing tendency towards aggression and an insatiable sexual appetite. To compensate, Daisy herself became controlling, uncompromising, and increasingly violent. She was a formidable figure, a large woman who wore a thick leather belt around her waist – as Walter did – and wouldn't hesitate to use it on her children. Fred remembered years later that 'Whatever mother said went. You didn't answer mother back or she grabbed you and wapped you a bit quick ... She was very dominant, like, and you didn't get a chance to get a word in. She would tell you and that was the story, like.'

Despite her fierce temper, however, she adored Fred. He was her first child, and had survived where Violet had perished. The other children remember how Daisy was always on Fred's side in an argument, and how she used to go to his school to confront his teachers when he had been disciplined for bad behaviour. Although it was never confirmed by Fred or Daisy, it was generally accepted within the family that when Fred reached puberty, at around the age of twelve, Daisy decided to teach her son about sex. It is alleged that she and Fred remained lovers throughout his teens. Walter apparently encouraged Fred's 'education', and used to give his son fatherly advice, telling him, for instance, that it was perfectly acceptable to have sex with young girls. Everybody did it, he said, but it wasn't something that people talked about, and Fred should ensure that he never got caught.

As a child, Fred was at his happiest in the company of his family, where there was undoubtedly a lot of closeness. Daisy adored Fred, and Fred adored Walter who was his hero and mentor. He later said, 'My father was a fantastic man', 'the most understanding man you'd ever meet'. But the family were inordinately, unhealthily, close. Like many Much Marcle families, the Wests were a closed unit who defended each other against outsiders unquestioningly. What went on behind closed doors was the family's business and theirs alone.

At Much Marcle school, Fred was always scruffy and badly behaved, and was often given the slipper or caned. He did not make friends with the other children in his class, who used to laugh at him behind his back because he smelt of manure. They didn't dare do it openly as Daisy and John were aggressively protective of Fred, who never stood up for himself. His brother Doug remembers that 'He wasn't a fighter and whenever there was a dust-up he would stand there and take it. If John didn't arrive in time, he would go running home crying. If he did, John did the fighting for him.'

School was a waste of time, for Fred hadn't the slightest interest in anything academic. His daughter Mae later wrote, 'Dad left school by the time he was fourteen, but he hardly ever went anyway. He wasn't educated and could hardly even write.' Fred was remembered as a stupid boy at school, 'as thick as two short planks', as he himself put it. Walter and Daisy didn't care, for they didn't see the point of reading, writing and spelling and so in 1956 Fred left school to work on the land as his father, and his father before him, had done.

Aside from farming, Fred's principle interest was sex. The sexual abuse by his mother, and his father's prurient advice, had not inhibited his sexual growth, but ignited his lust. Like many children prematurely initiated into sexual activity, his fascination with sex became obsessional and incapable of real satisfaction. From the age of twelve, Fred was driven by his sexual needs, and he was constantly seeking out new partners with whom to experiment. His approach was direct and crude: if he liked the look of a girl he would tell her so and suggest that they go off to one of the fields; sometimes he would not even bother with words, and simply grab the girl, waiting to see if there was any resistance. Even if there was, this would not necessarily deter him. Leo Goatley, Rose West's solicitor, later said that Fred and his brother John would often go out 'wenching' together and they both 'shared a dirty attitude to sex ... There is this rural colloquialism of calling women "it" as in "I wouldn't mind giving it one". Fred and John had a similar attitude; the idea that women said no, they meant yes.'

It was later to emerge that as an adolescent, Fred West had

raped several women. His sex drive was never satisfied, because it was not like an appetite (which peaks, ceases with satisfaction, and slowly peaks again) but an obsession and fixation – a mental state incapable of gratification, demanding constant enactment, and unlike normal sexual behaviour, needing an expanding range of fantasy material in order to produce excitement. He didn't like to experiment, he *needed* to.

The year after Fred finished school, he left home for the first time. Without telling his family, he decamped to Hereford, where he got work on a building site. He hadn't left Much Marcle for good, he just wanted to earn enough money to buy the motorbike that he had dreamt of for so long. After a month working away from home, Fred returned to Moorcourt Cottage, and Daisy allowed him to buy the bike on the strict condition that if he had an accident he would sell it immediately. The accident that his mother had been fearing happened in November 1958, when Fred collided with a local girl who was riding her bicycle. The girl was not seriously hurt, but Fred remained unconscious for a week at Hereford Hospital. He sustained a fractured arm and broken nose, and his leg was so badly broken that he had to wear a metal brace for months after the accident. All his life he would walk with a (barely perceptible) limp.

Although the accident was certainly nasty, it was to take on increasingly fantastical proportions whenever Fred recounted the story. Fred's son Stephen later wrote that his father 'lay unconscious in a gully for eight hours until a passer-by spotted him ... He was taken to hospital where his heart stopped beating and a doctor pronounced him dead. To everyone's amazement, Dad came round on the mortuary slab and was resuscitated.' Fred said that the surgeons had to rebuild half of his face from plastic. Some of his family believe that the accident significantly altered Fred's personality, and that afterwards he was moody, taciturn, and bad-tempered. Fred himself denied that any changes took place.

When he had recuperated, Fred moved to Gloucester, nearly twenty miles away, where he did a bread round and worked on the ships for just over a year. In 1961 he returned to Much Marcle where, in April, he had his first criminal conviction, for the theft of a watch strap and two cigarette cases. The first serious charge against him came just two months later, when his thirteen-year-old sister fell pregnant. Fred didn't even bother to deny that he was the father. Yes, he had had sex with his sister, and with other young girls too: 'Doesn't everybody do it?' he asked the police. Certainly he had been brought up to think so, but Walter's tales of the pleasures of incest and sex with under-age girls had been accompanied by the strict warning not to be found out. It was a lesson that Fred would carry with him into later life. For now, he had been caught, and exposed the family's secrets. Daisy decided that he had to go.

And so, in disgrace, he was sent to his Aunt Violet's house. When his trial came up in November, however, Fred walked away without a criminal record as a sex offender. When his sister was put in the witness box, she steadfastly refused to divulge who had made her pregnant. Even at the age of thirteen, the concept of family loyalty was deeply imbedded in her, and without her evidence the case was thrown out of court. Yet Fred was not one to learn from his mistakes: over thirty years later, a woman came forward to say that on the very night that Fred had been acquitted, he had taken her out for the evening and raped her on the way home.

By the next summer Fred's family had forgiven him, and he was welcomed home to Moorcourt Cottage. In the autumn of 1962, Fred met Catherine Costello, or Rena as she was popularly known, who had recently come down to Hereford from her home in Glasgow to visit a friend. She had been in and out of approved schools all her life, and had been involved in gangs, drugs, and prostitution back in Glasgow. Fred took an instant liking to her: she wasn't like the Much Marcle girls, she was tough, exciting, and didn't care what people thought of her. More sexually experienced than Fred, she was initially more than happy to indulge his expanding sexual appetite, even teaching him a thing or two he didn't already know.

Rena undoubtedly liked Fred, but she also had a hidden agenda. She had, she confessed, left Glasgow pregnant by an Asian bus-driver. Fred took the news well, telling Rena that if she didn't want the baby he could perform an abortion for her.

The 'operation' was unsuccessful, however, so Fred proposed that they should get married and raise the baby as their own. It all happened very quickly, and in November 1962 the couple were married at Ledbury Register Office. Apart from John, their families did not attend. Walter and Daisy had both refused their invitations, as they knew that Rena was pregnant, and were convinced that she was using their son.

In view of the hostilities from the West family, Fred and Rena moved to Glasgow, where, over the next three years, the marriage steadily deteriorated. Fred was increasingly infuriated by Rena's anarchic spirit, which ironically was what had first attracted him to her. Although she was pregnant, he had started to beat her, and she didn't hesitate to hit him back, and had taken to carrying weapons. 'You didn't mess with Rena. Nobody did,' Fred later said, in a comment reminiscent of his description of his mother, Daisy. Both Fred and Rena continued to take other lovers, and Rena began working as a prostitute. Yet despite the violence and the infidelity, a strong bond and a baffling respect remained between them.

When Charmaine was born in March 1963, Fred was too busy in bed with another woman to go to the hospital. He took an instant dislike to his new step-daughter. Every time he looked at the girl, her half-caste appearance reminded him that she was not his; he wanted a baby of their own, and although Rena didn't, she became pregnant again shortly after Charmaine's birth. When she went into labour in July 1964, Fred was (again) in their bed with a lover. Unperturbed, Rena walked in and announced that they had better move, as she was about to give birth. Fred delivered his daughter into the world himself, and they named her Anna-Marie, though she was later to rename herself Anne Marie. Fred was entranced by his first natural daughter, and while he would not hesitate to beat Rena or Charmaine, he would never raise his hand to Anne Marie. She later wrote of her father that, 'As a small child I worshipped him – he was everything to me. In the early days he was never cruel or violent ... We were a team, me and Dad. I was his little girl and he was my handsome dad.'

In 1965, Fred and Rena decided to return to Much Marcle,

where they bought the first of several caravans they were to own. The mobile-home would have been cramped even with just the four of them in it, but Rena had also brought two friends with her from Glasgow: Isa McNeill and Anne McFall. Fred and Rena's marriage was now becoming increasingly unstable as Fred's moods seemed to vacillate constantly, and he was beating Rena on the slightest pretext. Underneath the violent exterior, however, was cowardice, as Fred would always shy away from physical confrontations with other men, just as he had as a boy. Rena's Scottish lover, John MacLachlan, remembers that Fred 'couldn't tackle a man, but he was not so slow in attacking women'. The sex that Fred and Rena had together had always been brutal, and now Fred was developing a new taste for bondage, which gave him control as he had never known it. It seems an inevitable extension of fantasy into reality, and suggested an escalation of his sexual obsessions, which were unrestrained by the normal curbs of self-restraint, shame, or feeling for others.

It is no wonder that Rena was growing weary of his demands, and she soon rang her lover to ask him to rescue her. While Fred was indifferent to Rena's leaving, he refused to let her take their children, and Anne McFall offered to stay as their 'nanny'. In fact, the seventeen-year-old girl was already Fred's lover. He later wrote that 'Anne was not hard; she was gentle, kind and pleasant. She was my angel' whereas 'Rena could be the devil when she wanted to be'. Of course it was this toughness that had first attracted him, and therein lay the dilemma. Although Fred claimed to love Anne, he could not get Rena out of his system, and when she returned in the summer of 1966 he promptly took her back, and Anne was forced to find somewhere else to stay. They kept seeing each other, however, and in November 1966 she became pregnant.

The next eight months were spent in a state of constant flux. When Rena and Fred's fights became too frequent and violent, Rena would go back to Scotland, and Anne would move back into the caravan. When Rena returned, as she inevitably did, Anne would have to leave again. Sometimes, when Rena's absences were too lengthy, the children would be taken into care, to be returned when their mother came home. When Anne was eight months pregnant the situation finally became intolerable to her, and she decided to return to Glasgow to give birth. In early August Anne told Fred that she was leaving. It was soon after this that she disappeared.

Anne McFall's remains were not found for almost thirty years, buried in Fingerpost Field on the edge of Much Marcle. Her naked body had been carefully dismembered, and numerous bones, including fingers, toes and kneecaps, were missing. There was binding on her hands and arms. Anne's unborn baby had been removed, and buried alongside her body.

Fred claimed that Anne had returned to Glasgow. It is unclear whether he told Rena of the murder, but Fred did tell Walter, who told Daisy. Although they were shocked, their strong sense of family loyalty held: the secret was safe with them. Rena and Fred continued their stormy relationship, and Fred returned to his old pattern of constantly seeking new sexual partners.

Rose Letts was ideal. Born on 29 November 1953, she was disadvantaged from the start, conceived and raised by mentally unstable parents. Her father, Bill, was a schizophrenic who suffered from severe mood swings, paranoid delusions, and outbursts characterized by sudden and unpredictable violence. Her mother, Daisy, had suffered a severe nervous breakdown as a consequence of her husband's behaviour, following a bout of post-natal depression after the birth of her fourth child. At the time of Rose's conception she was an out-patient in a psychiatric hospital where she was receiving ECT treatment.

Even as a baby there was clearly something not quite right about Rose. She would move her little body repetitively – nodding, rocking – silently for hours, as if the movement were calming to her. When she wasn't rocking she would simply sit and stare at the walls, as if she were in a state of semi-consciousness. Her siblings lost no time in cruelly, if aptly, dubbing her 'Dozy Rosie'. When she was old enough to go to the village school she was unable to pick up even the most rudimentary concepts in her lessons. She was no better socially, unable to form friendships with the children of her own age, who were mentally more advanced than she. At home she liked to play with her younger siblings, whom she would 'look after', almost as if she were their mother. All her life she was to adore babies, because of their helplessness. But her own daughters remember that as soon as the babies became toddlers, with some will of their own, she lost interest in them.

Rose was the fifth child of Bill and Daisy's unhappy union. When the first three children – Glenys, Patricia, and Joyce – were born, Bill was away serving in the Navy. Returning to civilian life in the early 1950s, he was frustrated to find that he couldn't get any work, which further unbalanced his delicate mental state, and he began to take his anger out on his wife. Their neighbours in the village of Northam in Devon remember that Daisy sometimes had black eyes, although Bill was usually careful to confine his beatings to parts of her body that were not on public display. The beatings were frequent, unwarranted and unpredictable. Bill insisted that their house be sparkling clean at all times. If there was anything out of place Daisy would be punished. If the house was clean he would think nothing of emptying the dustbins over the kitchen floor to generate more work for his wife.

The children were also treated like slaves in the house, and were not allowed to play with their friends after school. When they disobeyed their father, they were beaten. Daisy remembers that 'the regime at home was terrifying'; 'we lived under terror for years', it was like 'hell behind closed doors'. Bill took immense delight in depriving his family of their few pleasures. If they were watching a television programme he would turn it off, yet he often forced them to sit silently while he watched sport on television. He was known to turn off the electricity when the mood took him; sometimes he would lock the children out if they were late coming home, making them sleep in the garden.

The only child not to feel the full force of Bill's violent temper was Rose, which was surprising as he could easily have been infuriated by his daughter's ineptness. In fact he found her funny ways endearing, and compared to the rest of them, Rosie could get away with anything. Rosie was daddy's best little girl.

In 1960, shortly after the birth of their seventh child, Graham,

Bill and Daisy decided to move to Plymouth, a decision precipitated by the local gossip that Bill had an unhealthy interest in young girls (a rumour which was never confirmed). Within two years they were again on the move, this time to Stratford-upon-Avon, and shortly after to Bishop's Cleeve, where they settled. Under the strain which a new, and demanding, job provoked, Bill's violence towards his family was escalating dangerously. As well as beating them with his fists, he had also begun threatening them with a variety of deadly weapons. Although he still did not beat Rose, his violence had nonetheless begun to influence her behaviour, as she began to ape her father's manner of dealing with anger and conflict. Rose had always been the quiet one at school, but as she grew older an aggressive streak began to appear, and she was no longer ignored, but feared, by the other children. If her brothers were ever in trouble she would not hesitate to come to their aid with physical violence.

Around this time, Rose found herself experiencing another new sensation. Like Fred, her sexuality was awakened precociously. Whether this was initiated by her father we cannot say for sure, but Fred later alleged that Rose and Bill had had a sexual relationship which began when Rose was a girl and lasted until Bill's death. Fred and Rose's daughter, Mae, later wrote 'I think that there was some abuse in the family but mum won't ever really talk about it, all she says is that her dad hurt her once.' Whatever the reason, Rose was fascinated by sex. As the boys were frightened of her at school, she began to play sexually with her brothers, and started to masturbate Graham as they lay in bed at night, an activity that continued for some years.

By 1969 Daisy had had enough. Taking fifteen-year-old Rose and the younger children with her, she moved in with her first daughter, Glenys, and her husband, Jim. Rose left school that year, and was given a job by Jim working in his mobile snack-bar. He remembers her constantly flirting with the customers, and on several occasions he caught her emerging from a lorry-driver's cab looking flushed and ruffled. In her spare time, she would often wander around the village, flirting with any men she encountered, for like Fred, her major preoccupation was to seek new sexual encounters. She later said that she had lost her virginity at the age of fourteen, and further claimed that a year after this she had been raped by a stranger.

Later that same year, Rose suddenly decided to move back in with her father. The move seemed inexplicable to her family at the time but, with hindsight, it made sense. She was, after all, the only child her father had favoured, and it is not unlikely that, if they did have a sexual relationship, it was one that Rose both enjoyed and encouraged.

At the time of their first meeting, Fred West and Rose Letts (unlike Ian Brady and Myra Hindley) were already strikingly similar people. Their childhoods had been characterized by sex and violence, associated with patterns of dominance and submission. Relationships, they had learned, were rarely equal: there was usually a taker and a giver, a bully and a victim. Both had been introduced to sex early: Fred was almost certainly sexually abused by his mother, Rose by her father. Both were fascinated with sex, and both shared a craving for more sexual experience and held the dangerous assumption that if you want sex you simply take it. Sex was ultimately about power and satisfaction, which were gained in, and through, preying upon a weaker party. Having both been abused as children – and having learned, as abused children often do, that the way to endure the pain is to convert it into a form of pleasure – in their adult incarnations they became the hunters rather than the hunted. They preyed on whoever was available and weaker than themselves, including children and emotionally or physically vulnerable young women.

They met on a bus in the late summer of 1969. Fred was on his way back from the hospital, where he'd been treated for a minor accident at work; Rose was returning home from working at the bakery. When he saw Rose, who was not quite sixteen, Fred, typically, thought he'd chance his luck, and they were soon seeing one another regularly. Rena was away at the time, so Fred soon invited Rose to the caravan and introduced her to Charmaine and Anne Marie. When Rena returned she was unconcerned to find yet another young girl with her husband, and she continued to live at the caravan when it suited her. Fred employed Rose as a nanny for the children, and they became lovers.

Bill and Daisy, who were now reunited, weren't happy about the relationship. Fred was, after all, twelve years older than their daughter (who was still below the age of consent) and more importantly, he was a married man. They banned Rose from seeing Fred, but she wilfully continued, and by the end of 1969 she was pregnant. Bill issued an ultimatum: she could either live at home, have an abortion and never see Fred again, or she could go and live with Fred and have his baby. If she chose the latter, the family would disown her. In fact, if he ever saw them together on the street, Bill said, he would 'stab' them. Rose went to live with Fred.

A couple of months later, when Rena was once again in Scotland, Fred and Rose moved to Gloucester with the two girls, where they rented a modest bedsitter, first at 10 Midland Road and then at number 25, a short walk from the centre of town. During Rose's pregnancy, while Fred worked on a milk-round, she started work as a prostitute, just as Rena had done. Rose was only sixteen, but she was eager to give Fred everything that his wife could, and more. Besides, it excited her. Rose's sexual appetite was still blossoming and the couple would both enjoy the occasions when Fred watched her having sex with other men. Fred later said that Rose 'didn't want foreplay, she wanted rough sex', and as his own sexual tastes were becoming increasingly violent, they were perfectly compatible.

Rose quickly usurped Rena's role, and Fred even told his daughters to call her 'mum', although Rena continued to visit them. Soon, however, just as Daisy West had done, Rose ran into problems. She was only a girl herself, she was pregnant, and had two small children to look after. Already possessing a marked tendency towards aggression, Rose quickly found that violent punishment was the most effective way to keep the children under control. Old enough to resent Rose for replacing Rena, Charmaine was a constant annoyance to her. As a woman, Anne Marie remembers how her half-sister was always 'voicing her obsession that her real mum would be coming back to claim her any day' and how she 'would go out of her way to antagonize and aggravate our volatile step-mother'.

When Charmaine was particularly outspoken, Fred – who

rarely punished the girls himself – encouraged Rose to chastize her with a wooden spoon or a belt. Anne Marie remembers that, 'Our new step-mother didn't try to hide the beatings from Dad. It was rare for him to lose his temper with us or hit us himself, but he never, ever objected to Rose doing so. In later years his only comment would be: "Make sure you hit them where it doesn't show".' Fred thrived on the conflict, playing the girls off against Rose, and Rose against Rena.

In October 1970 Rose gave birth to their first child, whom they named Heather. When the baby was not yet two months old, Fred was found guilty of theft, and sent to Leyhill Open Prison where he served seven months. In Fred's absence, the violence in the house escalated. With the exception of baby Heather, Rose subjected the children to increasingly violent, unpredictable and unprovoked beatings. Both Charmaine and Anne Marie were treated at Casualty for 'domestic accidents' during this time: Charmaine for a 'puncture wound' which almost certainly came from a knife; Anne Marie for a head wound which had been inflicted by Rose when she smashed a plate over the girl's head. One of Charmaine's friends at the time (a girl called Tracy who lived upstairs), later remembered how she had walked in unannounced one day to find Charmaine with her hands tied behind her back with a leather belt. Rose was standing beside her, preparing to beat her with a wooden spoon.

Unlike Anne Marie, Charmaine refused to be silenced or reduced to tears by Rose, something which only incensed her step-mother. Rose wrote to Fred at Leyhill telling him, 'I would keep her for her own sake, if it wasn't for the other children. You can see Char coming out in Anna now. And I hate it.' In future letters and visits they talked of sending Charmaine away, and Rose wrote, 'Let me know about Char, yes or no. I say yes, but it is up to you darling.' Fred wrote back agreeing that she should go. Rose West's defence would later allege that when the couple spoke of Charmaine going away they meant that she should live with Rena. The Crown would suggest that they were discussing a more final departure for the girl.

Fred was released in June 1971. Some time that summer both

Charmaine and Rena were murdered. Charmaine's remains were found in May 1994, in a hole under the kitchen of 25 Midland Road. Her naked body had been cut in half, and once again a number of bones were missing. Rena's dismembered remains were found in Letterbox Field, next to Fingerpost Field where Anne McFall had been buried. Again, there were bones unaccounted for, and there was also a length of metal tubing buried with her.

Fred and Rose told anybody who asked, including Anne Marie, that Charmaine had gone to live with her real mother, Rena, in Scotland, 'and bloody good riddance' said Rose. Rena, who was always on the move anyway, was never reported missing. Now, Fred and Rose decided, they could get married. On the marriage certificate Fred described himself as a bachelor.

It was not long before Rose was pregnant again, and three months after Mae was born the Wests moved to 25 Cromwell Street, in September 1972. Cromwell Street was, indeed is, a slightly run-down road, the houses often spilt into bed-sits, builders' vans and skips littering the street. Number 25 stood at the end of the row next to a church. (Today there is no Number 25. It has been pulled down. Instead there is a walk-way, unremarkable in itself, but chilling to contemplate when one knows what once lay underneath.)

As the house was too big for them alone, the Wests began to advertise for lodgers almost immediately, and soon there were up to six young people renting rooms. The arrangements were casual: if somebody needed a room and there was space, they could move in, without references, and for a minimal amount of rent. Number 25 was considered something of an open-house locally, and one visitor recalled that it was 'well known as a place where drifters and drop-outs and teenagers who had been kicked out of home could look for bed-sits'. On the surface the atmosphere was relaxed, friendly, and liberal: many of the lodgers took drugs, and Fred and Rose were known for their sexual permissiveness. Permissiveness is actually something of a misnomer. If the Wests seemed to permit sex, it was only when they ultimately controlled it. Rose may have been a prostitute, but unlike most prostitutes, she was doing it for her own excitement. The house was the setting for the Wests' sexual pleasures, and its other inhabitants were to become mere functions of their desires, to be played with, used, and on too many occasions, disposed of.

Fred would often tell his children that people should have sex several times a day, and ex-lodger Elizabeth Brewer remembered that 'Rosemary said when she retired [from being a prostitute] she was going to spend all her time having sex.' Rose would frequently walk around the house naked or with no underwear, sitting with her legs splayed in front of her children and their friends. When the children complained that she was embarrassing them she would snap, 'If they don't like what they see, they shouldn't be looking.' Fred would think nothing of parting his wife's legs at the dinner table, putting his hand up her skirt and offering his children 'a smell' of their mother, laughing at their discomfort.

Rose needed little encouragement from Fred to begin work as a prostitute from her upstairs 'quarters', and she soon began advertising her services. She even had her own bell outside for clients to ring, and she would frequently interrupt her evening meal to entertain a 'guest' who had called. If a client phoned during the day, the children were required to take their name and number for 'Mandy', who would ring them back. She claimed to enjoy the sex just as much as her clients, who bought her presents of alcohol, chocolates or cigarettes, as she didn't ask for money. Sometimes Fred would swap his wife's favours in exchange for a job he needed doing. He once had his van fixed through this kind of bartering. At Fred's request, but apparently with relish, Rose diligently collected her semen-stained knickers in a jar with labels on each noting the details of that particular encounter: name, date, marks out of ten and penis size.

When she was not with clients, Rose would have sex with the various lodgers and visitors to the house, both male and female. Ben Stanniland and Alan Davis, who both lodged at Number 25, remembered later that Rose crept into their beds just the day after they moved in. The lodgers knew that Rose was working as a prostitute from the house, and that both of their landlords were obsessed by sex. This agreed with them, and they were willing to participate to a certain extent. But some things made them distinctly uncomfortable. One ex-lodger, Jayne Hamer, remembers how one night 'I heard the children screaming and shouting "Stop it, daddy"'; another, Gillian Britt, recalls that at times the noises of sex at night 'didn't sound like pleasure', so she would turn up her radio to drown them out. An ex-boyfriend of Anne Marie vividly recollects lying in bed at night hearing 'No, no, please' being screamed for up to twenty minutes. But they all thought that Fred was 'a nice bloke', and couldn't believe that his young wife could really be hurting anyone, so they were unwilling to interfere.

The range of Fred West's sexual fantasies and behaviour was expanding alarmingly. The mere act of penetration had become disappointingly ordinary to him, and he now needed extra stimulation. Voyeurism particularly excited him: he had drilled holes in the bedroom and bathroom doors, through which he would watch his daughters undressing, and his wife with her clients. After watching Rose with other men, Fred would customarily demand to have sex with her immediately afterwards.

Pornography and sex toys were frequently used at Cromwell Street. Not that this is unusual in itself, but the Wests' collection included a large assortment of dildos and vibrators, many of them huge in size, designed solely to bring pain to their recipient. The couple also harboured an enormous range of bondage equipment: whips, rubber suits, masks, various restraints and harnesses. Their obsession with sex was becoming increasingly, and disturbingly, sado-masochistic in nature. Their imagination was Sadean: it increased geometrically, as they constantly needed further and more exotic stimuli. While some of their pornography was home-made and inherently harmless, depicting Rose masturbating or 'playing' with the gear-stick in Fred's van, it is probable that these were early efforts. Later material was of a far more foreboding nature, centring round images of women gagged, bound, and suspended from ceiling beams being beaten, clearly in agony.

Another sinister aspect of their sexual profile was Fred's growing obsession with the gynaecological workings of the female body. He used to boast that he knew how to and had performed abortions, and he liked to look inside women's vaginas and to take pictures of them internally. Also interested in the possibilities of artificial insemination and cross-breeding, he would ask Rose to save sperm from her clients in condoms and then try to inseminate her using a syringe. He also encouraged his wife to have sex with black men in order to produce half-caste children, a desire which Rose was happy to accommodate, as she said that (true to the cliché) black men were better endowed, and made good lovers. Fred was also intrigued by the idea of breeding Rose with a bull. Laughing, he told his children that it was the only way their mother could ever be satisfied.

There is one woman who particularly remembers Fred's interest in female anatomy. Caroline Owens (née Raine) moved into Cromwell Street in October 1972, where she was employed as a nanny for Anne Marie, Heather and Mae. She stayed only a matter of weeks, however, as her employers' constant sexual innuendoes were making her uncomfortable. Rose would stroke her hair in a suggestive manner, and Fred was always making 'smutty' comments. The month after she had moved out, Caroline encountered the Wests as she was hitchhiking, and they stopped to offer her a lift. Although she had been disturbed by their behaviour while she was living at Cromwell Street, she didn't seriously think that the couple were any threat to her, and she accepted their offer.

Almost as soon as they had pulled away, however, Rose began to grope Caroline's breasts, as Fred crudely inquired, 'What's her tits like?' In spite of Caroline's protests, Rose had soon progressed to touching her between the legs. When Fred saw a quiet spot on the road, he pulled over at a lay-by and punched Caroline several times, rendering her unconscious. When she came round, her hands were tied and she was gagged with tape. The Wests took their victim back to Cromwell Street where she was stripped, bound, blindfolded, and then subjected to a horrifying joint sexual assault by her captors. Rose performed oral sex on her, Fred whipped and raped her, and they both inquisitively probed and explored her vagina. Caroline later told the court, 'It was like being examined in the genital areas. I could feel fingers inside me and they were discussing my genitals. I was scared they might operate in some way.'

Caroline said that it was Rose who seemed to be the dominant partner and the initiator of the assault. When Rose was not in the room Fred apologized to Caroline for raping her, and told her that the abduction had been entirely his wife's idea. Yet it was Fred who said 'that he would keep me in the cellar and let his black friends use me and when they were finished with me they would bury me under the paving stones of Gloucester', as (he claimed) hundreds of other girls already were. It seems that Fred and Rose West were 'in it together'. Which of the Wests was the dominant partner seems to depend on which victim or witness tells the tale. There is certainly no question here of one dominant partner leading another, weaker and inadequate partner astray: no *folie à deux*. Each of the Wests was independently a fully fledged sexual psychopath. Each was extremely dangerous. Together they were lethal.

By agreeing to come back to work for them, as they had asked, Caroline finally made her escape, telling the Wests that she would go home to get her belongings. Instead, she went to the police. The rape charges were eventually dropped, and the Wests were only charged with actual bodily harm and indecent assault. They were fined just £50 each. Astonishingly, the judge said that imprisoning them would serve no purpose. There might have been some reluctance to allow the children to go into care, although in retrospect that would have been the best place for them. Twenty years later the judge would publicly say that he wished he had not been so lenient. He had made a mistake that was to be repeated over the forthcoming years by law-enforcement officers and social workers: he had underestimated the Wests. Had anyone actually believed what was virtually in front of their eyes, numerous lives would have been saved, and enormous suffering on the part of grieving families whose children were yet to be murdered would have been averted.

The Wests' appetite for bondage and sado-masochism was escalating, and it was not long before they involved Anne Marie, who was then just nine, in the enactment of their fantasies. In early 1973 they took their daughter down to the cellar, which had been turned into a make-shift torture chamber, and tied her to a metal frame, naked and gagged. They used a vibrator on her, mauled her breasts, and (as Rose laughingly watched) Fred raped her. Claiming that she ought to be thankful to them for giving her such a good education, they told her it would teach her how to keep her husband satisfied when she was older. It was something that Rose's own father, Bill, might easily have said to her; or Fred's mother, Daisy, to him.

After the assault they left Anne Marie bound and bleeding, alone in the cellar. When they returned some time later, they inserted something into her vagina which she thought looked like frogspawn. What she was describing was one of Fred's 'experiments'. She remembers 'the pain was so bad I almost lost consciousness' and 'I wished I was dead'. Poignantly, she further recalled that 'I also felt I shouldn't be ungrateful because they were doing this to help me'. After they had violated their daughter, Rose handed her a sanitary towel to mop up the blood and told her, 'Everybody does it to every girl. It's a father's job. Don't worry, and don't say anything to anybody. It's something everybody does but nobody talks about.'

From this time onwards, Anne Marie was regularly abused by Fred and Rose. 'I had no choice but to suffer it', she later wrote in her book *Out of the Shadows*, 'I was a victim of my parents' sexual fantasies. To complain was to increase my torture and provoke severe beatings.' The assaults were often joint, but both parents also abused their daughter independently of their partner: Fred would regularly take Anne Marie out in his van and rape her, giving her sweets afterwards; Rose would force the girl to satisfy her orally and digitally. When she was just twelve, she was made to have sex with Rose's clients while Rose watched. One man bought Anne Marie a box of chocolates as payment, and Rose took them from her and ate them all herself. Then, at the age of fifteen, Anne Marie was impregnated by her father. When the pregnancy turned out to be ectopic, she was never told why she was in hospital, nor why she had to have her operation.

Although Anne Marie was undoubtedly abused the most severely, her half-sisters Mae and Heather were also systematically sexually harassed and beaten by their parents. They were never actually raped by Fred, but the threat was always there. He would make their lives a misery by constantly leering at and groping them, watching them as they undressed and showered, telling them it was their turn next. Rose's abuse of the children was of a different nature to her husband's, and it is she whom the children remember as the physically vicious one. She would frequently beat the girls and their brother Stephen, once slashing Mae with a knife, leaving cuts over her chest. On another occasion she strangled Stephen until he lost consciousness.

The escalating sexual violence, and the fact that the Wests had killed before, made murder at 25 Cromwell Street almost inevitable. It happened just months after they had moved in. Lynda Gough was friendly with some of the lodgers at the house, and had been visiting them there since the beginning of 1973. As she became a more frequent visitor, nineteen-year-old Lynda was drawn into the promiscuous sexual activity in the house, and began to have regular sex with several of the lodgers. She also embarked upon a sexual relationship with both Rose and Fred, and apparently shared bondage and S&M sessions with the couple. In April, when the Wests asked her if she would like to move in and become a nanny to the children, Lynda accepted. After writing her parents a short note, saying that she had found a place to live and asking them not to worry, Lynda packed a bag and left home.

After two weeks had passed and the Goughs had not heard from Lynda, her mother, June, traced her daughter to Cromwell Street, and called round to see her. The Wests told her that Lynda had been staying there looking after the children, but they had recently asked her to leave as she had hit Anne Marie. They told June that they believed her daughter had gone to Weston-super-Mare. When June Gough noticed that Rose was wearing Lynda's slippers and that her daughter's clothes were hanging on the line, the couple told her that the girl had left some of her belongings behind. The Goughs never saw or heard from their daughter again. In March 1994 Lynda Gough's remains were found buried under the ground floor bathroom at 25 Cromwell Street. Although her body was in a full-size grave, it had been dismembered, the head and legs cut off. One hundred and twenty bones were missing, including fingers, toes and kneecaps.

Just a few months after Lynda's murder, on 10 November the Wests lured fifteen-year-old Carol Ann Cooper to Cromwell Street. Carol – or Caz, as she preferred to be known – had spent much of her life in various care institutions and sleeping rough on the streets, and in 1973 she was living at a children's home in Worcester. On the night of her disappearance she had gone to the cinema with her boyfriend and some friends. After the film, she got on a bus to return to her grandmother's house, where she was staying for the weekend, and was never seen again. It is believed that she must have encountered Fred, either alone or with Rose, as she got off the bus. Violent abduction was not the Wests' usual MO, and as it has been suggested that Caz had met the couple and visited Cromwell Street previously, it is not unlikely that she willingly accompanied them back to the house. When her remains were found two decades later, her head and her legs had been separated from her body, and many bones were missing. There was an elasticated length of cloth around her jaw.

The Wests didn't wait long for their next victim. Lucy Partington was a twenty-one-year-old undergraduate in her final year at Exeter University, where she was reading medieval English and history. In contrast to many of the Wests other victims, Lucy, who was Sir Kingsley Amis's niece, was a studious, religious, sensible and emotionally stable girl. On 27 December she had been to see a friend in Cheltenham, whose house she left at about 10.15 in the evening to get the bus back to her mother's home, where she was staying over the Christmas holidays. Everybody who knew her later agreed that it would have been completely out of character for Lucy to have accepted an invitation to a stranger's house, as some of the other victims may have done. Her friends and family can only conclude that she missed her bus and accepted a lift from Fred West, who would almost certainly have had Rose with him, which would have made Lucy feel safe in accepting the ride.

When Lucy's dismembered body was found in 1994, there

was cord and tape wound around her head, and many bones were absent. Horrifyingly, it seems that she may have been kept alive in the cellar for up to a week. She disappeared on 27 December, but it was not until 3 January that Fred went to Casualty to be treated for fresh cuts to his hand, which were surely sustained during her dismemberment. The knife used for this purpose had been buried with her.

The fourth victim at Cromwell Street, and the seventh in all, was twenty-one-year-old Thérèse Siegenthaler, a Swiss sociology student in Woolwich. On 15 April 1974 Thérèse had been to a party in South London, and the next day she set out for Holyhead, where she was meant to be catching a ferry to Ireland. Despite a friend's warning, she had decided to hitchhike from London to Wales, assuring her friend that she could look after herself. At some point on her journey, Thérèse was picked up by Fred West, who may have been accompanied by his wife. When her remains were found in the cellar at Cromwell Street, they exhibited the same distinctive features as there had been in the other cases: the nakedness, the dismemberment, the missing bones, and the binding.

That same year, in November, fifteen-year-old Shirley Hubbard was to become victim number eight. On 14 November, Shirley had been on work experience at Debenhams in Worcester, and that evening she and her boyfriend, Daniel, sat by the river and had something to eat. Daniel put Shirley on a bus at 9.30, but she never arrived home that night, nor did she keep the date that she had made with him the next day. At some stage on her way home, Shirley met one or both of the Wests who probably offered her a lift, and then took her back to Cromwell Street. When her body was found in the cellar twenty years later bones were missing, and she had been decapitated. Her skull was completely ensconced in tape, with breathing apparatus – a U-shaped plastic tube – attached.

The last victim to be buried in the Wests' charnel house of a cellar was eighteen-year-old Juanita Mott. After leaving school at the age of fifteen, Juanita had become a frequent visitor to Cromwell Street and even lodged there for a time, as she was unhappy at home. By 1975, however, she was staying with a friend of the family, a woman who lived in a village outside Gloucester. The woman, Jennifer Baldwin, was getting married on 12 April in Gloucester, and Juanita was meant to be looking after her children that day. The night before the wedding Juanita had decided to hitchhike into Gloucester, as she frequently did. But she didn't turn up to babysit Jennifer's children the next day, and she was never heard from again. Her dismembered body was eventually found at Cromwell Street buried alongside a harness and a plastic clothes-line. A pair of tights had been wrapped securely around her head, and again bones had been removed from her body.

There is no evidence that any murders occurred at Cromwell Street over the next three years. Yet given the rate at which the Wests had been killing, and the psychology of the serial killer whose lusts invariably accelerate, not diminish, there is strong reason to suppose that there were more victims during this time. If there were, however, they were not buried at Cromwell Street. Shirley Robinson was different to the other Cromwell Street victims. Her murder – like those of Anne McFall, Rena, and Charmaine – was primarily a matter of convenience. Shirley had moved into Cromwell Street in June 1977, where she stayed for over a year, during which time she began a sexual relationship first with Rose and then with Fred. The relationship between Rose and Shirley soon turned sour, however, when Shirley became pregnant by Fred and started to talk of becoming his wife. Friends and lodgers recall that Fred would unabashedly introduce Rose as his wife and Shirley as the lover whom he had impregnated. Rose's brother-in-law, Jim, remembers how Fred told him that Shirley 'wants to get between me and Rose ... I'm not having that. She's got to fucking go'.

Shirley was more than eight months pregnant, in May 1978, when she was murdered. Her body was dismembered and bones were again missing, yet this time there were no bindings. Her baby had been removed from her body, just like Anne McFall's. As the cellar was now full of bodies, Shirley and her unborn baby were buried beneath the patio.

The next body to be buried under the patio was that of Alison Chambers. In 1978 Alison was living at Jordan's Brook House, a children's home near Cromwell Street, where she was very unhappy and regularly ran away. To make her life more bearable, she would escape into a fantasy world, dreaming that she lived in the countryside in a beautiful farmhouse. Some time in the summer of 1978, a friend introduced her to the Wests, and Alison started calling round to Cromwell Street on a regular basis. She thought that the Wests were very kind, as they fed her and let her stay the night, and on one occasion they even gave her a necklace with her name on it. One day she told Rose of her fantasy farmhouse, and to the girl's delight Rose showed her a photograph of a farmhouse which she claimed that she and Fred owned, telling the girl that once she had left the children's home she could go and stay there.

On 5 August Alison ran away from Jordan's Brook House and was reported missing. Her mother received a letter from her shortly afterwards, saying that she was living with a family, looking after their children and doing some of the housework. This was the last that she heard of her daughter, until her dismembered body was found underneath the patio of Cromwell Street fifteen years later. A wide leather belt was tied around her skull.

The last known victim of the Wests was their first daughter, sixteen-year-old Heather. There was a gap of eight years between the murder of Alison Chambers in 1979 and that of Heather in 1987, a period of time too long for serial killers who have been regularly satisfying their lust to go without a murder, though no other victims have been identified. Like the Wests' other daughters, Heather had been subjected to abuse from her mother and father for as long as she could remember. Fred was continually sexually harassing Heather, but she and her sister Mae had made a pact that they would not accede to their father's demands, which prompted Fred to call his daughter a lesbian. Under the constant pestering and pressure from both parents, Heather became increasingly withdrawn, secretive and sullen.

In the summer of 1987 she finished school, having passed eight GCSEs, and applied for work at a holiday camp in Torquay for the summer. When she was offered a job she was ecstatic, as she would finally be able to escape Cromwell Street. When, inexplicably, the job fell through, Heather was inconsolable and sank deeper into depression. Unable to bear the parental abuse any longer, she confided to one of her friends what had been happening. Tragically, when the friend relayed the story to her parents they didn't believe it. When the Wests discovered that Heather had been divulging the family's secrets, they were furious, and she received a vicious beating. That summer the girl went missing. To their family and friends, the Wests maintained that she had left home, and that they had given her £600 to start her adult life. A woman in a red Mini – probably her lover, they said – had come to collect her.

Having described the circumstances of the disappearances of the Wests' victims, and considered the couple's sexual practices, we are now in a position to consider exactly how the murders took place. To aid us in understanding the Wests' crimes, a study from America, carried out by Dr Park Dietz, Dr Janet Warren and Special Agent Robert Hazelwood (1990), which looks at thirty incarcerated sadistic sexual offenders will be used as a model. This study found that sadistic offenders tend to conform to a certain pattern of behaviour in the preparation and execution of their crimes. The crimes 'often but not invariably' contained a set of recognizable elements. For example, an overwhelming 93 per cent of offenders, some of whom were working with a partner, had meticulously planned their murders. In 90 per cent of cases, strangers were chosen as victims, and lured using a 'con approach', rather than violence. The victims were then taken to a site which had been chosen in advance by the offenders, and which had often been specially prepared for the crime.

These findings fit the Wests' MO almost exactly: in general, their victims were not forcibly abducted, but approached on buses or while hitchhiking and invited back to Cromwell Street. Many of their victims may have accepted the offer, as they were unhappy young girls, who were in care, and had no family to go back to. Once they were at the house they were taken to the cellar, which had been specially equipped for the Wests' purposes.

Dietz *et al* found that once the offenders had their victims in captivity, the next stage of the crime was invariably the use of

sexual bondage, which they define as the 'restriction of movements or use of the senses to enhance the sexual arousal of the
offender'. Gags were put over the victims' mouths, their eyes
were blindfolded, their wrists and ankles were tightly bound
with rope, masks were put over their heads, and full body
harnesses were used.

The Wests were deeply aroused by bondage: they watched
pornographic videos depicting women being tied up and
degraded, and they had a large collection of equipment, including full body-suits made of rubber, and body harnesses which
Fred made himself. Furthermore, we know that they put their
interest into practice, as Caroline Owens and Anne Marie were
both rendered immobile by their bindings while they were being
sexually assaulted by the couple. The Wests' victims were found
with tape wound around their skulls, bindings on their arms,
and masks covering what had been their faces.

After the bondage, the sexual torture began. Dietz *et al* found
that the most frequent practice was forced anal sex, followed by
oral sex, vaginal sex and then foreign-object penetration. Nearly
70 per cent of the offenders performed at least three out of these
acts. The victims were also intentionally tortured in any number
of other ways, including beating, burning, whipping, electric
shocks, and biting. We know that the Wests committed forced
vaginal and oral sex, and penetration with a vibrator, upon Anne
Marie and Caroline. Fred was also later charged with having
forced anal sex with one of his younger daughters. Therefore, it
is almost certain that their victims were subjected to similar acts.

Dietz *et al* define sexual sadism as 'a persistent pattern of
becoming sexually excited in response to another's suffering'.
Anne Marie and Caroline both remember that their fright and
pain were no deterrent to the Wests, on the contrary, they
enjoyed it. Further proof of the pleasure that the Wests took in
protracting their victims' suffering is discernible from the
remains of the bodies. Dietz *et al* found that, 'the importance of
the victim's terror is underscored by the caution taken by several
offenders to ensure that their victims retained consciousness
while being tortured'. A length of metal tubing was found with
Rena's remains and Shirley Hubbard's skull was entirely

ensconced in tape, a U-shaped tube where the nostril would have been. The tubes were breathing apparatus, used to ensure that the victim was kept alive. As criminal psychologist Paul Britton said, after looking at photographs of the Cromwell Street victims' remains, 'It was clear to me that the pipe had been used to keep the victim alive and to open up the possibilities of what they could do to her. Unable to see or to cry out, she would be totally under their control.' The evidence points to Lucy Partington having been kept in the cellar for up to an entire week. Unlike Peter Sutcliffe or Dennis Nilsen, the Wests had no use for a victim who was dead, because she would not be able to feel the pain that was being inflicted upon her.

The victims would eventually be killed by asphyxiation, Dietz *et al* found. As Dr Robert Brittain says of serial killers:

> The method of killing, except when gross and mutilating violence or multiple stabbings is used – the less common forms – is almost always asphyxial ... in asphyxia, by increasing or decreasing the pressure, they have it in their power to give their victims their lives or take their lives from them. They can feel this as a God-like power.

Although he was known to be a liar, Fred did admit that on several occasions he strangled his victims.

Each victim's body was found with a number of bones missing, usually kneecaps, finger and toe bones, and also, on two occasions, a shoulder-blade and a collar-bone. Dietz *et al* observed that 'Personal items belonging to the victims are kept as trophies of the offenders "conquests" or as stimuli to facilitate arousing recollections.' Just as Jack the Ripper took a victim's kidney, the Wests may have removed bones from their victims after their deaths purely as mementoes. However, there is the more sinister possibility that the bones were removed as part of a sadistic ritual, before the victim's death, and then kept afterwards as trophies.

Another common factor was that the young women were dismembered before burial. Fred West later told the police that the victims had been decapitated and their arms and legs removed, in order that they could be buried in smaller, more discreet, spaces. But Lynda Gough's dismembered remains were found in a full-size grave that could easily have accommodated her whole body. This implies that the dismemberment was done not for utility, but for pleasure. It was an important part of the post-mortem ritual. As Paul Britton said to the police, 'You are dealing with people for whom the limits and features of what you and I would regard as ordinary sex have long ago dissolved. Enough is never enough. Even the act of dismembering the bodies is going to give these people pleasure.'

Fred and Rose West began by rehearsing sadistic sex in their fantasies, but soon it wasn't satisfying enough to merely fantasize about an act, they had to perform it, with each other, and then with real victims. Caroline and Anne Marie were almost like experiments, trial-runs, and they were bound, gagged, blindfolded and sexually assaulted in a variety of ways. Eventually this was insufficiently exciting to the Wests, who had to keep inventing and enacting more extreme ways to make their victims suffer. It was almost inevitable that death would occur, as they became inured to lesser forms of torment and degradation. In some instances the Wests may have had other reasons for their murders, such as the eliminating of a threat or an inconvenience (as was the case with Charmaine, Rena and Heather), but even in these cases the evidence shows that the victims were killed during sado-masochistic sex sessions in which murder provided the ultimate arousal.

Five years after Heather's murder, in the summer of 1992, a policeman walking down Cromwell Street was approached by a concerned local woman who related to him some of the chilling stories her daughter had been told about what went on at number 25. The social services were duly informed, and because of the deeply disturbing nature of the allegations of child abuse, the Wests' youngest children – Tara, Louise, Barry, Rosemary and Lucyanna – who were all under ten, were taken into care, pending inquiries. On the basis of what the children told the authorities about their parents, which was verified by the findings of the doctor who examined them, Fred was charged with three counts of rape and one of buggery involving one of his younger daughters. Rose was charged with cruelty and 'causing or encouraging the commission of unlawful sexual intercourse with a child'. They came to trial on 7 June 1993, but as their children refused to testify against their parents, through a combination of fear and grossly misplaced family loyalty, Judge Gabriel Hutton had no choice but to return verdicts of Not Guilty. The Wests had cheated justice once more.

Although the Wests had been acquitted, their youngest children were not allowed back into the family home as the police had found evidence of unhealthy sexual interests in it, including the Wests' huge collection of pornography and bondage paraphernalia. Additionally, the social workers had heard the children joke about their sister Heather, who had not been heard of since 1987, being 'under the patio'. Although the story might have been put down to childish gossip, the recent allegations against the Wests had aroused considerable suspicion, and Detective Constable Hazel Savage was assigned to investigate Heather's 'disappearance'. Of course, her diligent trawl through unemployment agencies, doctors' surgeries, hospitals, and tax records drew a blank. DC Savage's fruitless search lasted over a year until, at the beginning of 1994, she finally persuaded her senior officers to apply for a warrant to search Cromwell Street for a body.

On 24 February 1994, Detective Chief Inspector Terry Moore, Detective Inspector Tony James and Police Sergeant Tony Jay arrived at Cromwell Street and informed Rose that they had a warrant which entitled them to dig up the patio to look for her daughter Heather's body. At just before two o'clock Fred was rung at work and he promised to come straight home. In his absence, despite Rose's profanities and allegations of police harassment, the police began their excavation. When Fred finally arrived home, over three hours later, with an improbable story of having fallen asleep in his van, he voluntarily accompanied the police to the station, while Rose was questioned at home. Fred was released later that evening, claiming to have been in contact with Heather on several occasions since she left home in 1987. That night, Fred and Rose stayed up talking until the early hours, presumably trying to synchronize their stories.

When the police came to resume the digging the next day, Fred told his son Stephen to look after Rose and Mae as he would be 'going away for a bit'. He then asked the police to take him down to the station to make a statement. On the way there he confessed to the murder of Heather, telling them, in addition, that they were digging in the wrong place for her body. The motivation for his confession was probably the knowledge that if the police continued in their thorough excavation they would find the remains of both Shirley Robinson and Alison Chambers, as well as those of Heather. That day he was placed under arrest for Heather's murder and Rose was questioned and released. Like Myra Hindley, she was not arrested until some time after her partner.

The study by Dietz *et al* notes that as sadistic murderers 'enjoy attention, the interviewer should be prepared for an exhausting and lengthy interview'. Fred now embarked upon the first of his accounts of his crimes, which would eventually fill 145 tapes. He was eager to talk, although his 'confessions' were largely false and he expressed himself in long, rambling stories. Fundamentally an insignificant little man, whose only purchase on the world was through preying on the weak, he had finally found an audience who wanted to listen to him. He was important at last. Fred explained that Heather's murder had been an accident which had taken place during an argument. He claimed that he 'just went to grab her, to shake her, and say take that stupid smirk off your face'. He 'lunged at her ... grabbed her throat ... held her for a minute' and 'the next minute she's gone blue ... I never intended to hurt her', he told officers. Realizing that she was dead, he then tried to put her body in the dustbin, only to find that it wouldn't fit. Nonchalantly, he told the police that he 'cut her legs off' first and then 'cut her head off' to fit her inside the bin. He later buried his daughter's dismembered body.

After his confession Fred West was taken back to Cromwell Street to enlighten the police as to the whereabouts of Heather's remains. When the police had still not found her body by the next day, however, Fred decided to change his story. He now told them that Heather wasn't under the patio at all, but was, in fact, working as a drugs runner in Bahrain and he heard from her regularly. 'Nobody or nothing's under the patio', he insisted. Just hours later, in the late afternoon of 26 February, the police found Heather's remains. But there was something wrong with the picture: three thigh bones had been found. There were at least two bodies buried beneath the patio.

When confronted with the fact that Heather's remains had been recovered, Fred reverted to his original story of her murder. He insisted, however, that 'there was no sexual motive in it at all' (although she had been found naked), and also that hers was the only body they would find. However, when told of the mysterious third thigh bone – 'Heather didn't have three legs' noted DC Savage ironically – he reluctantly confessed that it might belong to Shirley Robinson. He patiently, and falsely, explained that Shirley had been a drug-dealer, and was a bad influence on Heather. Knowing that the body of Alison Chambers would also be unearthed, Fred confessed to her murder as well. He told the police that Alison had precipitated her own death by blackmailing him, threatening to show Rose a revealing photograph of Shirley and him together.

Having now confessed to three murders, Fred insisted that there were no more. When questioned about the whereabouts of Rena and Charmaine, he said, 'I have no idea where they went.' But when the police informed Fred of their intention to explore his entire house, starting with the cellar, he decided, on 4 March, to confess to all twelve murders. In his subsequent statements, however, he continued to lie to the police about the details of their deaths. All his life he had been a fantasist, constantly embellishing and fabricating details, often concocting entirely fictitious accounts of events. In an affable manner, obviously enjoying himself, Fred West offered the police multiple versions of the murders, each at odds with the last. On one occasion he told them that Charmaine was alive and well; on another he said that he had killed her, but buried her body fully clothed and intact. He insisted that he had had a year-long affair with Lucy Partington, had got her pregnant, and that when she demanded money for an abortion he had killed her. He gave two versions of the murder of Thérèse Siegenthaler. In the first he claimed that she had died by mistake as they were experimenting with bondage; in the second he maintained that she had told him that she was pregnant, and was going to inform Rose. Shirley Hubbard had allegedly demanded money from him for sex, and had refused to work for him as a prostitute; Juanita Mott was going to expose their affair to Rose. Fred West's stories of his irresistibility to women are reminiscent of John Christie's insistence that many of his victims died after having demanded sex from him.

Fred West was particularly unforthcoming about the missing bones of his victims, which he maintained, contrary to all evidence, that he had never intentionally removed. He further claimed, although he later retracted this, that none of the girls in the cellar had been dismembered. In his more candid moments however, he did allude to the fact that 'kinky sex gone wrong' had played a part in the deaths of the girls in the cellar. But since the death of the Wests' victims was part of the ritual, the ultimate in sadistic pleasure, nothing had 'gone wrong'. In their own private language it was ghoulishly 'right'.

Using Fred like a gruesome tour-guide, over the next two months the remains of all twelve victims were gradually uncovered. Given the time which had elapsed, the identities of the victims in the cellar were difficult to determine. They were, by now, merely sets of bones, and incomplete ones, at that. And while Fred West, like Dennis Nilsen, was willing to help police with identification if he could, he had only a vague recollection of some of his victims. Fred's (sporadic) memory and the recollections of the rest of the family and lodgers, as well as missing persons' files and forensic analysis were used to identify the victims. Unlike Nilsen's victims, where there were often not even bones with which to work, the identities of all twelve women were finally established.

By July 1994 Fred West had been charged with all twelve murders. Thus far he had denied that Rose was involved in any of them, claiming that 'Rose didn't have a violent nature at all'. However, he had already proved himself to be an incorrigible liar. In any case, there was ample evidence that Rose was as predatory and sexually violent as her husband. She had, after all, been jointly charged with the vicious sexual assault on Caroline Owens back in 1973. Police and public opinion concurred that it was inconceivable for a husband who was so intimate with his wife to have such profound secrets. Could he really have tortured, killed, dismembered and buried so many girls in their own house, which Rose rarely left, without her realizing anything was amiss? It stretches credulity to think so. Even supposing that Rose might not have been the one to actually terminate the girls' lives, her complicity, her knowledge and her participation would make her – like Myra Hindley – as guilty as her partner.

On 24 April, Rose was charged with the murder of Lynda Gough. By July she was jointly charged with nine of the murders, excluding those of Anne, Rena and Charmaine. Rose steadfastly insisted that she was innocent, answering many of the questions put to her with 'No comment'. As Paul Britton told the police, 'She's a woman who thinks that if she holds her nerve she'll get through. She doesn't have the same need for reinforcement and approval as Mr West.' She implied that Fred might have committed the murders on the nights that she was out working as a prostitute.

When Fred West discovered that his wife had been charged with the murder of Lynda Gough, he changed his story yet again. He now flatly retracted all his previous confessions – 'I had nothing to do with these girls' deaths at all' – maintaining that what he had told the police had been an elaborate series of lies, designed to cover up for another 'person or persons' whom he refused to name. 'For God's sake put it together', he implored police officers. Although he had not initially intended to implicate Rose, now that an opportunity had been presented for him to exonerate himself, he seized it. Fred West told his solicitor that he was innocent of all charges, including that of Heather's murder, of which he had given a detailed description. 'Rose fucking ruled me', he now claimed. He said he was quite ignorant of the bodies in the house until Rose told him about them on their last night together: 'When Rose told me where the bodies were and everything, I died at that moment.' But Fred, by his own (new) account, magnanimously elected to take all the blame: 'I swore on the kids' lives that I wouldn't shop Rose for what she did.'

Accusations were shifting from one partner to the other, but it seemed obvious to the police that Fred and Rose West were in it together. The Wests saw each other for the last time at Gloucester magistrates' court in December, as they were charged. As they stood in the dock she shied away from his touch, refusing even to look at him.

On New Year's Day of 1995, Fred West was left alone in his cell at Winston Green Prison for an hour, to eat his lunch. He used the time to strip and sew together his blankets, hanging himself from a bar above the door. His biographer Geoffrey Wandsell called his death 'a bizarre if unconscious salute to the young women whom he had caused to suffer a similar fate.' Fred West was found hanging behind his door by prison officers at just after one o'clock. They cut him down, but could not revive him.

There was a note found in his cell, intended for Rose on her last birthday on 29 November: 'The most wonderful thing in my life was when I met you. Keep your promises to me. You know what they are. You will always be Mrs West all over the world. I have no present. All I have is my life. I give it to you. Come to me, I'll be waiting.' He may have thought that by ending his life there would be insufficient evidence to convict Rose, and that they would both be free. He was wrong. Indeed, in light of her husband's death, Rose West was actually charged with another murder which had not previously been attributed to her: that of Charmaine West.

The trial of Rose West opened at Winchester Crown Court on 3 October 1995. It was Brian Leveson's job for the Crown to prove either (1) that Rose West was actually a murderer herself, 'in it together' with her husband, or (2) that she had taken some more passive, collaborative part in the murders, even if it was just that she 'must have known' they were occurring. The jury might be forgiven if they were slightly confused about which alternative Leveson was opting for, for as the trial progressed his position patently decreased in its gravity, as he gradually downplayed her role.

Part of the reason for this may have been that the evidence presented by the Crown for Rose having had a direct hand in the murders was primarily evidence of similar fact, and thus of a controversial nature. 'Similar fact' evidence, such as that used in the trial of Robert Black, is the submission of past convictions used as evidence for the charges at hand. As there could be no direct evidence as to exactly how the Cromwell Street victims died, there was considerable difficulty in establishing who had killed them. Rose was obviously not the sole offender, as Fred West had killed Anne McFall before he had even met Rose, and the signature which marked the murder – the dismemberment, the binding, the missing bones, the hole as a grave – was present in the cases of future victims. And Fred had confessed to the murders, often in detail, and pointed out the sites of the graves. There was thus no disputing that he was directly involved in the young women's deaths. What the Crown *did* dispute was that he committed the murders at Cromwell Street alone.

The similar fact evidence in this case came from the testimony of Caroline Owens, whom the Wests had been convicted of assaulting in 1972. Caroline was a young woman, as were all of the Cromwell Street victims; she was picked up by Fred and Rose while hitchhiking, as many of the other victims were alleged to have been; she had been taken back to Cromwell Street, like the others; and had been bound and sexually assaulted in a sadistic manner, *by both Fred and Rose*. Mr Leveson told the court that apart from the fact that Caroline escaped with her life, the assault was a virtual carbon copy of what we know of the murders. 'Think for a moment,' Leveson said of the murder of Lynda Gough, 'about the absence of clothes and the presence of tape ... and the picture becomes clear.'

Going through the charges, Leveson built up a compelling, if circumstantial, case. Even omitting the similar fact evidence – that Rose must be involved in the murders as she was involved in the assault – there was strong evidence for the weaker argument that she must have played *some* indirect part in, or at least had knowledge of, the murders occurring. 'She must have known about those who were brought to Cromwell Street and buried there,' said Leveson:

> Consider how much time it must have taken after death to deal with the remains, dismember the bodies, dig the hole, fill in over the remains, dispose of the excess soil, clothing and belongings, tidy up, and clear up the mess ... even assuming Rosemary West did not, in fact, participate in the disposal and hiding of the bodies, she must have known it was going on.

Leveson asked the court to look at the case of Lucy Partington, where the evidence suggested that she was kept in the cellar for up to a week. Surely both Fred and Rose must have been party to that? It is simply not plausible that Fred could have kept her there for a week without his wife's knowledge and complicity. Similarly in the case of Thérèse Siegenthaler, Leveson alleged it 'unthinkable that Rosemary West would not have known of it [her abduction and subsequent murder] and been involved in it.'

Rose West's lies also implicated her. She had given conflicting stories of Heather's disappearance and falsely claimed to have spoken to her daughter on the telephone, which suggested that 'she participated in the murder of her own daughter. Why else the lies?' As for the case of Shirley Robinson, Rose had 'a much stronger motive for ending the life of Shirley Robinson than did her husband', as Shirley was about to have Fred's baby.

The principal witnesses for the Crown were Kathryn Halliday, a woman identified only as 'Miss A', and Rose's stepdaughter, Anne Marie. Kathryn Halliday had been a neighbour of the Wests at Cromwell Street and had had a lesbian affair with Rose. She contended that Rose's role in the affair had become increasingly sadistic, and that she had finally ended their relationship through fear for her own safety. 'Miss A' testified that as a girl of just fourteen, one of her visits to Cromwell Street ended in a vicious sexual assault by both Fred and Rose. This assault was very similar to their assault on Caroline Owens. Anne Marie then told the court of her years of physical and sexual abuse at the hands of her step-mother. If the testimony was to be believed, it proved that Rose West was a sexual sadist.

A succession of witnesses were also called to testify with regard to the nature of life at 25 Cromwell Street. Lodgers told of regular sex with Rose, and of hearing occasional screams in the night, which Rose would attribute to her children's bad dreams. One of Rose's clients testified to having rung social services, after Rose told him of the incest going on in the house. An acquaintance, Elizabeth Agius, told the court how she had babysat for the Wests one night and, on their return, Fred told her, in Rose's presence, how they had been out cruising for young girls.

After days of such evidence, the Crown had made their point: Rose West was a sexually promiscuous, predatory, violent and sadistic woman. Leveson charitably, if rather disingenuously, pointed out that 'What she did with her husband and what she did with others who consented, is, of course, entirely up to her and does not of itself mean that she was involved in sexually abusing anybody, either to the point of death or otherwise.' But the likelihood of Rose's involvement in some way was becoming increasingly compelling, 'the evidence that Rosemary West knew nothing [is] wholly unworthy of belief'. That a sexually sadistic woman, living with a similar partner, had lived in a house for over twenty years in which sexually sadistic murders were regularly being carried out and of which she had no knowledge, was simply inconceivable.

'I want to tell you as loudly and clearly as I can that Rosemary West is not guilty', opened Mr Ferguson, for the defence. Not guilty of committing, participating in, or having knowledge of, any of the murders. Rose West's defence responded in a similar way to Robert Black's, accusing the Crown of having no evidence and arguing that the fact that his client was a sexually peculiar individual – a 'pervert' even – did not necessarily make her a murderer. 'The Crown must prove guilt beyond all reasonable doubt but all they have are allegations, accusations, and a superficially attractive theory.' Ferguson said that Rose West might be a lesbian, have sex with her lodgers, work as a prostitute and have a large collection of sexual aids, but 'that does not make her a murderer'.

The defence contended that it was Fred West alone, unaided in any way by the defendant, who committed the murders in question. Ferguson began by undermining the testimony of the women who claimed to have been victims of assault by the Wests. He told the court that Caroline Owens, Anne Marie, 'Miss A' and Kathryn Halliday were all promised large sums for their exclusive stories from newspapers. 'You may think,' he said, 'consciously or unconsciously, they are aware that the more sensational the evidence, the more the media will pay for their stories. No paper is going to ... pay out large sums if Rosemary West is acquitted.' In addition to this, the witnesses were unreliable in other respects: Miss A had long suffered from mental problems and had only come forward with her complaint after two decades; Caroline Owens had reported that she had been left physically unmarked by the allegedly brutal attack on her; Kathryn Halliday had testified that she had been frightened during her sadistic sex sessions with Rose, but she had continued to go to Cromwell Street to see her lover; and Anne Marie had always disliked Rose for usurping her father's affections.

Ferguson then attacked the Crown's contention that Rose must at least have known about the murders, as they were occurring in her own house. For 25 Cromwell Street was simply not like most houses, Ferguson said. As lodgers were constantly moving in and out, with their friends staying with them for unspecified lengths of time, Rose would not necessarily have noticed absences. And the digging of graves could easily have been attributed to Fred's constant DIY activities around the house and garden. In the light of these facts, argued Ferguson, it was perfectly plausible that Fred could have gone about his clandestine activities unnoticed by his wife.

A succession of witnesses were then called to tell the court how they had been subjects of sexual assault by Fred West alone. The defence's main witnesses were then Rose West herself, and the taped confessions of Fred West, speaking, spookily, as if from the grave. Rose West did not prove to be a sympathetic witness. Aside from when she was talking of Heather, she was cold and petulant, and her answers were often vague. She was also caught in obvious lies on several occasions. She flatly denied having ever abused Anne Marie, although Anne Marie's testimony had been obviously, and painfully, truthful. She similarly denied having assaulted 'Miss A'. In the case of Caroline Owens – against whom she had been convicted of assault – she stubbornly answered questions about the episode with 'I don't know' and 'I can't say either way'.

Four of Fred's 145 taped interviews were then played to the court, in which he described the murders of Heather, Charmaine and Rena, which he said he committed alone. However the tapes also contained examples of Fred's obvious fantasies and lies, such as his claims to have been conducting affairs with all of the victims at Cromwell Street. In rebuttal of the evidence of Fred West, the prosecution asked to be able to call Janet Leach, the 'appropriate adult' that Fred had been assigned while in custody. Undermining the taped 'confession', Janet told the court that Fred had told her that he and Rose had made a 'pact' that he would take the blame for the murders, to cover up her participation. Janet said that Fred had told her, 'He was always at work when Rose killed, though he sometimes helped to dispose of the bodies afterwards.'

Ferguson reduced the defence to its most basic argument in his closing:

> Rosemary West is not accused of cruelty to children, or being party to rape, but of the crime of murder ... Her conduct as a woman and a mother falls far below the standard you would expect. One fact remains stark and clear – at the end of it all, when it comes to proof, they have not got the evidence. You cannot convict without proof ... You are not being asked to acquit in the teeth of the evidence but because there is no evidence.

Ferguson said that it was not Rose West, but her late husband, who should have been standing trial, 'a man devoid of compassion, consumed with sadistic lust... someone you may think was the very epitome of evil.'

On 20 November the jury returned verdicts of guilty on three counts of murder, for those of Heather, Charmaine and Shirley Robinson. Before retiring again to consider the other seven counts, they asked the judge whether 'the total absence of direct evidence other than the presence of the remains linking the victims to 25 Cromwell Street [is] an obstruction to bringing in a guilty verdict?' The judge replied that it wasn't. The next day they returned guilty verdicts on the remaining charges. Judge Mantell told the defendant that 'if attention is paid to what I think, you will never be released'.

Rose West has inevitably been compared to Myra Hindley. When both women were incarcerated within Durham Prison the tabloid press immediately reported an – entirely fictitious – bond between them, with Hindley portrayed as West's role-model. Yet Rose West claimed the lives of more victims than Hindley, and the murders were palpably more sadistic. And unlike Hindley, the case of Rose West admitted of no extenuating circumstances: there was no *folie à deux*, little doubt that West was a principle, not an accessory. Yet Myra Hindley retains her title as the most hated and vicious woman in Britain, her image indelibly imprinted in the public mind. As Joan Smith observed, when a picture of Rose West was released to the public:

The police photographer had snapped West full-face, staring expressionlessly into the camera, in an obvious echo of the infamous mugshot of the Moors Murderess. Yet while West had just been found guilty of some of the most horrific crimes ever described in British judicial proceedings, her picture was something of a disappointment; this was no Hindley, all bleached blonde hair and pitiless lips, but a middle-aged woman with badly cut brown hair and old-fashioned glasses. Where Hindley appeared a woman of her time in the photograph taken shortly after her arrest in 1965, hard as nails and icily sexy, Rose West was plump and homely, someone who wouldn't attract attention in a crowd of mothers.

Rose West's appearance has saved her from inheriting Hindley's demonic mantle.

10

SERIAL KILLING: SOME TENTATIVE CONCLUSIONS

No one believes, these days, that men are wholly the products of determinative forces: of the will of God, the power of evil, the effects of society or politics, the programming of genetic structure. Any – or all – of these, depending on your view, may have profound effects on the way individuals develop, but none of them could seriously be argued to be the sole determinant of why one person becomes a serial killer, and another does not. Human behaviour is too complex for any reductive explanatory system to be imposed upon it, and our understanding of our fellow human beings is always sketchy, contingent, and prone to error.

That doesn't mean, however, that it isn't worth trying to understand why people behave as they do, and that understanding ought to begin with how they were treated as children. We are all profoundly influenced by the way that we are treated in our early years – both in our societies and, crucially, in our families – and are in some complex way inevitable products of that experience. The child comes into the world unformed, a little package of potential dispositions and capacities, equally able to learn to trust its new environment or to reject it as hostile and loveless. It is largely a question of what is on offer. The kind of adult that the child will become can best be understood in terms of the ways in which early patterns of love, trust, dependence and independence are laid down.

We have now compiled, largely without comment, a considerable amount of information concerning the childhoods, backgrounds, and subsequent crimes and trials of British serial killers. So what have we learned? What patterns and similarities can we distinguish in the early lives of these offenders? What, if anything, do they have in common? The attentive reader will already have noticed refrains running through the accounts of the childhoods of this group of killers, and will also have observed differences between them. Their upbringings and personal histories are not carbon copies of each other, and their lives do not match step by step. Why should they? What we do find, however, are overlapping sets of similarities, which are consistent within the group: childhood experiences, relationships and events which, while not identical, breed the same types of feelings and responses to the world, to produce a recognizable, dangerous and unstable type of person. (Henceforth, for ease of reference I shall refer to the child, in the developing model of the serial killer as 'he', as the vast majority of such people are men.)

In general, the offenders were born into working-class families, with their parent(s) employed either in low-income, unskilled jobs or in the services. John Sutcliffe worked at the mill and the bakery, Kathleen was a cleaner; Walter and Daisy West both worked on the land; Colin Ireland's mother was a newsagent's assistant; Peggie Stewart, Ian Brady's mother, was a waitress; Jessie Black worked in a factory; Olav Nilsen, Bill Letts (Rose West's father), and Bob Hindley were all in the army. Only Ernest Christie had a skilled job (as a carpet designer), and the Christies were, as Ludovic Kennedy puts it, 'a solid Victorian middle-class family'.

Other than the Christies, the families were all of poor socio-economic status. Often they struggled to provide adequately for their children: Fred West was given home-grown turnips in his lunch-box; until Rose West was ten, her father was constantly in and out of employment and the family was always impoverished; Colin Ireland and his mother were evicted from one of their first homes for non-payment of rent; Dennis Nilsen remembers his mother as 'self-reliant in her daily struggles to make ends meet'.

Thus, on the whole, the children were brought up in small, overcrowded accommodation. Five of the offenders – John

Christie, Peter Sutcliffe, Fred West, Rose West and Dennis Nilsen – came from families with six or more siblings, which meant both that they experienced little privacy, and that they were unlikely to be given adequate attention by their parents. For some years, Dennis Nilsen, his mother, and his brother and sister shared just one room at his grandparents' flat; Fred West shared a room with his two brothers in a small cottage; Peter Sutcliffe used to lock himself in the bathroom in order to find some privacy in his bustling household.

But large working-class families with low incomes are common, and are often a source of considerable closeness. How these families differed from the norm was that they were all dysfunctional in some important way, the children becoming deprived of adequate love and nurturing. Ian Brady, Robert Black and Colin Ireland had the most conventionally difficult childhoods. All three were unplanned illegitimate births, born to young mothers who were in no position to care for them. The mothers' partners all left before the birth of their sons, and never made any contact with them again. Brady's and Black's mothers couldn't cope with the responsibility of raising children on their own – financially or emotionally – and gave up their babies for fostering almost immediately.

Black's mother never saw her son again after relinquishing him. He was placed first with foster parents and then, after their deaths, in numerous care institutions, in one of which he was sexually abused. Brady's mother, having given her son to foster parents to look after when he was a few months old, visited him regularly until he was twelve, and then had no further contact with him until he was sixteen. Although Brady's foster parents were decent people who tried hard to provide him with a good home, he always had the feeling he didn't belong, that he was an outsider with no real family.

Ireland's mother, although the youngest at seventeen, kept her baby, and was fortunate enough to have her parents to help her. Yet she still struggled to bring up her child and they were forced to stay at a shelter for homeless mothers, after which the boy was placed in care for some months when he was ten, and later spent time in a special school, and in three borstals. In

291

common with Brady, Black and Ireland, Dennis Nilsen never knew his natural father, who divorced his mother when Nilsen was four. His mother, also, was too young to cope with a child by herself, and like Colin Ireland's mother she lived with her parents, who helped her with the boy.

Though these rejections are of different kinds and orders, involving one or both of the natural parents, we are dealing with children who, in every case, were given inadequate care and protection. Usually no malice towards the child was intended; poverty, youth and inexperience impose their own harshness. However from the point of view of a child emerging into consciousness, the upbringings may well have taught the lesson that one was unworthy, unloved and unwanted, not deemed important enough for the parents to wish to stay and provide. And while this would have caused grief and withdrawal on the part of the child, it would have caused resentment too, and an anger that may have been impossible, or unsafe, to express.

The other offenders – John Christie, Peter Sutcliffe, Myra Hindley, Fred and Rose West – grew up in families which were intact, with both their natural parents present, yet there were grave underlying problems. All of the households were characterized by what Dr Robert Brittain, in his study of sadistic murder, calls an 'authoritarian and punitive' father. Christie, Sutcliffe, Hindley and Rose West all had aggressive, tyrannical and violent fathers: Ernest Christie allegedly ran his family as if it were a regiment, and administered beatings regularly; Bill Letts thrashed his wife and children (with the exception of Rose); one of Sutcliffe's brothers recalls that they were all terrified of John, who used to hit them; Hindley remembers her father beating her mother while he was drunk.

So we are dealing with children whose father was either absent or dangerous, which is particularly damaging for boys. Such a child, notes Anthony Storr, 'has less chance of developing into a confident male than a boy whose father lives at home and is actively concerned with him'. As the child developed he had no adequate male model, no figure with which to identify himself.

To compensate for their husbands' aggression, the mothers of these offenders tended to become over-protective towards their children, which had the effect of turning them into 'mummy's boys', a term which has been used to describe both Peter Sutcliffe and Fred West. Gordon Burn comments that Sutcliffe was still 'clinging limpet-like to his mother's hems' when he was of school age; Daisy West was renowned for marching up to her son's school and loudly voicing her complaints when Fred had been caned by teachers, or picked on by other children.

In a study of sex killers, Donald Lunde found that 'normally there is an intense relationship with the mother'; similarly, in a study of murderers, Dr Abrahamsen found that as children they were frequently 'alienated both physically and emotionally from the father' and thus became too close to their mothers. Sutcliffe and Christie were constantly silenced and repressed by their fathers, their masculinity undermined and diminished. In escaping to the soft but (understandably) anxious hyper-protectiveness of their mothers, they were further emasculated. As Dr Abrahamsen notes, the child's reliance on the mother, owing to his fear of the father, led to 'distorted identification which weakened his feelings of masculinity and made him vulnerable to any threats against his virility and manliness.' The boys became 'unable to develop a firm and constant male identity'. And this, of course, leads to a kind of emotional, and sometimes physical, impotence, and intensifies burgeoning feelings of powerlessness.

The mother instinctively wants to protect her child, yet she too is frightened of her violent husband, reluctant to confront him, and to stop him abusing her children. Instead, she does what she can to protect the child in other areas of his life, and thus begins to smother him with her constant affections. And although she means well, unlike the bullying father, she too harms her child. For a good mother not only protects; at the same time, and progressively, she encourages separation. As Anthony Storr says of children in general, 'There is the need to cling to the mother, to be sure of her affection and support. But there's also a drive to explore and master the environment, to act independently… wise mothers encourage their children to do as much as possible for themselves.'

Kathleen Sutcliffe, Hannah Christie and Daisy West, in cosseting their children, stunted their growth (interestingly, each of the boys was runtish) and inhibited their autonomy. To force dependency on a person, which is a form of imposing one's control, is also to encourage the growth of resentment, however subliminally. In attempting to make up for a failure of love from the physically or emotionally absent father, the mother overcompensates, and becomes to the child yet another figure of resentment.

Yet this model of family life, with a violent father and overprotective mother, is hardly an unusual one. As criminal psychologist Paul Britton says, 'Lots of children have raw deals or grow up in difficult circumstances, and they don't turn out to be sadistic murderers.' These children, however, 'catch up because there are wider influences such as school, or important friendships which socialize them and make them frightened of doing things they know are wrong.'

In the cases we have looked at, further factors hindered the development of a separate and strong ego. As the children began to grow up and go to school, we find that they were mostly unsuccessful in forming relationships with others. With the exception of Myra Hindley, the children are remembered as socially hesitant and largely friendless throughout their school years. One phrase recurs throughout the different accounts we hear of each killer's childhood: 'He was a loner'. John Sutcliffe used to find his son standing alone in the corner of the playground; Christie's peers found him fussy and odd; Fred West preferred the company of his own family; Colin Ireland remembers how at school 'I would often be on my own'; a contemporary of Robert Black remembers how 'Bobby didn't mix in with the normal playground games'; Brian Masters describes Nilsen as a 'quiet, withdrawn, intensely private' boy.

As the process of openly relating to family members has never been encouraged, such children have never learnt how to form and maintain positive human relationships, and thus do not make friends as other children do. The child – isolated within the family or put into care, silenced by violence and smothered by love – now becomes even more self-reliant and private, as he withdraws further from the world. As ex-FBI Agent Robert Ressler notes, serial killers as children were 'nurtured on inadequate relationships in their earliest years, had no one to whom they could easily turn, were unable to form attachments to those closest to them, and grew up increasingly lonely and isolated.'

All of these children (with the exception of Robert Black), were also physically weak or unprepossessing. Children notice differences in others quickly – particularly those of a physical nature – and mercilessly exploit them: Ireland remembers himself as a 'puny little runt' who was bullied for his appearance; Nilsen and Christie were both physically small and frail, and reluctant to join in with the other boys' games; Sutcliffe badgered his mother for a pair of long trousers to hide his scrawny legs, about which the other boys taunted him; both the girls, Rose West and Myra Hindley, were almost masculine in appearance, and were teased about it.

Friendless and withdrawn, their academic performances were also uniformly poor, which would have further lowered their self-esteem. Rose West was nicknamed Dozy Rosie; Fred West was 'as thick as two planks'; Ireland, Nilsen and Hindley had some creative talent, but little else; Sutcliffe's teachers had trouble even remembering who he was. Some of the children had above average IQs, yet none were motivated enough to stay on at school beyond the age of fifteen, and left school without taking any exams, and with no prospects for further education.

We now have a child who, feeling unloved and resentful at home, is sent to school where he makes few friends and performs poorly in all areas. Who, he may think, would want to befriend him? And so the child becomes increasingly emotionally fragile, unsure of himself, lacking in self-esteem. Essentially, he feels powerless: he feels that he has never had any control over the way in which he has been treated, he has never been taken seriously, and he progressively retreats into his own misery. This isolation, Ressler says, and Storr agrees, is 'the single most important aspect of their psychological makeup'.

As the child turns into an adolescent he begins to grow curious about sex, and to have sexual impulses, but because of his isolation, and lack of self-confidence, it is hard to find partners in normal ways. He has been raised to feel insignificant, unattractive, and inadequate; he is neither clever, popular, nor physically attractive: why should anyone find him sexually appealing? Why should he be worthy of love? His upbringing has taught him that he isn't – and even when he has received love, it has been overbearing and diminished his sense of his own power. And so he feels more isolated. But now that loneliness is not only familial and social, but sexual as well. The lesson of early life is underscored: nobody wants me (as a child this means 'nobody loves me', as an adolescent, that 'nobody desires me'). The adolescent begins to feel both sexually inferior and angry. All of the latent resentment at being improperly loved as a child is now allied to being improperly loved as an emerging adult: thus the subterranean power of the repressed rage of childhood is conjoined with the anger of adolescent rejection. There is now some danger of this anger being acted out upon those who refuse to provide their love.

Anthony Storr says that the result of the adolescent's feelings of sexual inadequacy 'is to increase the importance of an inner world of phantasy'. A private world has probably been important to the child for some years, as unhappy children often retreat into a world of make-believe, and though the mechanism is not in itself unhealthy, it is now intensified. The child begins to invent that alternative reality where he can be in control of events, and life can be manipulated to produce one's own ends: in his own head he can be powerful, sexually confident and fulfilled, even happy. In the realm of fantasy others behave as you wish, they become a function of desire. 'His fantasy life', says Dr Robert Brittain, is 'in many ways more important to him than is his ordinary life, and in a sense more real, so diminishing the value he puts on external life and on other people'. As the adolescent becomes increasingly engrossed with his inner world he becomes progressively estranged from what is happening, and what is acceptable, in the real world.

At this point, when the adolescent is estranged from family and peers, sexually curious but unsure, living increasingly in a fantasy world, he is susceptible. The retreat into fantasy is not in itself dangerous, and can provide escape from the intolerable realities of the external world. Fantasy can lead to art, to literature, to self-fulfilment. It is a primary mode of creative self-expression. But if the wrong stimulus or catalyst comes along, it can all too easily lead to an unhealthy fixation and obsession, as the child has inadequate emotional resources to cope with a powerful but potentially dangerous impulse or image. The reality to which he has been exposed – often involving violence and the extremes of rejection – does not allow him to test his inner world for healthiness or soundness.

In almost all British serial killers we find that during their childhoods the themes of death, sex and violence have somehow become distorted and entwined. All are experiences that are intense and powerful, but hard to assimilate or to understand. Dennis Nilsen saw his beloved grandfather's dead body, and subsequently the images of death, love and sex became complexly intermingled. At a time when he was lacking in direction, and sexually inexperienced, Ian Brady 'discovered' sexual sadism and Nazism, and they excited him, and made him feel powerful. Robert Black, who was already precociously sexual, was sexually abused by a man who was meant to be caring for him, implicitly suggesting to Black that sex and aggression were connected. Fred and Rose West, similarly, were both almost certainly sexually abused as children, by their parents – their primary caretakers – and thus deduced that sex was something there to be taken, by force if necessary. From the time of his first inept attempt at penetration, John Christie often found himself unable to perform sexually, a problem which worsened until he felt unable to contemplate sex unless his partner was entirely passive, or unconscious.

These people are still a long way from becoming murderers, however. But the seed – the fusion of sex and violence, or power – has been planted and left to grow. For now, they begin to enact their growing feelings of anger, isolation, frustration, powerlessness and rejection in lesser ways. Thus far they have successfully repressed their negative feelings, and turned them inwards, but this is a dangerous process, leading in some cases to clinical depression, but in others to the acting out of the repressed rage.

In his Freudian analysis of murder – which makes perfect sense in describing the development of the serial killer – Dr Abrahamsen says:

> When as a child we feel hurt by people's rejection or criticism, we either give vent to it or push away from our mind our real resentment and dislike until we 'forget' about them. They become unconscious. When we continue to repress and it becomes a pattern of behaviour, without finding any outward expression or release, these hateful emotions accumulate within us.

The feelings build and demand release, because they have found no healthy and constructive outlet, as they do in the 'normal' child. Normal children are encouraged to reasonably exert their own power over the world without fear of the consequences; in other children, where autonomy and control have been consistently denied, leading to feelings of intense powerlessness, the child will withdraw even further into himself. Dr Joel Norris notes that:

> One of the early signs that a child is reaching emotional adolescence is that he begins to exercise power. Sometimes that power takes the form of a direct confrontation or challenge to adult authority, but this challenge is normal … The powerless adolescent, however, will not seek to challenge authority directly. Nor will he seek confrontations.

In our sample, aside from Robert Black and Rose West, the offenders shied away from physical confrontations, with both family and friends, even when provoked. None of the children struck back when on the receiving end of violence or sexual abuse: Fred West's brother was constantly fighting on Fred's behalf; Peter Sutcliffe and Colin Ireland simply skipped school entirely. It is a sad irony that it is not the bullies, but the bullied, who can grow up to perpetrate the most extreme forms of aggressive behaviour.

Instead of exerting their own power and confronting the source of the problem – the inadequate, violent or sexually abusive parent, or the school bully – the child's behaviour, says Dr Norris:

> will be abnormal, even criminal ... The powerless adolescent will adopt a demeanour of camouflage but will cross swords with authorities in oblique ways. Eventually he will seek invisibility and will finally express himself in bizarre or abnormal behaviour ... in the form of deviant sexual behaviour, attacks on physically weaker members of the same or opposite sex, petty crimes, extreme cruelty to animals, and even attempted suicide.

Colin Ireland, Ian Brady, Fred West and John Christie all began their criminal careers by committing theft and burglary as teenagers. Unable to strike back at those older and more powerful than themselves, the child begins in small ways to take revenge, and seeks empowerment through crimes perpetrated on those weaker or more vulnerable than themselves.

But these relatively minor acts of rebellion are not sufficient to satiate the deep anger that they feel. They need more. They still feel essentially powerless and unwanted. And the conflation of sex and power – both of which they have always been denied – intensifies: sex, they think, can be obtained through power; and feelings of power are obtainable through sex. And so sexual acts in which the offender is in control, where he cannot be rejected, become inevitable – as they serve the dual purpose of sexual gratification and self-empowerment. The acting out of sexually perverse imaginings, drawn from the escalating fantasy life, becomes the means to self-esteem: it is the only way in which the potential killer feels whole.

Fred West and Robert Black began to force themselves upon young girls; John Christie started to visit prostitutes whom he could use and abuse as he liked; Peter Sutcliffe initiated a sexual relationship with a younger and meeker girl; Ian Brady took Myra Hindley, a girl who adored him unquestioningly, as his lover; Rose West began to masturbate her younger brother at night; Dennis Nilsen turned to men for one night stands. In these 'relationships' the offender fulfils his sexual desires, and becomes, for the first time, the dominant party, the initiator rather than the victim: in control at last, somebody to be reckoned with. As Dr Abrahamsen further observes: 'When a person resorts to violence, it is, in the last analysis, to achieve power. By obtaining power, he enhances his self-esteem, which fundamentally is rooted in sexual identity.'

Throughout their lives these people have never felt valued, their needs never treated as important. And now that they are older they begin to treat people in the same way that they were treated: they take without regard to others, they use, they depersonalize, they deny others the power which they themselves have been denied. The figures in their fantasies now become actual. Real people are used as objects in the enactment of desire, in the living out of a fantasy that has always been empowering and satisfying. And these fantasies, as we have sometimes seen (but often had to infer), involve a dangerous, and virtually inevitable, conflation of images of sex and death. If a would-be sexual partner is not going to give herself willingly to one so weak, unattractive, and unloveable, then she will have to be made to acquiesce. Occasionally, the potential killer can find a partner with whom to share his fantasies, as Fred West found Rose, and Brady found Hindley. But usually this is not the case, most can't find consenting partners and thus have to force consent upon the unwilling or the unaware.

Although there is much controversy over the term, it seems relatively clear that the person we are describing – the sexual serial killer – is a psychopath. The term is, however, frequently criticized for being a criminal catch-all, as it includes (as defined by the Mental Health Act), any personality disorder which makes a person behave in a 'seriously irresponsible or abnormally aggressive' manner. As criminologist Dr Eric Hickey says, the all encompassing term psychopath 'serves adequately to describe serial killers mainly because there appears to be a variety of serial offenders'; yet, he continues, 'this "variety", however, may be more of style then substance. The underlying pathology of serial killers typically is frustration, anger, hostility, feelings of inadequacy, and low self-esteem.' All serial killers, arguably, are psychopaths, although obviously, not all psychopaths are serial killers.

The psychopathic personality is typically marked by intelligence, charisma, manipulativeness, the absence of life-time plans, a façade of normality, emotional deadness, egotism, inability to relate to others and a lack of remorse. Other people, for the psychopath, are to be used as objects to fulfil his personal desires. When he has obtained what he wants from his victim, he will cast him aside, with neither thought, nor remorse. As Storr says:

> The psychopath announces by his conduct 'I care for nobody, no, not I, since nobody cares for me'. Since he does not believe that anybody really values him, he has little to lose by anti-social conduct, nor any motive for telling the truth. Deprivation of society's approval means nothing to a man who has never felt that it was accorded him.

Thus, the psychopath – and the serial killer – seems incapable of feeling guilt. Why should he? Nobody ever felt guilty about treating him as an object.

And so it begins. The fantasies, bred from isolation and powerlessness, start to be acted out. But, as with most types of fantasy, they become less satisfying as they are brought into reality, and as the fantasist learns from experience. The childhood fantasies of power may have started in small and essentially harmless ways, but they have elaborated over time, and continue to develop. Initially the person may be satisfied with an abusive relationship with a weaker partner, but they will soon need more control and violence, which may eventually lead to an attack and a murder. And the fantasies will continue to grow, even after the first murder. Peter Sutcliffe was interrupted in his attack on his first victim, and she didn't die, so he was left unsatisfied; of his subsequent victims, some died and some didn't, but his attacks grew more vicious as he went along, the mutilation of the bodies more elaborate. The lust continues to build and the hunger becomes unassuageable.

We now have a model of the development of the British serial killer from childhood. Extrapolated from our case histories, it is based upon empirical data, and has some, if limited, explanatory value. Such a model has to be used with great care: it cannot account, in any exact way, for how a child turns into a serial killer, much less predict which child might do so. It can provide some of the conditions that seem to pertain in the majority of cases, but often it is based on inference when facts are unavailable. Thus we have made certain assumptions about the fantasy lives of the serial killers, which are based on the evidence of how they have behaved, but we have – except in the case of Dennis Nilsen, and perhaps Peter Sutcliffe and Robert Black – no confirmation that the killings were enacted fantasies.

Some might say that we do not know enough. Access to the English serial killers – even to the records of the trials – is severely limited, and no comprehensive study has been attempted. What information we have about the English sample is largely limited, therefore, to what may be gleaned from secondary sources, as only a few serial killers have given full accounts of themselves.

Yet this lack of information obscures a problem. Even if we had more information, even if every serial killer was willing and able to give a full and honest account of himself, this would still result in a complex conjectural muddle. For it is clear, even on the basis of what we know now that, while we can construct some model of the childhood of the serial killer – a sort of profile – none of the elements of that model are strictly necessary. There is no single over-riding and essential factor in their backgrounds or psychology, save the indisputable fact that they become serial killers. That is what defines them, just as what defines teachers is that they teach.

If this seems a methodological, and definitional, impasse, it is a useful and constructive one. It has never been the purpose of this book to define the essence of a – or even the – serial killer, to demarcate that set of necessary and sufficient conditions whereby one person becomes a serial killer, and another does not. And it is the absence of such a set of necessary and sufficient conditions that seems to undermine much of the available literature. Thus one unhappy child, abused and mistreated, may become a serial killer in adult life, while another, equally appallingly raised, does not: one child becomes a serial killer, while his brother becomes a priest. What, then, say commentators, accounts for the difference?

Too often, at the conclusion of long and serious studies of murder, the authors are left to postulate the presence of some other factor – environmental, or genetic, or psychological, perhaps only a knock on the head – they do not know, some factor X which has to be present before someone with the necessary qualifications becomes a killer. But to come to such an unsatisfying conclusion one must either have asked the wrong question (searching for essences, attempting to describe conditions both necessary and sufficient) or provided the wrong sort of answer.

Let us turn, for a moment, to a theme found in Wittgenstein's *Philosophical Investigations* in which he argues powerfully against an attempt to reach definition through location of essence, understood as a set of necessary and sufficient conditions. There is a western tradition, for instance, which has, since the Ancient Greeks, sought to define the essence of, let us say, beauty, or of goodness. The literature attempting to answer the question – what is the nature of the good? or the beautiful? – would fill a library, and be inconclusive. But the problem will simply vanish, says Wittgenstein, if we deny, in the first instance, that the right way to define a concept or category is by attempting to locate its essence.

His example, characteristically, is a homely one: let us consider, he says, the Churchill face. Scanning the portraits at Blenheim, it is clear that there is a family resemblance (a key term in its metaphoric implications) between the Churchills: they look alike. Scrutinize any given face, and it is palpably a Churchill face. But when you ask what qualities make up this family resemblance – large chins, oval heads, reddish or blotchy skin tones, dark hair, bulbous noses, and so on – it is clear that you do not need all of these qualities to be a member of the group. A certain number of them, combined, give the result. None of the features is even necessary, much less sufficient, but a combination of an adequate number prompts the viewer to say: 'Oh, that is a Churchill'. In the same manner, there is no single defining criterion of what constitutes the beautiful, just a number of overlapping instances in which we use the concept. There is no factor X, simply this overlapping set of similarities, as we may find in a Venn Diagram.

The implications of this are clear, and helpful. If we ask, not what is the essence or nature of serial killing, but instead wonder what set of combined and recurring factors may be located in the lives of people who become serial killers, then we will avoid any fruitless search for a mythical factor X. Consequently, the results we have observed in the British offenders is useful and interesting, rather than frustrating. There are isolatable factors which occur in the backgrounds of these offenders, yet no one condition is necessary to the development of a serial killer. It has been assumed, because two children may grow up in almost identical circumstances, yet have radically different lives, that there must be another mysterious force at work. Thus it is thought that we simply do not know enough, that human beings, and life itself are so complex as to render our limited knowledge negligible or meaningless. But it may not be the case that we simply do not know enough, rather that what we are seeking does not exist.

We have gone some way towards describing not the set, but the overlapping sets of conditions, which prevail in the backgrounds of serial killers. This undoubtedly has some predictive ability – we probably know enough to claim that child X is more likely to become a serial killer than child Y. That we cannot guarantee that X will, or, indeed, that Y will not, does not mean that we know nothing at all.

Human beings are so infinitely complex and unpredictable, their freedoms so various, that we cannot be described as simple products of our own inheritance. On balance, this complexity is a good and exciting thing, if frustrating to those of us who would wish comprehensively to map and to predict human behaviour. We will never succeed, nor could we in principle. We shall always, unpredictably, with results both edifying and tragic, have our saints, and our sinners.

SELECT BIBLIOGRAPHY

Much of the research for this book has, inevitably, been carried out using newspaper articles, which are too numerous to mention individually.

Chapter 1

- Abrahamsen, D., *Confessions of Son of Sam*, New York: Columbus University Press, 1985.
- Caputi, J., *The Age of Sex Crime*, London: The Women's Press, 1988.
- Dibdin, M., *The Last Sherlock Holmes Story*, London: Faber and Faber, 1990.
- Fox and Levin, *Overkill: Mass Murder and Serial Killing Exposed*, New York: Plenum Press, 1994.
- Gaute, J.H.H. and Odell, R., *The New Murderers' Who's Who*, London: Headline, 1989.
- Gresswell and Hollin, 'Multiple Murder: A Review', *The British Journal of Criminology*, 34, 1, 1994.
- Harris, T., *The Silence of the Lambs*, New York: St. Martin's, 1988.
- Holmes and DeBurger, 'Profiles in Terror: The Serial Murderer', *Federal Probation*, 49, 1985 .
- Holmes and DeBurger, *Serial Murder*, Newbury Park, CA: Sage Publications, 1988.
- Lane, B. and Gregg, W., *The New Encyclopedia of Serial Killers*, London: Headline, 1992.
- Masters, B., *On Murder*, London: Coronet, 1994.
- Masters, B., 'True Crime', *The Author*, Spring 1998.

- Orwell, G., *Decline of the English Murder and Other Essays,* London: Penguin, 1965.
- Sugden, P., *The Complete History of Jack the Ripper,* London: Robinson, 1994.
- 'The Lust Murderer', *FBI Law Enforcement Bulletin,* 49 (4), 1980.
- 'The Men who Murdered ', *FBI Law Enforcement Bulletin,* 54 (8), 1985.
- 'The Split Reality of Murder', *FBI Law Enforcement Bulletin,* 54, (8), 1985.
- Rappaport, R.G., 'The Serial and Mass Murderer', *American Journal of Forensic Psychiatry,* IX, 1, 1988.
- 'Violent Crime Scene Analysis: Modus Operandi, Signature and Staging', *FBI Law Enforcement Bulletin,* 61 (2), 1992.
- Wilson, C. and Seaman, D., *The Serial Killers,* London: W.H. Allen, 1990.
- Wilson, C., *Casebook of Murder,* London: Leslie Frewin, 1969.
- Wilson, C., *A Plague of Murder,* London: Robinson, 1995.

Chapter 2

- Britton, P., *The Jigsaw Man,* London: Bantam, 1997.
- Canter, D., *Criminal Shadows,* London: HarperCollins, 1994.
- 'Crime Scene and Profile Characteristics of Organized and Disorganized Murderers', *FBI Law Enforcement Bulletin,* 54 (8), 1985.
- Douglas, J., Ressler, R., Burgess, A., and Hartman, C., 'Criminal Profiling from Crime Scene Analysis', *Behavioural Sciences and the Law,* 4 (4), 1986.
- Douglas, J. and Olshaker, M., *Mindhunter,* London: Heinemann, 1996.
- Egger, S. A., 'A Working Definition of Serial Murder and the Reduction of Linkage Blindness', *Journal of Police Science and Administration,* 12, 1984.
- Hickey, E., *Serial Murderers and Their Victims,* Pacific Grove, CA: Brooks/Cole, 1991.

- Holmes, R., *Profiling Violent Crimes: An Investigative Tool*, Newbury Park, CA: Sage Publications, 1989.
- Jenkins, P., 'Serial Murder in England 1940-85', *Journal of Criminal Justice*, 16, 1988.
- Leyton, E., *Hunting Humans*, Toronto: McClelland and Steward, 1986.
- Leyton, E., *Men of Blood*, London: Penguin, 1997.
- Lowenstein, D.F., 'Homicide – A Review of Recent Research', *The Criminologist*, 13, 1989.
- Mactire, S., *Malicious Intent*, Ohio: Writer's Digest Books, 1995.
- Oleson, J.C., *An Analysis of Offender Profiling* (a short thesis), Cambridge: Institute of Criminology, 1995.
- Ressler, R., Burgess, A., Hartman, C., Douglas, J., and McCormack, A., 'Murderers who Rape and Mutilate', *Journal of Interpersonal Violence*, 1 (3), 1986.
- Ressler, R., Burgess, A., and Douglas, J., *Sexual Homicide: Patterns and Motives*, Lexington, MA: Lexington Books, 1988.
- Wilson, C., *Written in Blood*, London: HarperCollins, 1995.

John Christie

Much of the research on Christie was done at the Public Record Office (PRO) at Kew, London. Other sources include:

- Camps, F., *Medical and Scientific Investigations in the Christie Case*, London, 1953.
- Furneaux, R., *The Two Stranglers of Rillington Place*, London, 1961.
- 'John Christie', *Murder in Mind*, Marshall Cavendish Partworks, 10, 1997.
- Kennedy, L., *Ten Rillington Place*, London: Victor Gollancz, 1961.
- Simpson, K., *Forty Years of Murder*, London: Grafton, 1980.
- Traini, R., *Murder for Sex*, London: William Kimber, 1960.

Myra Hindley and Ian Brady

Much of the research on Ian Brady and Myra Hindley was done at the PRO. Other sources include:

- Dostoyevsky, F., *Crime and Punishment*, London: Penguin, 1970.
- Harrison, F., *Brady and Hindley*, London: Grafton, 1987.
- Lucas, N., 'Monsters of the Moors', in *The Child Killers*, London, 1970.
- Ritchie, J., *Myra Hindley: Inside the Mind of a Murderess*, London: Angus & Robertson, 1988.
- Smith, J., *Different for Girls*, London: Chatto & Windus, 1997.
- Sparrow, G., 'The Passion of Perversion', in Jones, R. G. (ed.), *Couples Who Kill*, London: True Crime, 1993.
- 'The Moors Murderers', *Murder in Mind*, Marshall Cavendish Partworks, 4, 1996–7.
- Williams, E., *Beyond Belief*, London: Hamish Hamilton, 1967.

Peter Sutcliffe

- Bland, L., 'The Case of the Yorkshire Ripper: Mad, Bad, Beast or Male?' in Scracton and Gordon, *Causes for Concern*, London: Penguin, 1984.
- Burn, G., *Somebody's Husband, Somebody's Son*, London: Heinemann, 1984.
- Cross, R., *The Yorkshire Ripper*, London: Grafton, 1981.
- De River, J. P., *The Sexual Criminal*, Charles Thomas: Springfield, Illinois, 1956.
- Jouve, N., *The Street Cleaner*, London: Marion Boyars, 1986.
- O'Gara, N., *The Real Yorkshire Ripper Revealed*, Athlone: Noel O'Gara, 1989.
- Podolsky, E., 'The Lust Murderer', in *Medico-Legal Journal*, 1966.
- Smith, J., 'There's only one Yorkshire Ripper', in *Mysogynies*, 1989.
- 'The Yorkshire Ripper', *Murder in Mind*, Marshall Cavendish Partworks, 2, 1996–7.

- Yallop, D., *Deliver Us From Evil,* London: MacDonald Futura, 1981.

Dennis Nilsen

- 'Dennis Nilsen', *Murder in Mind,* Marshall Cavendish Partworks, 8, 1997.
- Fromm, E., *The Anatomy of Human Destructiveness,* London: Penguin, 1977.
- Listners, J., *House of Horrors,* London, 1983.
- Masters, B., *Killing For Company,* London: Coronet, 1985.
- McConnell, B. and Bence, D., *The Nilsen File,* London: Futura, 1983.

Robert Black

- Church, R., *Well Done Boys,* London: Constable, 1996.
- Clark, H., *Fear the Stranger,* Edinburgh: Mainsteam, 1994.
- 'Robert Black: Evil Child Killer', *Real-Life Crimes,* 108, Eaglemoss Publications, 1995.
- Wyre, R. and Tate, T., *The Murder of Childhood,* London: Penguin, 1995.

Colin Ireland

- Most of this chapter was written using Colin Ireland's replies to the questions that I sent to him, with newspaper reports filling in the details of his crimes. The only book used was: Ressler, R. and Shachtman, T., *I Have Lived in the Monster,* London: Pocket Books, 1998.

Fred and Rose West

- Dietz, P., Hazelwood, R., and Warren, J., 'The Sexually Sadistic Criminal and his Offences', *Bulletin of the American*

Academy of Psychiatry and the Law, 18 (2), 1990.
- 'Fred & Rosemary West', *Murder in Mind*, Marshall Cavendish Partworks, 1, 1996–7.
- Masters, B., *She Must Have Known*, London: Doubleday, 1996.
- Sounes, H., *Fred and Rose,* London: Warner, 1995.
- 'The Criminal Sexual Sadist', *FBI Law Enforcement Bulletin*, 61 (2), 1992.
- Wansell, G., *An Evil Love*, London: Headline, 1996.
- West, Anne Marie, *Out of the Shadows,* London: Express Newspapers, 1995.
- West, Stephen and Mae, *Inside 25 Cromwell Street,* London: News Group Newspapers, 1995.

Chapter 10

- Abrahamsen, D., *The Murdering Mind*
- Brittain, R. P., 'The Sadistic Murderer', *Medicine, Science and the Law*, 10, 1970.
- Bruhns, Bruhns and Austin (eds), *The Human Side of Homicide*, 1982.
- Fromm, E., *The Anatomy of Human Destructiveness*, London: Cape, 1972.
- Inglis, R., *Sins of Fathers*, 1978.
- Lunde, D., *Murder and Madness,* San Francisco: San Francisco Book Company, 1976.
- Ressler, Burgess and Douglas, *Sexual Homicide: Patterns and Motives*, Lexington, MA: Lexington Books, 1988.
- Ressler, R. and Schachtman, T., *Whoever Fights Monsters*, New York: St. Martin's, 1992.
- Storr, A., *Human Aggression*, London: Penguin, 1992.
- Storr, A., *Human Destructiveness*, London: Routledge, 1991.
- Storr, A., *Sexual Deviation*, London: Penguin, 1965.
- Toch, H., *Violent Men*.
- Willie, W.S., *Citizens who commit murder*.
- Wolfgang, M.E., *Patterns in Criminal Homicide*.